Our Preposterous Use
of Literature

Our Preposterous Use of Literature

Emerson and the Nature of Reading

T. S. McMillin

University of Illinois Press

Urbana and Chicago

© 2000 by the Board of Trustees of the University of Illinois
All rights reserved
Manufactured in the United States of America
∞ This book is printed on acid-free paper.

Library of Congress Cataloging-in-Publication Data
McMillin, T. S. (Tracy Scott)
Our preposterous use of literature : Emerson and the nature
of reading / T. S. McMillin.
p.   cm.
Includes bibliographical references and index.
ISBN 0-252-02538-5
1. Emerson, Ralph Waldo, 1803–1882—Criticism and interpretation—History. 2. Emerson, Ralph Waldo, 1803–1882—
Knowledge—Literature. 3. Literature—History and criticism—Theory, etc. 4. Criticism—United States—History.
5. Reader-response criticism. 6. Books and reading. I. Title.
PS1638.M38   2000
814'.3—dc21   99-6662
CIP

C 5 4 3 2 1

In memory of my mother, Margaret,
and for my father, Henry,
my wife, Laurie Hovell McMillin,
and my sons, Liam and Jack

The learned and the studious of thought have no monopoly of wisdom. Their violence of direction in some degree disqualifies them to think truly.

—"The Over-Soul"

Contents

Acknowledgments *xi*

Introduction: What's the Use of Literature? *1*

1. The Consumption of Emerson *13*
2. Writing in the Name of *Emerson* *34*
3. Waldo, Inc. *51*
4. Foolish Consistencies *72*
5. American Scholars and the Objects of Criticism *97*
6. Toward a Natural Philosophy of Reading *122*

Notes *151*

Index *181*

Acknowledgments

The sources of inspiration, support, and instruction for this work are many; and because I have come to understand the acts of reading and writing as prompted and conditioned by diverse teachers, I wish to recognize here as many as I presently can recall, even though I am painfully aware that the list is terribly incomplete. In South Bend: Josephine Borror, Miss F, and espcially Mike Downey; in Northville: Pat Dorian, Bill Dennis, and especially Jack Townsley; in Ann Arbor: Lem Johnson, Mike Clark, and especially Herbert Barrows; in Syracuse: Bennet Schaber, Bill Readings, Tom Yingling, Robyn Wiegman, Steven Mailloux, and especially Steve Melville; in Oberlin: my students in courses on transcendentalism, nature writing, American literature, and theories of interpretation and also my colleagues in the Department of English, especially Pat Day and Sandy Zagarell; in sundry settings, from the unseemly to the sublime: Todd McGovern, Jeff Rowe, and especially Steve List; everywhere and always and extraspecially: Henry McMillin, Liam McMillin, and Jack McMillin; and most of all, for lighting my way these many years, Laurie Hovell McMillin—I am, as the Stranger informed me, "a lucky, lucky man."

I am grateful for the good offices of the reviewers at the University of Illinois Press, especially Leon Chai, whose broad knowledge and careful reading greatly influenced my revisions. And I am exceedingly thankful for the contributions of Emily Rogers; her suggestions and guidance have made this a better book.

A version of chapter 1 was first published as "Consuming Text: Transubstantiation and Ingestion in the Interpretation of Emerson" in *Criticism* (Winter 1996); a portion of chapter 4, with greater attention given to interpretive aspects of the connection between Emerson and Burroughs, was published as "'The Best Read Naturalist'? Burroughs, Emerson, and the Nature of the Text" in *Sharp Eyes: John Burroughs and American Nature Writing*, edited by Charlotte Zoë Walker (New York: Syracuse University Press, 2000); several ideas explored in this book were first pursued in "Reading Between: Time, Text, and the Preposterous" in *Layers* (Spring 1998) and "Reading Nature Writing" in *Surfaces* 4 (Spring 1994).

Our Preposterous Use
of Literature

Introduction:
What's the Use of Literature?

> This is bad; this is worse than it seems. Books are
> the best of things, well used; abused, among the worst.
> What is the right use? What is the one end which
> all means go to effect? They are for nothing but
> to inspire.
> —"The American Scholar"

Of the innumerable studies of Ralph Waldo Emerson, surprisingly few have treated the delicate issue of pie. Emerson was, as Holmes remarked, a "hopelessly confirmed pie-eater." James Thayer carefully documented the habit in his account of Emerson's 1871 train trip to California: "At breakfast we had, among other things, pie. This article at breakfast was one of Mr. Emerson's weaknesses. A pie stood before him now. He offered to help somebody from it, who declined; and then one or two others, who also declined; and then Mr.———; he too declined. 'But Mr.———!' Mr. Emerson remonstrated, with humorous emphasis, thrusting the knife under a piece of the pie, and putting the entire weight of his character into his manner,—'but Mr.———, *what is pie for?*'"[1] A haunting question, is it not? History does not record Mr.———'s reply, nor do we have Emerson's own thoughts on the matter. (One suspects that someday a dissertation will reveal the significance of the omission of pie from Emerson's essay "Circles.") For good or ill, the question of the uses of pie is left to the reader's imagination.

In my own ruminations on the subject, I have come to see a connection (albeit tenuous and only faintly analogous) between Emerson's concerns for pie and his worries, expressed above in the epigraph from "The American Scholar," over the "right use" of books. Although the potentially inspirational ends of pie no doubt merit attention, this book is devoted to the related question of the uses of literature. To what ends may literature be put? What ends might be deemed unwise or unjust, just or wise? What criteria, formulated by what authority, would yield the best or "rightest" ends? And, consequently, what methods of use would more successfully approach those ends? In what follows, I attempt to respond to these questions, taking the reception of Emerson as an example. That is, I am led by Emerson's pie to the question of literature, and this in turn prompts the question, What is Emerson for?

Since the midnineteenth century, Emerson and his writing have been used to stand for the true nature of America, for what is best (or sometimes worst) and most American in the nation's literary tradition, and for all that is good, just, moral, real, and genteel in the universe. In more material realms, we can find Emerson or select quotations of his works selling everything from insurance policies to tennis shoes.[2] Less favorable renderings have, since his own lifetime, depicted Emerson as too dreamy, a little foolish, maybe even insane. These sundry characterizations could indicate that the object in question—either the person of Emerson or his work—is, finally, all of these things, depending on the angle of vision applied. That one person or one thing could be so multifarious, so contradictory in nature requires further thought. Possibly the angles of vision—the modes of reading employed in identifying and defining Emerson—are responsible for producing different objects, all of which are called "Emerson." While I admit that a multiplicitous Emerson intrigues me from a philosophical perspective (is Emerson the same pie, regardless of how we slice him?), the effect of these angles of vision proves pressing enough to require sustained consideration.

That different "Emersons" arise from different ways of reading will surprise no one. Of course there will be good and bad methods of reading—some people do not read well or carefully or thoughtfully or at all. Accordingly, the bad or careless or thoughtless reader will proceed via an angle that distorts Emerson or simply gets him "wrong." I will suggest, however, that even "good" (or at least "better") methods of reading, even those knowledgeable of and respectful of their endeavor, even those intent on objectivity or judiciousness or broadmindedness or even generosity nullify reading. Such a suggestion necessitates explication of what we (i.e., American readers, American scholars, products and purveyors of American literary culture) have commonly called "reading," the methods by which we have practiced "reading," and especially the ends of our "reading." For it will become clear, in looking at serious and influential readers of Emerson, that certain ends yield certain Emersons and require the adoption of peculiar methods. Again, this may not be surprising. I hope, though, that by developing a clear enough picture of some of those ends and some of those methods, I will sufficiently startle or disturb readers into thinking again about their own means, their own purposes—into rereading, as it were, their own readings.

To do so, I will draw on and tease out Emerson's own provocations regarding the uses of literature. One use that approaches abuse, one end at which reading should *not* arrive, according to the essay "The American Scholar," is an end that stops at the limit of the author. Describing the sort of reading in which the "sacredness which attaches to the act of creation,—the act of thought,—is instantly transferred to the record," Emerson theorizes that such a reading mistakes the meaning of the text for the person of the author, which in turn imbues a text with the author's personal value: "The poet chanting, was felt to be a divine man. Henceforth the chant is divine also. The writer was a just and wise spirit. Henceforward it is settled, the book is perfect; as love of the hero corrupts into worship of his statue. Instantly, the book becomes noxious. The guide is a tyrant."[3] Although Emerson complains here about the corrupting deification of the author, the same results come from authorial demonizing. Both practices are based on an estimation of the author's personal worth and use his or her established status to settle the value and meaning of the book. Once the foundation of the book is set, certain edifices inevitably will follow, "hence arises a grave mischief." "Colleges are built on it. Books are written on it by thinkers, not by Man Thinking; by men of talent, that is, who start wrong, who set out from accepted dogmas, not from their own sight of principles."[4]

But if I am attempting to place Emerson's works in the service of challenging questionable reading practices, what prevents my efforts from operating under what could merely be deemed a different set of accepted dogmas, from simply saddling Emerson and his works with other values? In turning to Emerson's writing to think about reading, shouldn't I have already settled questions about his writing? These are serious questions that demand something other than answers; the nature of my study requires that these questions continually be asked, that my own principles, methods, and ends undergo repeated examination and revision.

Principles: Of Ridding and Reading

Our literary history makes clear that the *figure* of Emerson has created numerous problems for American readers of Emerson's *texts*. Accordingly, my first step is to suggest that to read Emerson we must rid ourselves of Emerson.[5] Ridding entails observing the cultural practice of settling on a singular meaning for Emerson and attempting to avoid it. This involves foregoing equations wherein Emerson = x or even "The American Scholar" = y. After ridding us of Emerson, the work of reading an Emerson essay includes such tasks as recognizing the questions the essay asks its would-be readers, suggesting possible responses to those questions, and reflecting on the consequences of being so questioned.

This line of questioning is necessary because all readers are subject to various institutions of interpretation—a subjection perhaps inseparable from the ways in which we have learned to experience texts. The institutional nature of interpretation is as much (if not more) the object of my study as are Emerson and his works. It is precisely this institutional or cultural settling that reading must challenge. In short, I plan to unsettle the literary institutions wherein the meaning of Emerson is kept. And this entails a persistent engagement with "the institution of any kind," from the popular to the biographical, the belletristic to the philosophical. Consider a complaint and response from "The American Scholar": "The book, the college, the school of art, the institution of any kind, stop with some past utterance of genius. This is good, say they,—let us hold by this. They pin me down. They look backward and not forward. But genius always looks forward. The eyes of man are set in his forehead, not in his hindhead. Man hopes. Genius creates."[6] Pinned down by academic assessments and nonacademic appropriations, Emerson's text has suffered a denaturing that has bereft the words of their ongoing, multiplying, and metamorphosing significance. These readings, far from inspiring, rest on a hindheaded "looking back" at Emerson, a stopping with his past utterance that disconnects the literary text from its relations to nature and to the reader. Looking backward at literature empties reading of the possibilities for hope and creation. Consequently, ridding ourselves of the retrospective settlement of Emerson may improve our prospects for reading.

A related principle regards questions of time. Hopeful, creative, inspiring reading must evolve from extended meditation on the temporality (in both senses of the word, "impermanence" and "pertaining to the nature of time") of interpretation. The problem with seeing that looks backward is precisely that it looks *backward,* metaphorically casts the eyes unidirectionally into the past. The modus operandi of institutionalist reading is linked on the one hand with talent and dogma, on the other hand with stopping or arresting the "natural flux" of the text (by which I mean an unpredictable movement inherent to the nature of textuality). Genius, then, as opposed to mere talent, means seeing in such a way as to overcome the backward fixing of one's gaze and means always reckoning time as a factor in textual and interpretive relations. Reading Emerson with regard to temporality will involve participating in the ongoing nature of interpretation, a participation contingent on foregoing the institutional, the past, the holding to and pinning down of Emerson within specific, unchanging, unnatural relations.

Methods: Of Nature and Scholarship

One of the many passages of Emerson's writing that directly challenges readers at the very moment of reading occurs in "The Over-Soul": "The learned and the studious of thought have no monopoly of wisdom. Their violence of direction in some degree disqualifies them to think truly."[7] The learned and the studious, the scholarly and the well read, it would seem, are especially prone to learning in a manner that removes thought—as if the activity of thinking was to be kept well away from the act of reading. In subsequent chapters, I will test the validity of this claim by examining the sort of thinking that goes on in readings of Emerson. If scholars—presumably among the best trained and most qualified of American readers—have disqualified themselves from truly thinking, we need to know why and whether something can be done to requalify our reading.

Judging from Emerson's own study of "The American Scholar," one surmises that studious violence of direction results from a neglect of nature. In that essay, Emerson observes that nature is a web (or weave or text, from the Latin *textus:* "that which is woven, web, texture" [*Oxford English Dictionary*], as it will appear in other essays) without end or beginning. He charges the scholar—commonly considered to be concerned with books—to study this boundless system, this "system on system shooting like rays, upward, downward, without centre, without circumference," primarily because

> the first in time and the first in importance of the influences upon the mind is that of nature. Every day, the sun; and, after sunset, night and her stars. Ever the winds blow; ever the grass grows. Every day, men and women, conversing, beholding and beholden. The scholar must needs stand wistful and admiring before this great spectacle. He must settle its value in his mind. What is nature to him? There is never a beginning, there is never an end to the inexplicable continuity of this web of God, but always circular power returning into itself. Therein it resembles his own spirit, whose beginning, whose ending he never can find,—so entire, so boundless.[8]

The scholar, regardless of academic discipline, must be mindful of the firstness of nature and must maintain an awareness of nature's primary influence on the mind. Nature, which has no first and no last, comes first, conditioning the mind and the phenomena by which nature itself is to be known.

This perhaps explains why it is the *relation* of nature to the mind of the scholar that warrants attention—the text does not ask, What is nature? but, "What is nature to him?" The distinction matters because nature (comprising suns and stars and days and nights and people conversing, etc.) has neither beginnings nor ends and cannot, therefore, be known in its entirety, cannot be comprehended. Nature can be known only relationally, through an endless process of observation, speculation, and adjustment of the means by which its measure is taken. And this is true for the scholar as well— that is, the mind or the spirit of the scholar, resembling nature, has no beginning and no end. It, too, needs to be considered a *textus,* or complex system. Thinking about nature or any of its constituents requires that two vast and intricate systems come into contact with one another. The scholar, situated in the multidirectional web of nature, must acknowledge this condition in order to properly perform her or his duties. It is because of this that "so much of nature as he is ignorant of, so much of his own mind does he not yet possess. And, in fine, the ancient precept, 'Know thyself,' and the modern precept, 'Study nature,' become at last one maxim."[9]

But how in the world does this pertain to the reading of books? "The American Scholar" announces that not until the value of nature has been acknowledged (and the similar value of the scholar's own mind been evaluated) can the scholar appraise the value or meaning of literature. Indeed, the essay situates the office of the scholar precisely between the study of the text of nature and the study of the texts of literature, which interstice the scholar must traverse. To eschew these traversals is to disconnect books from nature and thus disqualify oneself from truly thinking. Since this is our common practice, the notion of the American scholar as transcending the static noun (as a "mere thinker") and instead functioning as an ecstatic verb ("Man Thinking")[10] has not yet been realized, and "instead of Man Thinking, we have the bookworm. Hence, the book-learned class, who value books, as such; not as related to nature and the human constitution."[11] Hence the advent of scholars exempting themselves from relations with nature, out of time and out of touch. The bookworm burrows into and feeds on books, crawling away from its relations with the world and into an unnaturally literary existence. "Hence, the restorers of readings, the emendators, the bibliomaniacs of all degrees"—B.A., M.A., Ph.D.[12]

Emerson's essay accuses scholars of having abdicated their office, but also proposes a way out of the "grave mischief"[13] they have wrought. That way is through the cultivation of new methods, wise to the workings of nature and time and text, and to the bearing they have on whatever else one studies. Such methods are called for if one cares to *use* literature—read, write, or teach it—in a principled manner. "What is the right use? What is the one end which all means go to effect? They are for nothing but to inspire." Perhaps *inspire* means here something different from (or at least in addition to) infusing a reader with divine influence. Since the infinitive is not followed by anything specific, it could be that books are to be understood as breathing life into our relations with nature; and/or that readers are to breathe life back into books by reading them in relation to nature; and/or that reading should prompt us to relate to books and to nature in a different way. In any event, inspiration, Emerson writes, is the right use of literature, the end of reading.

How are we to attain such an elusive end? Given "our preposterous use of books,"[14] we have consistently ignored the nature of our business and have ended where we should have begun. Due to this untimely, unnatural, methodological violence of direction, our reading has seldom inspired but has, rather, expired. I try to redress this condition by a roughly threefold method: I examine the ways Emerson has been read, explicate those readings in connection with Emerson's writing, and extrapolate from these examinations and explications a general theory of (or what I will eventually call a natural philosophy of) reading. Throughout, I attempt to make my study answer to nature, to test my findings with larger questions of textuality, and to shun violence of direction in favor of a set of interpretations prompted by metaphors.

Chapter 1 begins with a study of the troping of Emerson's work as a "tonic" to be taken in by ailing subjects and follows the course of the trope from its prominent role in popular culture to its appropriation by formidable critics. The significance of the pharmaceutical encapsulation of Emerson is that his writing becomes something to be ingested, which means further that the act of reading is reduced to consumption for the sake of therapeutic care. Juxtaposing the prescription of Emerson as elixir with Emerson's own admonitions regarding literary consumptions, I adduce the problems involved in reading Emerson's texts and begin to speculate on a counterpractice to such problems. An instance of Emerson's early writing, "The Lord's Supper," metaphorically informs this counterpractice with its inquiry into ritualistic institutions of consumption. The next chapter examines peculiar uses of Emerson's name and his writing. Focusing on the essay "Self-Reliance" and its fate at the hand of success writers of the nineteenth century, I find that these writers forge a palimpsest of Emerson's work, altering the meanings of the text by employing it in the service of American business enterprise. After a comparison of this service to the work of scholars, "Self-Reliance" is then read against such uses, a reading that, by attending to the textual and contextual makeup of the paragraphs that constitute the essay, undermines the claims put upon it by its users. This results in the beginnings of a theory of interpretive responsibility, a crucial element in the natural philosophy of reading.

The third chapter discusses the various "Ralph Waldo Emersons" as portrayed in numerous biographies and ponders the extent to which the life of this "representative man" comes to account for and simplify the complexities of his writing. My analysis of the earliest biographies of Emerson reveals a process of "incorporation" of the Emerson text, in which the figure of Emerson is furnished with a body; his writing is made to cohere, to form one body or integral whole; and the body of Emerson and the body of his writings are synthesized to form another unitary body or uniform substance. Contrarily, Emerson's "Poetry and Imagination" brings into question prevailing notions of the author, the work of literature, and traditional methods of interpretation that permeate even our most current and theoretically informed approaches to reading. Comparing Nietzsche's *gaya scienza* with the *gai science* from Emerson's "Poetry and Imagination," I provide a figure for makeshift and mobile reading, a provisional version of ways in which a reader might experience textuality. This leads to an elaboration of the theory of the relations between literary texts and the text of nature. Chapter 4 proceeds with the hypothesis that attaching the person of Emerson to his writing arrests the movement of that writing. The chapter begins with a theoretical discussion of the conditions and consequences of biographical criticism and authorial intention. Next, returning to the specific case of Emerson, I bring forth a series of provocations regarding nature, vision, and textuality. This is followed by a comparison of the uses of Emerson in nature writing with twentieth-century biographers whose work constitutes a conquest of Emerson's nature.

The subsequent chapter examines the figure of Emerson in American studies in light of a critique of literary objectification. This critique is assembled at the beginning of the chapter through a reading of Emerson's *Nature,* a reading that espouses a theory of interpretation grounded in vision and textuality and is then applied to the work of influential Americanists. One set of these scholars is bent on overcoming so-called subjective reading practices in favor of objectivity, resulting in the creation of a certain version of Emerson that could then stand for a certain version of America. The other set, distraught over the state of art in America, calls for a different Emerson, one who would aid criticism in a quest for "inner standards" to replace the "outer standards" America had lost. The practice that creates these Emersons and these Americas, objectification, involves a radical separation of the self from everything else: the self as object and objectifier sees the world through a frame of practical diligence and conforms the objects of vision to its frame.

Ends: Of Preposterous Reading

In chapter 6, I further develop a natural philosophy of reading through an engagement with Emerson's essay "Experience." Such a philosophy is made necessary by the acknowledgment that reading, as commonly practiced, is a preposterous act, "preposterousness" itself. This odd word, set off by well-deserved scare quotes, contains two meanings that I wish to keep in circulation. One of these meanings involves contrariness, especially being "contrary to the order of nature, or to reason or common sense; monstrous; irrational; perverse, foolish, nonsensical; in latter use, utterly absurd" (OED). The other older sense comes from the Latin prae ("before") and posterus ("coming after") and means roughly "with the first last and the last first"—or, again as the OED has it, "having or placing last that which should be first."

The argument, in sum, is that preconceptions of the nature of interpretation and of the nature of the literary object prohibit reading, due mainly to tendencies toward one direction (the subjective) or another (the objective). Subjective reading posits that the subject who reads or writes comes before the text that is to be read; conversely, objective reading posits that the text comes first. In both, time is only linear, interpretation must comply to this linearity, and reading's object and subject positions go unquestioned. I suggest, following lines from Emerson's text (although, as the poet remarks in "Uriel," "Line in nature is not found"),[15] that subject and object are to be thought of as relational and that this thinking involves a rethinking of nature—nature's nature, reading's nature, our nature.

These lines have seldom been followed in the history of making sense of Emerson, which explains why much of my study is concerned with understanding where we go wrong as readers of the Emerson text and where we end up as a result of our wrong turns. The effects of attending to preposterousness are such that many renowned and beloved interpreters of Emerson, who have no doubt made important contributions to the conservation of Emerson's reputation, will be represented in a different light. I mean no disrespect to or belittlement of these contributions, nor do I mean to imply that I am better than those I am reading, that I have access to the "real" Emerson. I am subject to the same conditions, shortcomings, and missteps as those I am covering—indeed, this will be all too apparent in my use of Emerson and in my readings of his readers. But the hope for Emerson's text and the hope for reading arise from seeing (and learning to live with) the preposterousness that shapes our methods of interpretation. Thus my own approach, as misbegotten as it may be, is but a beginning, the end of which is to acknowledge that we commonly put the last first and the first last when we read—and to suggest other methods and principles of reading.

In conclusion, I am introducing here an investigation of the extent to which the act of reading Emerson, of making Emerson mean, has been and must be preposterous—an act in which the uses to which Emerson will be put come *before* reading, altering both the process of the textual encounter and the nature of the text itself. That the first and last have changed positions, however, is consistently forgotten or denied by preposterous practitioners. In such a schematic, reading must always be somewhat absurd, perverse, monstrous; it must be a memory of what has not yet happened, a rehearsing of the future, a prediction of the past. Interpretation's prospects lie in acknowledging preposterousness and in an attendant willingness to rethink the spatiotemporal dimensions of reading. If interpretation is, as the word indicates, a "movement between," perhaps it can be seen as a movement between the "post" and the "pre," between the conditions that cause and are caused by our methods of reading. These interpretive transitions, I argue, are called for in many of Emerson's writings and especially in his theories of the textual nature of nature.

By critically examining these transitions and speculating on their consequences, we can perhaps better understand the nature of text, the nature of reading, the text of nature, and the textual nature of our interpretation of the worlds in which we live. And I trust that this indicates something of what, in the end, I am finally after. I care much less about establishing or resuscitating the real Emerson than I do about finding a way of reading that might lead readers into a nature of which we are always a part but from which we commonly feel alienated. This nature is no mean woods or earthly garden or vast wilderness, but is rather a complex set of relations involving living beings, life itself, time, cosmos, *physis*... Nature, we read in "Spiritual Laws," may be simple, but it is a complex simplicity, the understanding of which requires earnest openness, tireless patience, endless self-scrutiny, and learning new relations between the myriad components of its text. "The simplicity of nature is not that which may easily

be read, but is inexhaustible. The last analysis can no wise be made."[16]
Living in relation to this nature—living up to new relations—demands a
certain transcendence, and I see this less as an "escape from" than as engaged "movement within," for the sake of initiating new relations (or what
Emerson calls "onwardness"). This would not be rising above our nature
but moving within it to gain a different perspective, time and time again:
"To make habitually a new estimate,—that is elevation."[17] To habitually
attempt to gain perspective on our present habits—such is transcendental
speculation.

In rethinking nature and natural relations and in allowing this new nature to inform new ways of thinking, we might be said to be readying
ourselves to read the texts that come before us. I guess this amounts to
learning from nature how to read, or learning from reading nature how
to think, and must constitute what "Spiritual Laws" calls a healthy mindfulness: "The intellectual life may be kept clean and healthful, if man will
live the life of nature, and not import into his mind difficulties which are
none of his."[18] Finding out which difficulties are native to reading and
which are imported is the first step in elevating our perspective—the necessary first step in learning to read naturally: "The wild fertility of nature
is felt in comparing our rigid names and reputations with our fluid consciousness. We pass in the world for sects and schools, for erudition and
piety, and we are all the time jejune babes."[19] My hope is that by comparing the rigid naming, reputing, and fixing of Emerson with the fluid text
of nature and consciousness, we will transcend scholarship that deadens
wisdom and uses of literature that destroy. Then might we be ready to begin
to read and to inspire.

1 The Consumption of Emerson

Did our own imaginations transfigure dry
remainder-bisquit into ambrosia?
—James Russell Lowell

In the preface to "the first selection of Emerson criticism ever made," Stephen Whicher lamented the "relegation" of Emerson "to the large shelf of moral tonics, from Plutarch to Tupper, whom past ages highly valued but for whom ours has lost the taste."[1] While this devaluation is undoubtedly worthy of note, that condition has been somewhat redressed, as attested by the flourishing of what Lawrence Buell has called the "Emerson industry."[2] Since the last half of the twentieth century Emerson has been repeatedly revalued by an array of assayers measuring with a compendium of scales. Nevertheless, two particular aspects of this devaluation warrant attention—the relegation of Emerson to a shelved vial of "moral tonic" and the subsequent loss of taste for that tonic. In some ways, the first of these is the opposite of a devaluation: instead of resulting from diminishing popularity, the bottling of Emerson as a moral tonic ensues from overpopularization. Sadly, for Whicher, Emerson has been overvalued for the wrong reasons and consequently has been converted into a popular panacea; more sadly still, that panacea is no longer taken and gathers a pharmacy's dust.

Both the preparation of Emerson into a restorative and the dwindling desire to partake of it indicate the notion that the writer and his work have a certain *flavor*. Whicher rues an age of damaged taste buds, an age of readers who not only have had the bad taste to reduce Emerson to a tonic but who also have lost the taste for that tonic altogether. By no means an uncommon trope for describing our likes and dislikes of writers and their work, "a taste of Emerson" has been particularly useful to commentators on American literature and culture and signifies a proclivity for the figurative ingestion of his writings. As early as Oliver Wendell Holmes's tribute, Emerson's words were found to be "in a high degree tonic, bracing, strengthening to the American."[3] With acerbic wit, H. L. Mencken registered his disgust for the ability of New Thought purveyors to appropriate and monopolize the "mellifluous [i.e., honeyed] obscurity" of Emerson's writings, which had resulted in "a debased Transcendentalism rolled into pills for fat women with vague pains and inattentive husbands."[4]

The tropic encapsulation of Emerson into a placebo was tampered with nearly a half century later, becoming a similar sort of potion in the writing of Kenneth Burke. Discussing the legacy of transcendentalism by returning to Emerson's *Nature,* Burke wrote that "an enemy might want to rate this early essay of Emerson's as hardly other than a Happiness Pill. But I admit: I find it so charming, I'd be willing to defend it even on that level, it is so buoyant."[5] Burke, instead of challenging the bottling of Emerson or the narcotic effect of *Nature,* defends the troping of the essay as a pill because that pill improves the mood of the person who takes it in: "If only like loving a pleasant dream, love him for his idealistic upsurge. For *it reads well.* It is medicine."[6] For Burke, *Nature* simultaneously reads well and makes one well. The emphasis in the second sentence subjoins the third to it, making the essay's medicinal quality a part of the fact that it reads well; or perhaps the italics indicate that a good read is more important than good medicine, but that the two undoubtedly are closely related. In any case, the aspects of the essay that Burke combines signify that reading and taking medicine have something to do with one another, might even be substitutions for one another. Most significantly, reading is posited as a form of therapy and as a process of internalization. In Burke's metaphorizing of *Nature,* Emerson's writing is to be internalized, taken in, *consumed,* for the therapeutic purpose of healing the sick self.

I stress the word above to move the discussion more quickly to the point: there is something consumptive in the way American readers have read Emerson. There is, however, something in Emerson's writings that, I will argue, attempts to resist such consumption; and yet, there is as well a quality to Emerson's writing that evidences the consumptive practices he otherwise would resist. To understand this argument and the stakes in making it, we must briefly look at the somewhat subtle definition of *consumption* on which such an argument is predicated. To consume something is to eat it, to ingest it, to take it into ourselves, from the Latin *consumere,* which means roughly "to take completely, to devour or destroy." We not only consume things but we are consumed by things: passion, fire, greed, desire, tuberculosis (which claimed the lives of several members of Emerson's family). There are thus two modes of consumption—eating and being eaten, taking in completely and being completely taken in. The ambiguity of the term makes it a viable trope for a peculiar if widespread mode of reading.

Eating has a long history of service as a metaphor for what we do to texts. Among investigations of this service, Steven Mailloux's "The Use and Abuse of Fiction: Readers Eating Books" begins with two epigraphs, the first from Francis Bacon's "Of Studies" (1597): "Reade not to contradict, nor to belieue, but to waigh and consider. Some bookes are to bee tasted, others to bee swallowed, and some few to bee chewed and digested."[7] The second, from a self-help book for girls in the 1890s (Annie H. Ryder's *Go Right On, Girls! Develop Your Bodies, Your Minds, Your Characters* [1891]), enjoins, "Do not read as a glutton eats. Digest your books, turn them into nourishment, make them a part of your life that lives always." In both cases, the metaphor of eating implies a parallel between the act of taking something into the body and the act of taking something into the mind: to paraphrase Yeats, one comes in at the mouth, one comes in at the eye. Certainly it is the very familiarity of this trope that prompted the *New York Times* to run ads for itself advocating consumption (e.g., see the book review of 26 January 1992). Those ads commenced with an eye-catching, bold, all-caps headline of one word: "DEVOUR." Below were four brief phrases: "Food for thought. Recipes for success. The world on a plate. Don't miss a day's worth." In this economy of information, reading is like eating, thinking is for success, and the world is our blue plate special.

This latter example, in particular, may seem innocuous—harmless ad copy employing a harmless metaphor. The metaphor, though, is far from harmless, for it indicates a propensity of American reading practices to destroy texts by internalizing them. This propensity originates from a larger tendency in Western thought (ceaselessly criticized by such writers as Emerson and Thoreau) to reduce constituent elements and aspects of the perceptual field to particularized *things*[8] and American consumers' culturally ingrained habit of appropriating—often unconsciously—objects for narrow and self-serving ends. Those ends, whether materialist or idealist in nature, are obtained through a practice that destroys the object. If reading must, by nature, involve a taking-in of the text, I propose, based on my own reading of Emerson and his consumers, that this may not necessitate the destruction of the taken-in. The matter turns precisely on the process of digestion or, to give the metaphor a rest, *use*.

In the history of the reception of Emerson texts, one can readily see how critics have neglected or disparaged or dismissed any value in those writings, for whatever reasons. If, however, taking a cue from Whicher, one looks at the various methods by which Emerson has been *conserved*, one can see diverse forms of appropriation at work, which, I will argue, are equally consumptive. By exploring some of the uses of Emerson's text and the ends to which Emerson has been put, we might better enable methods of interpretation that would make texts a part of our lives without destroying their nature and significance (rather actual or potential).

Calling on Emerson at the Address of Divinity

> The results are often astonishing, although I do not
> depend entirely on this form of counsel.
> —Napoleon Hill

An example of idealists' transfigurative use of the Emerson text occurs in what Mencken referred to as debased transcendentalism rolled into pills: New Thought. "A religious movement," as Richard Huber characterizes it, New Thought was "similar in many ways to Christian Science, devoted primarily to healing the sick in mind and body."[9] Getting its start at the end of the nineteenth century by combining success strategies with belief in mind cure techniques, New Thought grew into a vast amalgamation of creeds, viewpoints, and quasi-philosophical approaches to the maladies of everyday life.[10] This combination resulted in an impressive list of best-sellers, from Ralph Waldo Trine's *In Tune with the Infinite; or, Fullness of Peace, Power, and Plenty* (1897)[11] to Orison Swett Marden's more success-oriented publications to Norman Vincent Peale's *The Power of Positive Thinking* (1952).[12] "Eclectic in its borrowings from all types of speculation," New Thought relied heavily on textual consumption, developing a particular taste for the works of Emerson.[13] As Huber puts it, New Thought writers "permitted the complex simplicity of the American philosopher Emerson to speak to them most frequently and persuasively."[14] John G. Cawelti, who in his own history of the success gospel often reduces the work of Emerson to the "philosophy of self-reliance," reckons that Emerson's "conception of the Oversoul and his belief that the truly self-reliant individual could be transformed by uniting himself with powerful universal forces, were simplified and popularized in the 'New Thought' movement of the early twentieth century. In this movement, Emersonian self-reliance was metamorphosed into personal magnetism and made the key to a financial success available to all."[15] "In fact," observed Gail Thain Parker, "it is hard to find anything in the New Thought creed which Emerson did not say first."[16] This extensive borrowing and simplification leads Richard Weiss to employ an Emersonism to describe Emersonian appropriations: "In *The Transcendentalist,* Emerson stated that 'What is popularly called Transcendentalism among us, is Idealism; Idealism as it appears in 1842.' What was popularly called New Thought was idealism; idealism as it appeared in 1900."[17] What results from this simplification is an apotheosis of Emerson, an exaltation of his person and his writings that distorts the text of Emerson by enshrouding it in a mystical glow.

While New Thought authors drew frequently from Emerson's work, "well-intentioned plagiarism" dominated their writings.[18] "They had no scruples about adapting, quoting, and shamelessly borrowing the words of their own contemporaries."[19] A reviewer in *The Dial* commented that Orison Swett Marden's "labors, of the excerpting and arranging order, must have been something really appaling [*sic*]; and one is glad to reflect that his method was one which relieved him from the additional strain of severe and continuous thought."[20] Marden's *Peace, Power, and Plenty,* published a decade after Trine's *In Tune with the Infinite,* borrows chapter headings and concepts from Trine without citation, and thus in a sense consumes Trine's book.[21] Emerson, of course, is by no means neglected in this pillaging of words. *Pushing to the Front,* Marden's 1911 effort to combine the character building of success tracts with the spiritualism of New Thought, boasts over two score of acknowledged Emerson citations; as Parker has noted, Marden "took *The Conduct of Life* as gospel."[22] New Thought writers participated in a consumption of Emerson focused on his person and reputation, further obfuscating the complexity of his writing and worshipfully transfiguring the Concord Sage into a benevolent deity watching over practitioners of right thinking.

The best example of New Thought consumption, Trine's *In Tune with the Infinite* expounds a system of mind cure in which the self is responsible for illness and poverty. Disease must be exorcised by the self's affirmation of its identity with the Infinite: you are sick because you let your self "think sick." You are poor because you think poorly. If a man "holds the poverty thought," he will remain in poverty. "If he hold himself, whatever present conditions may be, continually in the thought of prosperity, he sets into operation forces that will sooner or later bring him into prosperous conditions."[23] The key to peace, power, and prosperity is to think one's way into union with the Infinite Spirit. "This Spirit of Infinite Life and Power that is back of all is what I call God," but it also goes by other names: "Kindly Light, Providence, the Over Soul, Omnipotence, or whatever term may be most convenient."[24] *The great central fact in human life, in your life and in mine, is the coming into a conscious, vital realization of our oneness with this Infinite Life.*"[25] Each of us, therefore, must be self-reliant and realize our oneness with the Over-Soul: "He who lives in the realization of his oneness with this Infinite Power becomes a magnet to attract to himself a continual supply of whatsoever he desires."[26] By appropriating elements of Emerson's writings and putting people to work on and for themselves, Trine describes an economy wherein we alone are our limitations; we, paradoxically, are never alone, full as we are with Infinite Life. In Trine's economy, it is the indisputably self-evident fact of our presence in the world that makes us responsible for taking care of ourselves. Health and wealth are made by the self's hard work, by its proper thinking, and by tuning into the Infinite.[27]

Although versions of self-reliance and the Over-Soul figure most prominently in Trine's work, numerous other Emersonian notions line the way to fullness of peace, power, and plenty. Circles, correspondence, the distinction between tuition and intuition, the Law of Compensation, the futility of traveling in search of peace, the dual nature of the world (the seen and the unseen, cause and effect, material and ideal)—each and all of these contribute to Trine's best-seller, to the realization of fullness, and to the deification of Emerson. Toward the beginning of *In Tune with the Infinite*, Trine relates a story that effectively situates Emerson in a pantheon of "God-men":

> While riding with a friend a few days ago, we were speaking of the great interest people are everywhere taking in the more vital things of life, the eagerness with which they are reaching out for a knowledge of the interior forces, their ever increasing desire to know themselves and to know their relations with the Infinite. And in speaking of the great spiritual awakening that is so rapidly coming all over the world, . . . I said, "How beautiful if Emerson, the illumined one so far in advance of his time, who labored so faithfully and so fearlessly to bring about these very conditions, how beautiful if he were with us today to witness it all! how he would rejoice!" "How do we know," was the reply, "that he is not witnessing it all? and more, that he is not having a hand in it all,—a hand even greater, perhaps, than when we saw him here?" Thank you, my friend, for this reminder.[28]

Witnessing it all, having a hand in it all, the illumined one is *here*, with us *right now*, watching over us and helping us help ourselves. The immortalizing of the presence of Emerson's being removes Emerson's words from the worldly realm of the readable. Such a removal effectually sacralizes the words, keeping them safe from critical analysis: Trine's work does not refer us to Emerson's, but rather insists that the true meaning of Emerson is always present. Consequently, Trine's access to Emerson's being makes him a channel for divine writing. Ralph Waldo the Son floats in the footsteps of Ralph Waldo the Father, and Trine becomes himself a divine writer. Offering advice to other aspiring scribes, Trine ties together writing, reading, and presence in a set of relations that houses all "true writers" at the address of divinity:

> Remember that an author can never write more than he himself is. If he would write more, then he must be more. He is simply his own amanuensis. He in a sense writes himself into his book. He can put no more into it than he himself is.
>
> If he is one of a great personality, strong in purpose, deep in feeling, open always to the highest inspirations, a certain indefinable something gets into his pages that makes them breathe forth a vital, living power, a power so great that each reader gets the same inspirations as those that spoke through the author. That that's written between the lines is many times more than that's written in the lines.[29]

To be your own amanuensis means, for Trine, that you let your pages breathe. Writing will be inspirational only insofar as it is respirational. Similarly, reading, instead of being a critical, an analytical, or even an interpretive act, becomes the immediate, respiratory reception of the breath of the eternal's dictation, a taking-in of the spoken Word: "each reader gets the same inspirations as those that spoke through the author."

This way of consuming a text allows the reader to internalize the writer's divine presence. That the writer is divine, especially *this* writer, is beyond question: "I had rather be an amanuensis of the Infinite God, as it is my privilege literally to be, than a slave to the formulated rules of any rhetorician, or to the opinions of any critic."[30] The Infinite God speaks through Trine; the words we read carry the breath of truth, unequivocal in their conveyance—we need only suck them up. To confirm this, Trine again calls on Emerson:

> It is this same spiritual power that the author of a great personality puts into his work, that causes it to go so rapidly from reader to reader; for the only way that any book circulates is from mouth to mouth, any book that reaches a large circulation. It is this that many times causes a single reader, in view of its value to himself, to purchase numbers of copies for others. "A good poem," says Emerson, "goes about the world offering itself to reasonable men, who read it

with joy and carry it to their reasonable neighbors. Thus it draws to it the *wise and generous souls,* confirming their secret thoughts, and through their sympathy *really publishing itself.*"[31]

Here Trine sanctifies consumption. To read is to inhale the truthful breath of Infinite Spirit (that "certain indefinable something" in the pages); to write is to exhale the truth into the mouths and down the throats of "reasonable neighbors." This strange practice of literary mouth-to-mouth resuscitation, Trine tells us, is condoned by the divine Emerson. Trine cites Emerson's "My book shall smell of the pines"[32] to warn off those who would read sacrilegiously: "Far better, gentle sage, to have it smell of the pines and resound with the hum of insects than to have it sound of the rules that a smaller type of man gets by studying the works of a few great, fearless writers like yourself, and formulating from what he thus gains a handbook of rhetoric."[33] The readers who will breathe in a book rather than study it will take in "something of vital value, something that will broaden, sweeten, enrich, and beautify their lives."[34] Consuming a book—taking it as gospel, taking its author as divine, taking its words as sacred, taking it *inside* and transmuting it into something else—allows us to be taken into the Infinite; any other method of reading leads us away, makes us "smaller men."

In Tune with the Infinite is thus a prototypic consumption of Emerson, one that deifies the author and renders the text of Emerson's writings knowable through mystical reception. Trine projects Emerson to an astral remove, whence the gentle sage watches over an economy of consumption. In this economy, we are to forego the frantic race for the accumulation of riches (although, as we will see, Emerson was used for these purposes by other writers) for the placid occupation of a "medium ground" of being: "When we come into the realization of the higher powers, we will then be able to give more attention to the real life, instead of giving so much to the piling up of vast possessions that hamper rather than help it. It is the medium ground that is the true solution here, the same as it is in all phases of life."[35] Trine envisions a middle-class happy land of serenity and "perennial joy" that everyone can inhabit. We do so, in Trine's economy, by consuming things: life, books, the world around us. "Wealth beyond a certain amount cannot be used, and when it cannot be used it then becomes a hindrance rather than an aid, a curse rather than a blessing."[36] "Using, wisely using, brings an ever renewing gain." "Then not by hoarding but by wisely using and ridding ourselves of things as they come, an ever renewing supply will be ours, a supply far better adapted to present needs than the old could possibly be."[37] Use and disposal are prescribed as a way of living, albeit one opposed to the accumulation of large fortunes, yet emphasizing the internalization of the world around us: the gathering up, the taking in, the discarding of the world for the sake of one's contentment. It is this very consumption, the wise using up of and disposing of something, that characterizes Trine's reading of Emerson.

And reading itself is figured as nothing other than mystical ingestion. Trine's *In Tune with the Infinite* gives scant attention to the actual text of Emerson's writing and to contexts in which passages occur. Instead, the gist of Emerson has been gleaned, cleaned, and transfigured into parts that fit happily with Trine's divine middle ground of satisfied being. What methods provide the gist, the grist for Trine's mill? This is a difficult question to answer satisfactorily, for methodology has been swallowed up in principles and ends. How particular aspects of Emerson's text occur inside Trine as "the truth" is nothing short of a mystery, for the intellectual exercise of interpretation is taken for granted, the nature of texts utterly neglected, and the contexts in which texts are produced and received dismissed as inconsequential. A nebulous notion of Emerson results from a misty encounter with his writing; through the mist, a divine Emerson emerges. The text of Emerson is to be understood through the deific dress with which the figure is now draped; thus clad, Emerson and his writings participate properly in the economy of consumption. Situated as God of the Medium Ground, as Grand Master of the Infinite, Emerson warrants reverence rather than reading.

While Trine's spiritualism brings with it a certain materialist increase— personal "Peace" is attractive because it promises "Plenty"—others obtain purely materialist ends through the spiritualist intake of the Emerson corpus. Both methods disfigure the text through an other-worldly consumption of Emerson's writing. This becomes strikingly clear in Napoleon Hill's 1937 classic success manual, *Think and Grow Rich*.[38] Cawelti, linking *Think and Grow Rich* to Dale Carnegie's *How to Win Friends and Influence People* and Norman Vincent Peale's *The Power of Positive Thinking*, sees these works as the "lineal descendants of nineteenth-century success books" in that "they stress the same central themes": the availability of success; the privileging of individual will over environment, heredity, or other conditions; and the view of America as "a land of uniquely unlimited opportunity and freedom."[39] Such books as Hill's differ from nineteenth-century success manuals in that while the latter asserted that the individual's will could change the individual's surroundings, these twentieth-century works no longer emphasize "the will's impact on reality. For them, the changing of the individual's mental outlook, the transformation of 'negative' into 'positive' thinking, has become more important than the control of external reality."[40] This form of idealism, turned toward material gain, concentrates mental energy on the self and its performance against a world viewed as always radically antagonistic.

Hill's *Think and Grow Rich* is remarkable among such works for many reasons: its insistence that "you can never have riches in great quantities *unless* you can work yourself into a white heat of *desire* for money, and actually *believe* you will possess it";[41] its putative possession of a secret for accumulating wealth, passed along to Hill personally by Andrew Carnegie and hidden in over a hundred places in the pages; and especially its extolling of "a few men of outstanding achievement, each of whom was known to have been of a highly sexed nature" and who were capable of "transmuting sex energy" into their particular geniuses.[42] Although these elements are worthy of discussion, it is a further service to which Emerson is called that merits my attention.

The final of Hill's thirteen "steps toward riches" involves what he terms the "sixth sense." This phenomenon, "the apex of the philosophy" of *Think and Grow Rich,* comprises "that portion of the subconscious mind which has been referred to as the creative imagination. It has also been referred to as the 'receiving set' through which ideas, plans, and thoughts flash into the mind. The flashes are sometimes called hunches or inspirations."[43] According to Hill, these flashes are the means by which one enters into communication with "Infinite Intelligence." Just as with Trine, the Truth comes through the Infinite's exhalation, which is to be inhaled or "received." It, too, is beyond analysis: "The sixth sense defies description! It cannot be described to a person who has not mastered the other principles of this philosophy. . . . Understanding of the sixth sense comes only by meditation through mind development *from within.*"[44] To better describe the sixth sense, to help readers take that thirteenth step toward riches, Hill records his personal method for tapping the Infinite Intelligence:

> Long before I had ever written a line for publication or endeavored to deliver a speech in public, I followed the habit of reshaping my own character by trying to imitate the nine men whose lives and lifeworks had been most impressive to me. These nine men were Emerson, Paine, Edison, Darwin, Lincoln, Burbank, Napoleon, Ford, and Carnegie. Every night, over a long period of years, I held an imaginary council meeting with this group whom I called my "invisible counselors."
>
> The procedure was this. Just before going to sleep at night, I would shut my eyes and see, in my imagination, this group of men seated with me around my council table. Here I had not only an opportunity to sit among those whom I considered to be great, but I actually dominated the group, by serving as chairman.

I had a very definite purpose in indulging my imagination through these nightly meetings. My purpose was to rebuild my own character so it would represent a composite of the characters of my imaginary counselors. Realizing, as I did early in life, that I had to overcome the handicap of birth in an environment of ignorance and superstition, I deliberately assigned myself the task of voluntary rebirth through the method I have described above.[45]

We can see in this astonishing passage the foundation for what is perhaps *the* prototypic consumption of Emerson. By reading Emerson in his way (acquainting himself with the "life and lifework" of Emerson) and subsequently employing "creative imagination," Hill is capable of summoning Emerson from his residence in the Infinite Intelligence, seating Emerson at his table, and "dominating" Emerson—along with Andrew Carnegie, Luther Burbank, Henry Ford, and the rest—all for the purpose of "voluntary rebirth" of the self. Reading, in this program, is not a critical interaction with text, and decidedly does not require a self-reflective analysis of the process of interpretation, but is rather a self-serving application of "flashes" or "hunches" to the writings and biography of an already elevated object. Through these means, Hill is reborn with a little bit of Emerson et al. *inside himself.*

Somewhat guardedly, Hill confesses, "This is the first time that I have had the courage to mention this," and "I have been emboldened now to reduce my experience to the printed page because I am now less concerned about what 'they say' [meaning critics? or disgruntled counselors, perhaps?] than I was in the years that have passed." And, while he insists, "Lest I be misunderstood, I wish here to state most emphatically that I still regard my cabinet meetings as being purely imaginary,"[46] Hill also observes:

My method of addressing the members of the imaginary cabinet would vary, according to the traits of character which I was, for the moment, most interested in acquiring. I studied the records of their lives with painstaking care. After some months of this nightly procedure, I was astounded by the discovery that these imaginary figures became apparently *real.*

Each of these nine men developed individual characteristics, which surprised me.[47]

Emerson is addressed according to a preconceived notion of the traits Hill is "most interested in acquiring." The strength of his desire and the persistence of his practice enable Hill the consumer to realize his dreams. Creative imagination brings Emerson and the others to life *inside of* Hill, who is startled by their presence. Hill, in making the counselors real and "dominating" them, becomes responsible for their reality. Asking them questions, he is given answers from the Infinite Intelligence—"It" speaks through them, they through him. The counselors begin to become so real to Hill that he temporarily discontinues the practice, fearing that they might somehow come to dominate him. Later, however, he is able to resume the confabulations, even upping the ante:

> My original purpose in conducting council meetings with imaginary beings was solely that of impressing my own subconscious mind, through the principle of autosuggestion, with certain characteristics which I desired to acquire. In more recent years, my experimentation has taken on an entirely different trend. I now go to my imaginary counselors with every difficult problem which confronts me and my clients. The results are often astonishing, although I do not depend entirely on this form of counsel.[48]

Reading and internalizing the object of that reading, Hill is able to acquire what he wants, receive the truths he seeks, and thereby think his way to riches. Consumption, then, is a way of taking texts that disengages select parts and draws those parts into oneself, for oneself. Hill's consumption of Emerson, his celebration of an Emersonian eucharist, enables him a rebirth and a growth toward wealth at the expense of an utter decontextualizing of and subsequent destruction of Emerson's writing, even though much of that writing calls into question the very uses to which it has been put. Such textual questioning, however, is nullified by Hill's refiguring of Emerson.

In the work of Ralph Waldo Trine and Napoleon Hill, we can see some of the uses of the divine Emerson in American popular culture. That figure results from a method of reading that consumes Emerson's writing. Consumptive reading destroys the complexities of a text through a process of internalizing, conserves the result of the simplification of the text, maintains that such a result is *the* meaning of the text, and employs that meaning to substantiate particular economic and/or metaphysical systems. Even if reading may be said to always involve internalizing texts to some extent, taking in or taking on texts need not result in textual destruction. What causes consumptive reading to destroy its object is that, acting on desires formed within a peculiar economy, such a practice seizes on the use-value of particular aspects of a text and invalidates aspects contrary to that use-value. Consequently the text has meaning only insofar as it answers to the desires of the reader. In terms of preposterousness, the desired meaning for a text *precedes* the text, hence the text *follows* a path laid out for it by the reader's desires. One might wish to argue that this seemingly "unprofessional" practice of consumptive reading is perhaps to be expected in "popular" works—works that, although purporting to be true and corroborated by many authorities, do not attempt to pass themselves off as necessarily "scholarly" or "critical." As I described earlier, however, the worry over the *flavor* of Emerson also marks "scholarly" and "critical" studies. Emerson's writing is put to use in these readings in a way different from—but no less consumptive than—that of *Think and Grow Rich* or *In Tune with the Infinite*. I will examine other popular uses of Emerson in the next chapter, hoping to better understand the mechanics of consumptive reading; for the moment, I will turn again to the critic and then to various approaches to consumption in some of Emerson's writing.

Discriminating Palates

James Russell Lowell, in his impressions after hearing an 1868 Emerson lecture, promotes a process of receiving Emerson similar to that described by Trine and Hill: the homogenization, distillation, and transubstantiation of the lecturer's speech and presence are depicted as necessary for feeding "the never-sated hunger of self-culture."[49] Observing that "few men have been so much to so many,"[50] Lowell portrays an already purified Emerson as himself a purifier: "Perhaps some of us hear more than the mere words, are moved by something deeper than the thoughts? If it be so, we are quite right, for it is thirty years and more of 'plain living and high-thinking' that speak to us in this altogether unique lay-preacher. . . . If ever there was a standing testimonial to the cumulative power and value of Character (and we need it sadly in these days), we have it in this gracious and dignified presence. What an antiseptic is a pure life!"[51] We are right, Lowell claims, to make Emerson's words into something else; those words are to be passed through the alembic of Emerson's life, where they are purified and might then purify us. The ejaculation regarding "an antiseptic" and "a pure life" can mean both that Emerson's reputed pure living has been an antiseptic and that he now can be taken *as* an antiseptic, a purifying potion. Homogenized, Emerson's words offer consumers their own homogenization. Lowell attaches this apothecary apotheosis to Emerson's person, characterizing the process as natural for adherents of self-culture and therefore laudable. In keeping with his metaphorizing of interpretation as consumption, Lowell attributes the metaphor and the process it describes to a form of distillation: "I suppose it is not the Emerson of 1868 to whom we listen. For us the whole life of the man is distilled in the clear drop of every sentence, and behind each word we divine the force of a noble character, the weight of a large capital of thinking and being. We do not go to hear what Emerson says so much as to hear Emerson."[52] His life distilled into his words and decanted into a chalice for self-cultural consumption, Emerson undergoes purification so that he might purify. The resultant admixture is so potent that we no longer need to listen to his "mere words"; rather, we need merely drink in his presence.

This "critical" homogenization—as opposed to the "popular" work of New Thought adherents—of Emerson's life and the distillation of that life into words combine in a multiform process that dilutes the significance of Emerson's writing. Reading Emerson becomes again an act of interiorizing the words. An intellectually dynamic interaction with the writing is deemphasized and replaced with a visceral experiencing of that writing within oneself. The interpretive process thus takes shape as a series of consumptions that ultimately limits or destroys much of the import of what the writer of "The Poet" referred to as "the double meaning, or, shall I say, the quadruple, or the centuple, or much more manifold meaning, of every sensuous fact."[53] In one part of the process, being is substituted for meaning—Emerson's life (after homogenization) replaces the "manifold meaning" of his writing. Accordingly, interpretation becomes hearing (or, by extension, reading) "Emerson," taking Emerson's life (distilled into his words) into oneself, possessing and being possessed by the pure being of Emerson.

The table is thereby set for a complete transformation of Emerson's words into a magical substance to be taken into one's body. In the paragraph following Emerson's distillation, Lowell exonerates the tendency to turn Emerson into a preternatural source of (spiritual) nourishment. After comparing the experience of hearing Emerson to receiving "unhoped-for food," he addresses unbelievers thus: "Cynics might say what they liked. Did our own imaginations transfigure dry remainder-bisquit into ambrosia? At any rate, he brought us *life*, which, on the whole, is no bad thing."[54] At any rate, the text of Emerson's mortal words no longer remain, having been replaced by transfigured food-of-the-gods. The critic's apology for Emerson becomes a transubstantiation of the writing into a holy, life-giving concoction of speech and presence, a divine comestible to be consumed by a needy public in difficult times. Hence the critical preoccupation with the figurative ingestion of Emerson's writings results in a transformation of those writings into a body of work that no longer needs to be read. Instead, readers are metaphorically encouraged to close their eyes, open their mouths, and receive the consecrated wafer.

The consumption of Emerson described in this critical transubstantiation has serious consequences for both the meaning of Emerson's writing and the act of reading. As we have seen, the transfigurative processing of Emerson fixes Emerson's writing with a certain consecrated meaning, which is less to be read than to be reverently received. The writing is reduced to a stable form (a tonic, a wafer, a pill) separable from contextual relations, a whole unto itself. Meaning thus is encapsulated, prescribable, ready for ingestion. As such, the act of reading Emerson becomes a eucharistic experiencing of the host instead of the active interpretation of a text.

The metaphorical transfiguring of Emerson results in the production of peculiar versions of Emerson the man and the destruction of Emerson's writing. Writing's manifold meanings are closed down, meaning is removed from context, and scrutiny of the text gives way to a passively reductive reception. Seen in this light, the consumption of Emerson is both the end of the play of signification in Emerson's writing and the end of reading (or at least the end of a critical, intellectually interactive approach to reading). If you are more familiar with the Emerson portrayed as an apologist for self-help and hard work or with the mystical, lanky "transparent eye-ball" Emerson, then perhaps the consumption of Emerson will strike you neither as particularly surprising nor as any great loss. If, however, you are aware of the threads running throughout Emerson's writing that call for "creative reading," that call for critical vision of texts (in their multiplicity of meaning), that deem the use of literature as the responsible investigation of the world around us and the active participation in changing that world, then you will be troubled by the implications of consumption. A substantial portion of Emerson's writing reveals his fears that our reading practices are too consumptive and posits suggestions for resisting consumption and reading differently. This can be seen as early as "The Lord's Supper," a version of which Emerson delivered on 9 September 1832.

Just before the beginning of his career as a writer and lecturer, which coincides more or less with the termination of his career as a preacher, Emerson delivered a sermon that provides us with a glimpse of the importance he put on a certain kind of interpretation, one that seriously questions the validity of transfigurative reading. He begins "The Lord's Supper" with these words from Romans 14: "'The Kingdom of God is not meat and drink; but righteousness, and peace, and joy in the Holy Ghost.'"[55] The sermon shares Emerson's doubts about the propriety of the ritualized eating of the body of Christ, effectively constitutes his resignation from his position with the Second Church, and gestures toward what becomes a significant aspect of his philosophy: the refusal of a way of reading, of a way of looking at texts that consumes them, and of a way of being read. Emerson will no longer take his place at the Lord's Supper. He justifies his

rejection by stressing the importance of a historically aware, metaphorically attuned, and critically attentive reading of the New Testament; reading
critically and resisting consumption thus become linked at this very early
moment in Emerson's writing.

The opening words of the sermon are found in the chapters of Paul's letter
to the Romans that admonish debauchery and licentiousness, insisting that
one "make no provision for the flesh, to gratify its desires" (Romans
13:14). But the letter also urges that one not cavil over the proper way to
live: "Let not him who eats despise him who abstains, and let not him who
abstains pass judgment on him who eats" (Romans 14:3). Emerson's use
of these words indicates both his refusal to consume and his lack of interest in legislating others' consumption. He appears willing to continue in
his office with the church, provided he be permitted to omit the celebration of communion with Christ through the symbolic eating of bread, citing indirectly as his justification a Pauline reminder: "If your brother is
being injured by what you eat, you are no longer walking in love" (Romans 14:15). "Do not, for the sake of food, destroy the work of God. . . .
It is wrong for any one to make others fall by what he eats; it is right not
to eat meat or drink wine or do anything that makes your brother stumble"
(Romans 14:20). The problem here for the writer is not that one eats or
does not eat the body of Christ, but that Jesus' consumption has been
understood literally and subsequently institutionalized: "Having recently
given particular attention to this subject, I was led to the conclusion that
Jesus did not intend to establish an institution for perpetual observance
when he ate the Passover with his disciples; and, further, to the opinion,
that it is not expedient to celebrate it as we do."[56]

Let me stress here several elements of the above quotation that seem
peculiarly pertinent. "Given particular attention": this marks out a way
of reading that Emerson describes in more detail later. It involves attending closely to the text and context of a passage, which requires the
affirmation of metaphorical meaning. "I was led to the conclusion": the
passive formation is telling. He has not concluded, but has been led to the
conclusion, seemingly by "[giving] particular attention," or reading: reading thus leads him to thinking. "Establish an institution": this was not
Jesus' intention; Emerson does not spend time trying to guess what Jesus
intended ("Without presuming to fix precisely the purpose in the mind of
Jesus"[57]), but tries instead to dispel the constrictive notions that such guess-
ing has begotten. He questions both whether Jesus intended to establish
an institution and whether Jesus *should be* an institution—again, he is
speaking here of the symbolic consumption of Christ's body. Institutions

obstruct the engaged living of life, substituting a prefabricated way of living. Emerson writes in his journal (10 January 1832), "The difficulty is that we do not make a world of our own but fall into institutions already made & have to accommodate ourselves to them to be useful at all. & this accommodation is, I say, a loss of so much integrity & of course of so much power."[58] Perpetuating institutionalized consumption permits institutions to consume us. "It is not expedient": from the Latin *expedire,* it does not "free one's feet from shackles or a trap." That we "celebrate" Christ (making Christ famous, making Christ a festival, feasting on Christ) shackles us to an institution; perhaps we will live more expediently if we "commemorate" Christ (Emerson's suggested substitute), if we are mindful of Christ instead of filling our stomachs with him. This is what comes of "having recently given particular attention to this subject": Emerson states that he can no longer be perceived by his audience as being in "sympathy with" the institution, that he can no longer be seen as being "interested in it."[59] Thus he no longer can let himself be read as faithfully consuming the body of Christ.

He has been led to this refusal, as I have remarked above, by reading, and it is in the practice of reading that Emerson finds the sources of the mistaking of Christ. A reductive reading of the New Testament, one that narrows the text selectively and makes use of passages narrowly selected, bears the mark of consumption and evidences the work of institutions. Of the four evangelists, only Luke mentions the words on which the rite is based ("Do this in remembrance of me"); that means, for Emerson, that to embrace the rite, one must read Luke literally and read only Luke. To this, Emerson offers an alternative reading practice that includes reading the other writings that make up the gospel together with the historical and cultural context of Passover:

> But though the words, "Do this in remembrance of me," do not occur in Matthew, Mark, or John, and although it should be granted us that, taken alone, they do not necessarily import so much as is usually thought, yet many persons are apt to imagine that the very striking and personal manner in which this eating and drinking is described, indicates a striking and formal purpose to found a festival. And I admit that this impression might probably be left upon the mind of one who read only the passages under consideration in the New Testament. But this impression is removed by reading any narrative of the mode in which the ancient or the modern Jews have kept the Passover. It is then perceived that the leading circumstances in the Gospels are only a faithful account of that ceremony.[60]

Instead of reading only the passages under consideration, one must consider other readings and examine the contexts in which not only the words themselves occur but also the cultural contexts to which the words refer. One must be referred by reading, led by reading, but by a reading that opens up meaning instead of closing it down.

As a further example of problems in interpretation, Emerson cites the misuse of Paul's first letter to the Corinthians. In the eleventh chapter, Paul rebukes celebrants for the manner in which the Last Supper has been kept, complaining that "each one goes ahead with his own meal, and one is hungry and another is drunk" (11:21). Emerson chooses this particular passage precisely because of its prominent service in the argument that the Last Supper should be observed. The writer finds in his reading of the epistle, however, that Paul does not "enjoin upon his friends to observe the Supper, but to censure their abuse of it. We quote the passage now-a-days as if it enjoined attendance upon the Supper; but he wrote it merely to chide them for drunkenness."[61] In the tradition of the discussion of the eucharist, this passage has been understood to prescribe the ritual and to sanctify the consumption of the body of Christ. Emerson, reading against this tradition, interprets it as an injunction against consumption. He goes on to say that, even if we construe Paul to be sanctioning the ritual, "there is a material circumstance which diminishes our confidence in the correctness of the Apostle's view."[62] That "material circumstance" is Paul's belief in the imminent Second Coming of Christ. This "prevalent error of the primitive church" results in the literalizing of the Word, in the belief in the trope made flesh. To Emerson, John's lesson to the people of Capernaum was precisely a warning against such literalizing:

> He here tells the Jews, "Except ye eat the flesh of the Son of Man and drink His blood, ye have no life in you." And when the Jews on that occasion complained that they did not comprehend what he meant, he added for their better understanding, and as if for our understanding, that we might not think his body was to be actually eaten, that he only meant we should live by his commandment. He closed his discourse with these explanatory expressions: "The flesh profiteth nothing; the words that I speak to you, they are spirit and they are life."[63]

Drawing special attention to the value of words indicates a way of reading—a way of experiencing a text, of experiencing the textuality of the word, or of living one's relation to a text—that resists a consumption of the text. Words—humans' words, humans' language—are not to be eaten, but attended to, read with care. If we do not attend to our words and our ways of reading, we will continue to merely celebrate ("make famous"), to merely consume (institutionally). "You say, every time you celebrate the rite, that Jesus enjoined it; and the whole language you use conveys that impression. But if you read the New Testament as I do, you do not believe he did."[64] Reading something as Emerson does in "The Lord's Supper" means reading in a manner that analyzes textuality, acknowledges metaphorical meanings, and situates context. Such a reading critically examines beliefs and the grounds on which beliefs are based, facilitating structural changes in the very ways we read. What we believe no doubt affects how we read; but changing the way we read may change what (and how) we believe by leading us to think.

As instructive as it may be regarding issues of interpretation, Emerson's early lesson in biblical exegesis does not present a clear distinction between consumption and a more careful reading. I do not wish to claim that Emerson, here or elsewhere, embodies the perfect reader. The writer of "The Lord's Supper" veers from his ability to look closely and consider broadly, sometimes toward an airy and unhelpful transcendence, sometimes toward a retrenched self-reliance. An uncritical transcendentalist or an unselfreflexive relier on the self do not, I presume, a good reader make. Indeed, one need only inspect Emerson's journal of 1840 for an example of the writer's own consumptive proclivity, in the form of a startling oneiric ingestion of the world: "I dreamed that I floated at will in the great Ether, and I saw this world floating also not far off, but diminished to the size of an apple. Then an angel took it in his hand & brought it to me and said 'This must thou eat.' And I ate the world."[65] Such a passage raises important questions regarding the writer's shifting epistemology. Attending to the text and context of the entry, we can see many aspects of the literary object that has come down to us under the sign of "Emerson." In the text of the passage, we find biblical imagery, Adamic characteristics, transgression, apocalypse, knowledge, mastery, a world idealistically diminished and made utterly knowable through introversion. As for the context of the passage, it occurs adjacent to sentences that find their way into such essays as "Circles," "Self-Reliance," and "Man the Reformer,"[66] sentences that call for manliness, valor, "selfrecovery," standing erect. Here are phrases extolling hard work and digging in the earth, complaints of an economy that removes some classes from the site of work and gives them instead the commodity, praise for the "self sufficiency" of those who do work; here is the optimism for which Emerson has been acclaimed and disparaged: "We are made for joy & not for pain."[67] "Every new thought which makes day in our souls has its long morning twilight to announce its coming."[68]

But here also—up against a happy, manly Emerson who sees the world as totally knowable through its incorporation into his person—is an

Emerson that vituperatively rejects those who would portray the world as a coherent, consistent, knowable whole: "What a pity that we cannot curse & swear in good society. Cannot the stinging dialect of the sailors be domesticated? It is the best rhetoric and for a hundred occasions those forbidden words are the good ones. My page about 'Consistency' would be better written thus; Damn Consistency.[69] And to how many foolish canting remarks would a sophomore's ejaculation be the only suitable reply, 'The devil you do;' or, 'You be damned.'"[70] While we see an Emerson eyeing the apple of the world, sizing it up for holy ingestion, we can just as well see an Emerson who looks critically upon any such epistemological totalizing of the world. Just before the record of his dream, the writer jots down this: "The method of advance in nature is perpetual transformation. Be ready to emerge from the chrysalis of today, its thoughts & institutions, as thou hast come out of the chrysalis of yesterday."[71] Such transformations pervade Emerson's writing and make any settlement of "the world according to Emerson" questionable.

In other words, there are innumerable ways of understanding Emerson's conceptions of the world and our means of knowing it. In American culture since around 1850 Emerson has been read as pragmatist, spiritualist, common-sensical businessman, Puritan, escapist, placater, poet of influence, prophet of individualism, philosopher of radical change, fool, tonic, pill, ambrosia. These readings claim to have encapsulated the truth—the real meaning of Emerson—despite conflicting opinions. I am proposing that if we pay closer and more thoughtful attention to the propositions for reading announced in Emerson's writing, we may find that a majority of American readings may not be reading at all. For instance, if we read Emerson as "The Lord's Supper" suggests we read the New Testament, those countless contradictions regarding the meaning of Emerson request that we think again about the Emersons we have read into being as well as the act of reading itself. Just as Emerson enjoins us not to take Christ at or as his word but to see, rather, where the words take us, I suggest that our reading of Emerson be allowed to lead us to resist consumption.

But then, one might ask, to what extent do these suggestions rest on my own consumptions of Emerson's texts? Is it possible, given the scope of the consumptive worldview I have described, to *not* consume when we read? What precisely are the differences between reading and consumption? Such questions are the very stuff of my investigation, and asking them is a crucial component of resisting consumption. My hypothesis, which I hope to revise and refine as the study unfolds, is that reading and consuming, although not cleanly separable, do differ. They may be part of a continuum of interpretation or a necessary dynamic or a matter of degree or a tension that will never go away but still must be confronted. Whatever the case, I posit that "reading" approximates attending to, cultivating, engaging with (in the senses of entangling or involving or participating in), finding one's position implicated in a text. "Consuming" assumes a strict division between the reader and the thing read, which is removed (or is considered already removed) from its relation to other things.

I will attempt to resist consumption by examining the methods by which we have made sense of Emerson and by learning from Emerson's texts how to read. The resultant methodology requires a fluctuating interplay of literary and cultural history, literary theory, and close reading. To read against consumption is to discern whether a reading of Emerson is possible that does not curtail or neglect inconsistent meanings of Emerson, but that rather turns to Emerson's writing in such a way as to open up those meanings. It is to try to understand how and why those meanings are produced, to discuss the consequences of that production, and to provoke possibilities for alternative meanings. Because these efforts involve persistent rethinking about the metaphors by which we approach texts, my own methods must avoid the tendency to consume Emerson's text (and Emerson's consumers' texts) by holding to one particular metaphor—such as consumption.

Consumption has its uses for understanding interpretation, but it is not, in and of itself, the answer to the problem of reading. My claim is that a crucial component for resisting uninspired and uninspiring uses of literature involves discerning the limits of and moving beyond (later I will say transferring from) the metaphors that inform our reading. To read on, to carry on with reading and thinking, we must be willing to exchange our metaphors for others, but not before we closely examine the nature of the metaphors by which we already think and read, the conditions and consequences of having (or being had by) this metaphor or that, and the potential for reading that these metaphors provide us. If reading is to lead to inspiration, we must learn how to follow—warily, wisely, watching every step.

2 Writing in the Name of *Emerson*

As the journals say, "the italics are ours." The profit of
books is according to the sensibility of the reader.
— "Quotation and Originality"

Moving on from consumption, I will shift to other aspects of the
American literary economy—to questions of the value of the name
of the author, the origin and limit of meaning, the "profit of books," and
the "sensibility of the reader." The chapter title bears two primary senses
to be addressed: writing under the sign of (on behalf of, sanctioned by, authorized to write by) Emerson; writing that name *in,* assuming the position of author and putting it on record, signing on the dotted line "Emerson"—thereby naming one's own writing by that word. The study thus
turns to the various marks readers make on texts, the traces left behind in
reading, and the import for such in the interpretive constitution of meaning. To understand the different "sensibilities" with which we have approached Emerson's writing, I examine the "profits" reaped from a peculiar (though popular and influential) set of American appropriations of
Emerson: nineteenth- and twentieth-century success manuals.

The hypothesis, informed by a theory of consumptive and preposterous
use, is that a certain economy of reading and writing practices enables success authors to become agents operating in the name of Emerson. While
it is clearly the case that others (e.g., Ralph Waldo Trine) have written in
Emerson's name, the success writers discussed below do not espouse the
divinizing transubstantiation of Emerson's *being* undertaken by the writers of New Thought tracts. More pragmatic, success writers attempt to
make and remake the meaning of success (and of Emerson's essays) by

manipulating the text of Emerson's writing and then strategically acting on and under the *signature* of the author. These writers forge a meaning of success and then forge Emerson's signature to authorize that meaning.[1]

An investigation of this aspect of American culture reveals less about Emerson than it does about popular writing and reading. In the late nineteenth century, the pervasiveness of the myths of success, the reproduction of highly individualized selves by those myths, and the various efforts to resolve the contradictory positions into which individualized selves were placed required a writing that broadcast the messages of the nascent power structure wrought by increased industrialization and the rise of corporations. This writing offered readers digested forms of philosophy, religion, economics, and psychology that assisted them in fitting themselves into the new order; it enabled them, that is, to become "proper" individuals. As Elbert Hubbard put it in his immensely popular "A Message to Garcia" (1899), "Civilization is one long anxious search for just such individuals."[2] The proper individual is the one who, when asked by his or her employer to accomplish a task, will unquestioningly comply. Hubbard, who considered himself a more flamboyant, modernized version of Emerson[3] (and whose Roycrofters published a handsome, handcrafted version of Emerson's "Self-Reliance"), took his essay's title and central trope of message-bearing from an incident in the Spanish-American War, in which "a fellow by the name of Rowan" delivered a message from McKinley to the Cuban revolutionary Garcia.[4] The message was an important one—"The President must secure his cooperation, and quickly"[5]—and Rowan is apotheosized because he "took the letter and did not ask, 'Where is [Garcia] at?'" Unlike the majority of American workers, who are portrayed as "frowsy ne'er-do-wells" marked by "this incapacity for independent action, this moral stupidity, this infirmity of the will, this unwillingness to cheerfully catch hold and lift,"[6] Rowan heroically does what he is told—carries the message from those in power to those whose "cooperation" is to be "secured." The hero does not read the message, does not criticize, does not ask questions; he simply bears the message. "The world cries out for such," Hubbard writes; "he is needed, and needed badly—the man who can carry a message to Garcia."[7]

While Hubbard uses the trope to alter workers' behavior on behalf of "the men who are striving to carry on a great enterprise, whose working hours are not limited by the whistle, and whose hair is fast turning white through the struggle to hold in line dowdy indifference, slip-shod imbecility, and the heartless ingratitude" of their employees,[8] I see it as paradigmatic of the roles filled by success writers and readers specifically and "proper" readers and writers in American culture more generally. Hubbard's "Message" was wildly successful itself with various corporate executives.[9] In it, we are told that "it is not book-learning young men need, nor instruction about this and that, but a stiffening of the vertebrae which will cause them to be loyal to a trust, to act promptly, concentrate their energies: do the thing—'Carry a message to Garcia!'"[10] Carrying the message is the summation of loyalty, prompt action, and concentration of energies. As such, it is the overarching rule governing how employees are to act. It is also a prescription for the proper manner of interacting with a message or piece of information. "Book-learning"—which comes from actually reading—is not needed, but the simple ability to transport text from sender to receiver is.

Of the typically incompetent worker, Hubbard asks, "Can such a one write a letter to Garcia?" And he adds, "Can such a man be entrusted to carry a message to Garcia?"[11] Thus writing and bearing a message are paired, not writing and reading a message. Further, the "writer" of the message is, in Hubbard's example, a stenographer (and one whose spelling and punctuation needs work); in this economy of information, the message is already produced (by the employer), is to be reproduced by the properly functioning worker, and is then to be transported by another properly functioning worker to the one whose cooperation is to be secured. What is to pass for reading becomes divisible into two classes—one class consists of taking the message unquestioningly, not looking at the message, carrying the message; the other regards a mysteriously total reception of the message that must conclude in the behavior desired by and prescribed by the initial sender, i.e., with the completion of the transaction. Writing is reduced to the production and reproduction of information relating to the construction, maintenance, and expansion of a system of economic dominance (as in the message of McKinley's imperialist efforts); reading is limited to the acceptance of the message's delivery and complete reception of neither more nor less than that information.[12]

Successful reading either transfers the message or gathers in the message in its entirety. The "message" itself—that one must fulfill one's proper function in the order of things (so that one might be happy, wealthy, healthy)—is conveyed within a system that attempts to ensure perfect circulation of prescribed information. The system consequently limits the possibilities of reading (through the systematization of information to be read and the transformation of the meaning of the very act of reading), converting it into a processing industry that operates more productively within the economy of information. Emerson's role in this economy offers an example for better understanding the modes of reading employed by success writers; more broadly, it sheds some light on the conditions of reading in America and on the figure of Emerson in American culture.

The Business of Palimpsest

Business interests have long made use of the Emerson of hard work and self-reliance. John G. Cawelti equates Emerson with Benjamin Franklin and Horatio Alger as "apostles of the self-made man," finding that "in his essays and lectures, most of which were originally created for that primary institution of self-culture, the lyceum, Emerson made an impressive synthesis of the diverse ideals of self-improvement, success, and self-culture which had developed in the early nineteenth century, shaping them into a pattern with his own transcendental philosophy."[13] While Emerson lived, chambers of commerce cheerfully sponsored his lectures to mercantilist societies and other young men's groups,[14] and antebellum success tracts employed Emersonian notions in their advice on how to get ahead. Freeman Hunt, the "leading pre-Civil-War authority on self-help"[15] and longtime editor of *Hunt's Merchants' Magazine,* put together his own writings and those of friends and other commentators in *Worth and Wealth: A Collection of Maxims, Morals, and Miscellanies for Merchants and Men of Business* (1856). Alongside such "practical" considerations as "Endorsing Notes," "A Trick in Trade to Recover a Debt," "How to Prosper in Business," "The Surest Way of Getting Rich," "Manners for Merchants," and "Credit or Cash Business," Hunt inserts the ethical perambulations of William Channing, Edward Everett, Henry Ward Beecher, and Theodore Parker. Included also is a brief chapter titled "Self-Reliance Important to the Merchant," which begins thus: "SELF-RELIANCE, to the merchant, and indeed to all who would succeed in the accomplishment of a laudible [*sic*] purpose or pursuit, is indispensable. It was this trait, perhaps, more than any other, that enabled an Astor, a Girard, a Gray, in our own country, to work out for themselves vast fortunes—to accumulate millions."[16] This introduction leads immediately into a lengthy passage from Emerson's "Self-Reliance," one that begins by deprecating the "young men" who "lose all heart" if they "miscarry in their first enterprises." Emerson extols the "sturdy lad from New Hampshire or Vermont, who in turn tries all the professions, who *teams it, farms it, peddles,* keeps a school, preaches, edits a newspaper, goes to Congress, buys a township, and so forth, in successive years, and always like a cat falls on his feet."[17] Hunt, foregoing quotation marks, puts Emerson to work in the service of business, reducing the notion of self-reliance to that "trait" which enables men to "work out for themselves vast fortunes,—to accumulate millions."

Using "Self-Reliance" to promote the "laudible pursuit" of making millions will not offend those readers of Emerson who reduce his work to that of an apostle of success, a gospeler "convinced that a man who had actually earned wealth through his own labors, and not through adventitious circumstance, had demonstrated a high cultivation of his worldly understanding."[18] Indeed, passages of the essay lend themselves to these reductions. Here Emerson insists that "welcome evermore to gods and men is the self-helping man."[19] He glorifies labor, especially the labor involved in making a self: "But do your work, and I shall know you. Do your work, and you shall reinforce yourself."[20] In the context of the essay, however, doing your work does not necessarily mean doing your job. Followed immediately by the harangue against conformity, "your work" might even be to *not* do your job. Using these words to make the claim that self-reliance simply means pursuing gainful employment requires either *not reading* the bulk of words that constitute the essay or reading them and destroying them while conserving only those deemed most useful. The textual discard—the essay's disjecta membra after Hunt's appropriative editing—controverts the new edition.

Concerned, somewhat, with issues of consumption, the writer of "Self-Reliance" defines the eponymous term as the "aversion" of society, that is, of a society that is no more than "a joint-stock company, in which members agree, for the better securing of his bread to each shareholder, to surrender the liberty and culture of the eater. The virtue in most request is conformity."[21] Liberty and culture are consumed by the joint-stock company of society—one's liberty and culture are eaten because one must eat. Emerson calls for the end of this joint-stock company through aversive self-reliance, through nonconformity, and through inconsistency.

The passage that Hunt cites for spurring young men on to accumulation is immediately followed in "Self-Reliance" (but erased in Hunt's "Self-Reliance Important to the Merchant") by a call to prayer, which Emerson describes as the "contemplation of the facts of life from the highest point of view."[22] Contemplation from this different perspective does not yield a worldview in which amassing vast fortunes is laudable: "But prayer as a means to effect a private end, is meanness and theft."[23] Instead of saluting an Astor, a Girard, or a Gray for building up enormous storehouses of property, Emerson concludes: "And so the reliance on Property, including the reliance on governments which protect it, is the want of self-reliance. Men have looked away from themselves and at things so long, that they have come to esteem the religious, learned, and civil institutions as guards of property, and they deprecate assaults on these, because they feel them to be assaults on property. They measure their esteem of each other, by what each has, and not by what each is."[24] The phrase "Men have looked away from themselves and at things so long" addresses what appears to be an important concern in the text of "Self-Reliance": vision, especially ways of seeing where we are. Hence it is significant that Hunt's selection ends with the need for self-reliance to "work a revolution" in, among other things, our "speculative views"; these are the very last words of Hunt's chapter.[25] Part of a separate paragraph in Emerson's essay, these words appear in Hunt's *Worth and Wealth* as the culmination of the same paragraph that begins with self-reliance's importance to accumulation. Thus, speculation, in Hunt's version, is associated with Astor, Girard, and Gray, that is, with *market* speculation.

Elsewhere in Emerson's essay we read that "a man must consider what a blindman's-buff is this game of conformity."[26] The man who conforms to the demands of the joint-stock company is blind; or, if he can see, "he is pledged to himself not to look but at one side,—the permitted side."[27] Instead of speculating (part of which, *specula,* is the Latin for "watchtower," which resonates with what Emerson calls prayer), "most men have bound their eyes with one or another handkerchief, and attached themselves to some one of these communities of opinion."[28] Later in "Self-Reliance," Emerson writes with disdain for those who will not look beyond the systematized "vision" afforded them by the authorities:

> It will happen for a time, that the pupil will find his intellectual power has grown by the study of his master's mind. But in all unbalanced minds, the classification is idolized, passes for the end, and not for a speedily exhaustible means, so that the walls of the system blend to their eye in the remote horizon with the walls of the universe; the luminaries of heaven seem to them hung on the arch their master built. They cannot imagine how you aliens have any right to see,—how you can see; "It must be somehow that you stole the light from us." They do not perceive, that light, unsystematic, indomitable, will break into any cabin, even into theirs.[29]

Idolizing the classification, we fail to see, for we look only through the lenses prescribed for us by "masters." Self-reliance, the aversion of the joint-stock company, provides the possibility that "the immortal light, all young and joyful, million-orbed, million-colored, will beam over the universe as on the first morning."[30] We must look *for* ourselves (i.e., attempt to find ourselves, but also to enact a vision on our own behalf that resists prescribed modes of seeing) before we might truly see. Failing to so look causes us to fail at reading: "Our reading is mendicant and sycophantic."[31] When we attempt that which passes for reading, we merely pass our classified eyes over a page, look to another for truths, look through another's sight; we do not look at the text before us (or, by extension, of which we are a part—the light would illuminate us also), but rather we overlook it. Just as, in looking through materials he could include in his compendium of maxims for merchants, Hunt overlooked what it means to look, overlooked looking for the sake of business.

My purpose here, however, is not to claim that Hunt simply mistakes or misses the real meaning of "Self-Reliance," but rather to speculate about what happens to the text of "Self-Reliance" under Hunt's consumptive gaze. By remorselessly rummaging around in "Self-Reliance" and removing the desired passage from its context, Hunt's editing both alters the meaning of the passage and creates a new frame by which the larger essay is to be interpreted, thus further altering the meaning of the text. This use of "Self-Reliance" leads to its demise, effectively rewriting "Self-Reliance Important to the Merchant" over or in place of "Self-Reliance." Such a treatment of the text scribbles over the traces of "Self-Reliance," an act that would cleanse the essay of potential significations that challenge its usefulness and meaning to merchants. For Hunt's text is, due to its effects on Emerson's, a palimpsest: traces of the old text—the title and the passage cited—are visible, but now signify within the boundaries of the new text. The bulk of the words of "Self-Reliance" have been erased, as has Emerson's name. Between Hunt's words (those consecrating the names and actions of the great capitalists) and the passage from Emerson's essay (which appears without quotation marks) is this: "An eminent writer has somewhere said . . ."[32] Hunt's erasures of the name of the writer and the larger text of the essay enact a rewriting *over* the name of Emerson, *in* the name of the "eminent writer." The new text is written under the name Hunt, and underwritten by the names of "merchants and men of business"—"an Astor, a Girard, a Gray." The business of the palimpsest forecloses on the meaning of "Self-Reliance."

I do not mean simply to imply that the "true meaning of Emerson" is to be retrieved from palimpsest by establishing and conserving the accurate or authoritative edition of "Self-Reliance." As Gary Taylor has shown, "every edition, every textual investigation, represents an assertion of value."[33] Even an authoritative version involves what Ralph Williams refers to as "a *tranche de texte,* the 'slice' being arbitrary with reference to the various criteria that might be privileged as basic to an edition."[34] To return to the epigraph that begins this chapter, when "the italics are ours," they are always symptomatic of the profit motive, always indicative of the *profit* to which we wish to put the material being quoted. "The sensibility of the reader" is a sensibility that enables that reader to make texts mean in a certain way based on the perceived value. In the case of Hunt's palimpsest, that value rests solely in the *tranche de texte,* allowing Hunt to write off the remainder of "Self-Reliance." Such a reading is based on what profit the sensibility of the reader seeks. The resultant value or meaning of Emerson indicates more about the desired ends of the reader than about Emerson's writing.

Hunt's *Worth and Wealth* demonstrates the fate of Emerson's text in the hands of various mendicant and sycophantic readers in this nation. Emerson's texts both invite and discourage palimpsestic treatment. The pithy aphorisms found amid the tangle of contradictions and incoherencies, the writer's own claims that he does not know who he was yesterday or what he meant in writing what he wrote, found alongside charges to know thyself, do your work, trust your instincts—these make for a many-layered text, a weave of myriad ideas, colors, confusions, visions, dares, and desires. Refusing to reckon with the complexity of these textual webs, the predominant method of handling such texts in American culture (popular and not) is a consumptive reading and palimpsestic rewriting of the text *in the name of Emerson*—as if calling upon that name could sanction any interpretation of and/or employment of the text. And this, I am proposing, forecloses on the significance of those texts in a manner that demarcates the end of reading Emerson.

Graft and Autograph

As success manuals proliferated after the Civil War, the body of Emerson's writings appeared ever more frequently in the form of disjecta membra—a piece of poem on this page, a half-sentence from that essay on another, a selection from an eminent writer there, quoting that shrewd American essayist here. As a result, when William Mathews writes in his *Getting on in the World* (1874) that "Emerson has startled the world by his Emersonisms,"[35] it is the apothegmatic and appropriated Emerson, the consumed Emerson, the *palimpsesticized* Emerson at work. Where New Thought promoters call on the benign figure of Emerson to found their idealist programs, success writers rely on practical application of select phrases.

Mathews, Hunt, and numerous other success writers remove Emersonisms and rework these fragments into new texts. These new texts are analogous to palimpsests in that traces of a text remain, but take on a different significance within the framework of the rewritten text, a rewriting which in turn revalues the texts from which the traces came. The meaning of the new text is to be read as written in the name of Emerson, who thus comes to authorize the abridged version of his writing. In sum, a new economy of meaning is produced from material resulting from the consumption of the Emerson text; the Emerson text is afforded a revised value within the new economy of meaning established by consumption and reproduction. In this economy, the end (worth and wealth, getting on in the world) of the new text bestows value or meaning on its parts. As a figure, the palimpsest enables us to begin to think about the ends to which Emerson is put, the methods by which those ends are to be attained, and the strategies by which such ends and methods might be recognized and resisted. But palimpsest is not the only applicable escritorial metaphor; consider, for example, the problem of the autograph—another instance of forging a new text in the name of Emerson, in which Emerson becomes a reader's secretary.

Edward Bok, the editor of *Ladies' Home Journal* from 1889 to 1919, remembers in his third-person autobiography how "the philosophy of the Concord sage made a peculiarly strong appeal to the young mind, and a small copy of Emerson's essays was always in Edward's pocket on his long stage or horse-car rides to his office and back."[36] Visiting Emerson as a teenager, Bok recalls Emerson at his desk—"the man whose words had already won Edward Bok's boyish interest, and who was destined to impress himself upon his life more deeply than any other writer."[37] That the impression was indeed deep can be seen in Bok's *Successward: A Young Man's Book for Young Men* (1895); in that guide to self-improvement, Emersonisms appear, but the name *Emerson* does not. *Successward*, Bok writes in his preface, is "not written by a patriarch whose young manhood is far behind him. It is written to young men by a young man to whom the noise of the battle is not a recollection, but an every-day living reality. He thinks he knows what a fight for success means to a young fellow, and he writes with the smoke of the battle around him and from the very thick of the fight."[38] Writing from the thick of youth's battle for success, Bok will take no prisoners and make no quotations. The writer claims authority by virtue of experience; but, in delineating a working philosophy for the working young man, he tinkers with and puts to use notions removed from that "small copy of Emerson's essays" forever in his pocket, thus writing over those notions.

Bok's philosophy is a tripartite injunction to young men that can be condensed thus: *Be/Have. Be* a success, *Have* a wife and home, and *Be-*

have. Emersonian notions of self-reliance are employed in the making of an autonomous individual, utterly accountable for assuming "his" place in the world: "I say all this because I want every young fellow to feel that, to a large extent, he stands alone for himself in the world."[39] Where Trine's seeker was to tune himself to the Infinite, Bok's young man must tune himself to *himself* and "follow where his instincts lead him. After a while what was at first a mere instinct or an unformed taste will develop and point him to something definite in the business world, and if he be true to himself he will sooner or later find himself in that particular position which he is best fitted to occupy and fill. His capacities will reveal themselves to him, and they will teach him his limitations."[40] Perhaps even as he wrote the above Bok clasped his copy of Emerson's essays, feeling Emerson's self-reliance emanate: "Trust thyself: every heart vibrates to that iron string. Accept the place divine providence has found for you, the society of your contemporaries, the connexion of events."[41]

But Bok's appropriative method of reading again fails to consider the manifold meanings in play. What, in the Emerson essay, is contextualized as an attempt at aversion—an attempt to figure out who or what one *is*, against the pull of the "common motives" of industrial society—becomes, in Bok's work, accepting one's place in the new corporate order. Where the writer of "Self-Reliance" urges a progress, through nonconformity, toward affirmation of what he calls "divine providence" or the Over-Soul, Bok finds that the "young man who progresses is he who enters into the spirit of the business of his employer."[42] One is what one must be. First by getting to know what one's capacities are ("by proper study of himself"), then by accepting one's place provided by an employer ("he will sooner or later find himself in that particular position which he is best fitted to occupy and fill"), the young man will truly *be* himself.[43] "Let a young man be thoroughly fitted for the business position he occupies, alert to every opportunity, and embracing it to its fullest possibility, with his methods fixed on honorable principles, and he is a successful man."[44] Finding himself, being himself, and making himself thoroughly fitted for his business position, the young man can now rely on himself. By reading every fourth sentence or so of "Self-Reliance," or half of the later essay "Fate," Bok has formed a philosophy of autonomous identity conforming to the needs of nineteenth-century corporations.

And what is most startling about this formation of a philosophy of conformity is that it has been authorized, according to a primal scene in Bok's autobiography, by Ralph Waldo Emerson. Returning to the scene of Bok's teenage visit to Emerson, we can see where acquiring Emerson's autograph provides Bok with a precedent for writing *Successward* in the name of Emerson. Bok describes the scene thus: visiting with the doddering Concord Sage in his last year of life, the teen has difficulties conveying his desire for Emerson's signature:

> "Please write out the name you want," [Emerson] said finally, "and I will copy it for you if I can."
>
> It was hard for the boy to believe his own senses. But picking up a pen he wrote: "Ralph Waldo Emerson, Concord; November 22, 1881."
>
> Emerson looked at it, and said mournfully: "Thank you." Then he picked up the pen, and writing the single letter "R" stopped, followed his finger until it reached the "W" of Waldo, and studiously copied letter by letter! At the word "Concord" he seemed to hesitate, as if the task were too great, but finally copied again, letter by letter, until the second "c" was reached. "Another 'o,'" he said, and interpolated an extra letter in the name of the town which he had done so much to make famous the world over. When he had finished he handed back the book, in which there was written:
> [Here Bok provides a replica of the signature, along with place and date.]
>
> The boy put the book into his pocket; and as he did so Emerson's eye caught the slip on his desk, in the boy's handwriting, and, with a smile of absolute enlightenment, he turned and said:
>
> "You wish me to write my name? With pleasure. Have you a book with you?"
>
> Overcome with astonishment, Edward mechanically handed him the album once more from his pocket. Quickly turning over the leaves, Emerson picked up the pen, and pushing aside the slip, wrote without a moment's hesitation:
> [Here Bok again provides a replica of the signature.]
>
> The boy was almost dazed at the instantaneous transformation in the man![45]

Note some of the more salient elements of this episode: As the scene opens, Emerson, due to senility, cannot grasp what is expected of him. He seems to understand that he has been asked to write a name and asks Bok to write the name for him. Bok writes *in* Emerson's name: i.e., he writes Emerson's name on Emerson's behalf. Emerson studiously copies Bok's writing of Emerson's autograph, writing his name at Bok's behest. (Something stirs him to add an extra o to Concord—in every word another circle can be drawn.) Bok copies Emerson's copy of Bok's writing of Emerson's name into Bok's autobiography. Emerson's eye is stirred by Bok's writing of his name into "absolute enlightenment." That he has enlightened absolutely the Concord Sage overcomes Bok with "astonishment"—they have both been deeply affected, even "transformed," by this uncanny series of writings of Emerson's name.

An economy has thus been established wherein Bok becomes the executor of the Emersonian pen, the transformative writer of and in the name. The founding act of this writing economy, however, is in many ways a forgery. In *Forgers and Critics,* Anthony Grafton describes several "great topoi of Western forgery." These include: "the motif of the object found in an inaccessible place, then copied, and now lost, as the authority for what would have then lacked credibility as the work of an individual"; "the claim to have consulted far-off official documents"; and the practice of oracles "producing relics and inscriptions that explained their origins."[46] The first two topoi call to mind Hunt's palimpsest—his fragment of "Self-Reliance" purportedly "somewhere said" by eminence. The third very much resembles Bok's use of Emerson's signature. The placement of Emerson's autograph in Bok's autobiography, the account of the writing of the name in the book, the reference to the ubiquitous copy of Emerson's essays on the person of Bok, and the use of digested Emersonisms in the writing of *Successward* amount to a case of forgery in the classic sense described by Grafton. Emerson's name is forged; a new philosophy of success is forged in Emerson's name.

I am willing to concede that "forgery" may be too strong to characterize Bok's writing in the name of Emerson; he most likely did not intentionally set out to write Emerson's name where Emerson had not written it. But Bok's representation of Emerson's signature functions as a metaphor for the appropriation of Emerson's name by success writers, which in turn functions as a metaphor for the use of Emerson by American readers more generally. Grafton allows that in some cases we may be encountering "not forgeries but pseudepigrapha—works wrongly ascribed but not intentionally deceptive."[47] Even if we view such uses of Emerson as pseudepigraphous, we can yet see that a new Emerson, a new meaning for "Emerson," is forged in the foundry of American success writers. This new meaning is ascribed to Emerson's texts, taken from those texts, and subscribed with the authorizing autograph of the Concord Sage. In Bok's case, Emerson's name is grafted into Bok's book, where the graft takes root and is to be seen as having flowered into *Successward.* Taking advantage of his position as the executor of Emerson's pen, Bok commits—however unwittingly—an act of interpretive graft, one of many misdemeanors of meaning perpetrated in and with the name of Emerson.

Closing Remarks: For Further Speculation

Graft, forgery, palimpsest—I have adduced the appropriative and consuming modes of interpretation deployed by success writers in order to trace the developments of a cultural reception of Emerson's writing. That writing, from the middle of the nineteenth century to the end of the twentieth, has often been used to promote the Business of America. As an inspirational apology for bootstraps and boosterism, "Self-Reliance" and other essays have been interpreted to have meaning only insofar as they stir readers to pick themselves up by their own suspenders and deposit themselves safely into their proper places in the order of things. The economy that structures such interpretations—an economy of consumption—sanctions the foreclosure of the text of Emerson on behalf of the propagation of the construed meaning of that text. Emerson comes to mean what the success writers say and this meaning is purportedly coined in the name of Emerson. Text and name are then rewritten and underwritten by Business's Emerson; a new Emerson is thus produced by consumption. Reproduced, repackaged, and ready for the market, Emerson means Business.

By proposing that success writers' uses of Emerson might function metaphorically for other modes of interpretation, I allude to questions that "writing in the name of Emerson" raises for the business practices of scholars, critics, and theorists. What profit system informs our sensibilities when we italicize (set off for particular attention) certain aspects of Emerson's (or other) texts? What texts and authors do we forge by our own interpretive methods? Grafton laments that "forgery and criticism resemble one another more closely than vice and virtue."[48] In differentiating between the two, however, Grafton claims that the forger "offers us a refuge from the open-ended reflection on our ideals and institutions that a reading of powerful texts may stimulate"; and yet, despite the best of intentions and "elegant techniques," the forger "is irresponsible."[49] I suggest—Grafton's differentiations to the contrary notwithstanding—that the well-intended, elegant offering of a refuge from the significant complexity of texts marks much of our modern criticisms, from historicist attempts to establish original texts to New Critical control of the self-enclosed text-as-universe, from psychoanalytic work by "purveyors of truth" to critics of psychoanalytic interpretations that forget or attempt to elude their own frames of reference. "Criticism," Grafton notes, "is, as we have repeatedly seen, inevitably fallible in its conclusions and deeply indebted to forgery for its methods."[50] Criticism, though, does not fail or come to fault, as Grafton hints, because it is partial, but because it so often refuses to acknowledge its fallibility and partiality. This refusal is an act of textual irresponsibility.

This chapter opened with speculations on the work of the name as an instrument of coherence, on coherence as an imposition of order and sense, on imposition as the manufacture of "true" meaning or value for a text within a certain economy. And this led to the exposition of two types of textual irresponsibility: one writes over the name and the text, creating a new text from bits and pieces of the old; the other writes in and writes under the name and the text. In both cases the text that is put to use is, in a sense, used up; the resultant palimpsest or forgery retains glimpses of the used text, but the latter no longer has the ability to signify differently—i.e., its significance arrives at a limit, framed by the new context, foreclosed by the palimpsest, or consumed by the autograph.

Such methods of interpretation are irresponsible in that they fail to respond to the complexity of the text, fail to respond to the text's questions of their readings, and consequently fail to acknowledge their part in the solemn engagement or entanglement with a text. This last failing, in particular, is truly a failure to interpret (from the Latin for "move between") the two sets of texts that make up interpretation—the text being interpreted and the texts/contexts that make up the perspective of the interpreter. And this, in turn, causes one's reading to fail. In this sense, the only bad reading or the reading that fails is one that does not *profit* (as in go forward, progress, advance, move), that curtails interpretive movement. "The profit of books is according to the sensibilities of the reader": a text profits or moves according to the ability of the reader to be sensitive to movement—the motion of his or her own thoughts and interpretive activities, the movement of a text's constitutive elements, the movement produced by the solemn entangling of text with reader. Texts move only according to readers' sensibilities and not at all if readers' insensibilities close them down.

Being insensible to a text's movements can cause us to make marks on a text that delimit it, stopping our reading in its tracks. In some cases, our methods of reading may even render texts illegible, our own marks covering the traces of the texts we would consider and to which our readings usually refer others. Besides the preposterous suggestion that all reading is also a writing, I am also proposing that this sort of interpretive marking can result in the closure of the play of possible meanings inherent to the nature of textuality and to the interaction of the different contexts in which reader and text operate. And this spells the end of the nature of the writing that is being read "in the first place." To read a text so that the text is rendered unreadable is to "unwrite" that text or to rewrite (write over) its potential significances. But if reading is also a writing, the answer to the text's precarious situation is not to *forego* reading it or to try to read in such a way that does *not* write. Rather, readers must own up to the consequences of Emerson's reminder that "the italics are ours," that our readings are writings and must be undertaken with an acknowledgment of the consequences of particular approaches.

To close this chapter, then, I return to the scene of the crimes—"Self-Reliance"—and specifically to the passage converted by Hunt into an exhortation for market success in the economy of consumption. I do so to speculate about the nature of textually responsible reading, hoping to re-open, as it were, the text of the essay: "It is easy to see that a greater self-reliance must work a revolution in all the offices and relations of men; in their religion; in their education; in their pursuits; their modes of living; their association; in their property; in their speculative views."[51] How might this passage mean, other than how it does in Hunt's version? What would it mean to read it responsibly? One method would involve responding or answering back with questions, speculating on some of the ways these marks signify. "A greater self-reliance," for example, refers to the trait that is aversive to conformity, consistency, the institutionalization of a self defined by a society of property and joint-stock companies. But perhaps it as well signifies a text greater than the one entitled "Self-Reliance."

It would indeed be "easy to see" that a greater text than the document in question would be required to work a revolution in all our offices and relations, including the office of the reader, the relations of reader to text. Assisting a greater "Self-Reliance" to work a revolution might then mean cultivating the texts produced by interpreting or moving between the reader's contexts and the text/context of the lesser "Self-Reliance" so thoroughly that speculative views are revolutionized (turned around or over)—one sense of this turning involves turning something over in one's mind, further reflecting on something. Speculative views, however, are concatenate with other offices and relations. Modes of living and association, religion and education, pursuits and property all must be reread, revolved, revolutionized. The earlier "Do your work, and I shall know you" thus comes to be a direct address to the reader, enjoining him or her to undertake the necessary labor of responding, of entering into new relations with a text that attend to the greater text that those relations produce.[52]

Another mode of responsible reading involves examining the economies wherein meaning is produced. Although the first chapter concerned itself with the figural ingestion of Emerson's text, the second has taken up a different set of issues regarding consumption. Here, as is the case with *Walden*, "the reader will perceive that I am treating the subject rather from an economic than a dietetic point of view."[53] What does fiscal economy (the system of the production, distribution, and consumption of wealth by which things are accorded value) have to do with textual economy (the system of practices of writing and reading by which things are accorded meaning)? To what extent does a particular fiscal economy produce a particular textual economy? What other economies obtain? What economies produce "Self-Reliance" as well as interpretations of "Self-Reliance"? To read that essay, it is perhaps necessary to study the economics of interpretation first. Such work would yield the possibility of considering the economies that structure a particular reader's version of a text. What makes up the contexts, the perspectives, the circles, the economies from which we read "Self-Reliance"? Would attempting to discern the reading economy in which we encounter the essay respond to the call for "a greater self-reliance"? "Economy," Thoreau reminds his reader, "is a subject which admits of being treated with levity, but it cannot so be disposed of."[54] Perhaps this is so because if we dispose of economy—remove it from our consideration—we dispose of the possibility for making sense of how we make sense of texts. Losing track of the way texts make sense, we are consumed by just that sense, forgetting that this sense is made by our disposals or consumptions of the texts themselves.

A third method would be to respond to specific strands of the text, speculating about the nature of the weave into which they (and our readings) are woven. How, for instance, are we to take the injunctions against that "foolish consistency" ("the hobgoblin of little minds, adored by little statesmen and philosophers and divines"[55]) and conformity (that which makes us "not false in a few particulars, authors of a few lies, but false in all particulars"[56])—lamentable traits that keep us in our places within certain economies and thereby prevent us from seeing? If, to enter into meaningful relations with the text, we must do our work, and if that work is reading, then it is our responsibility to abandon consistency and conformity, which taken together pronounce the capitulation to "badges and names, to large societies and dead institutions."[57] Capitulating our interpretations (i.e., surrendering them unresistingly to contexts, modes, schools, institutions of interpretation) surrenders the possibility of moving on. Conforming our readings to large societies and being consistent to interpretive strategies governed by dead or dying—or any—institutions cause us to profit (obtain advantage) from a text instead of allowing the text to profit (move on).

Yet another responsible reading, related to moving on, would involve perpetually making transitions back and forth between texts and contexts, truly interpreting, continuing to think through texts as well as the conditions and consequences of particular explications. Emerson's "Self-Reliance" teaches that "life only avails, not the having lived. Power ceases in the instant of repose; it resides in the moment of transition from a past to a new state, in the shooting of the gulf, in the darting to an aim."[58] Attending to these transitions requires, among other acts, reexamining the transfers we make between texts and contexts, the metaphors by which we carry (or that carry us) one to the other. This, in turn, means allowing oneself to transfer from one metaphor to the next—hence the move from consumption to palimpsest, from textual dietetics to contextual economics, from the preposterous history of reading Emerson to an eventual call for reading Emerson preposterously. Indeed, the proliferation of metaphor and the attendant will to move are part of a counterpractice to the mode of consumption. Consumption, marked by consistency, conformity, and coherence, submits to "the smooth mediocrity and squalid contentment of the times"[59] and ingests/puts to use/destroys "Self-Reliance." Its counterpractice responds to the text's injunction to "leave your theory as Joseph his coat in the hand of the harlot, and flee."[60]

In other words, the transfer of metaphors from, for example, consumption to palimpsest, does not entail gaining sight of one at the expense of losing sight of the other. Instead, it assists in making visible our ways of seeing by promoting necessary movement, by effecting the availing transitions. This sort of profit leads to a preposterous speculation: I can never be done reading "Self-Reliance." The end of my reading of the essay would signify the onset of consumption. "Self-Reliance" will always require being read once more, and my responsibility is to cultivate the ability to move on and read again and see differently.[61] Another preposterous speculation: I may not begin to read the greater text of "Self-Reliance" until I have read the essay, which I may not truly be said to have read until I have begun to consider the greater text.

And so on.

3 Waldo, Inc.

> To what extent can truth endure incorporation? That is
> the question; that is the experiment.
> —Friedrich Nietzsche

In the hands of success writers, Emerson's texts are an exploitable commodity, products to be repackaged and marketed anew. Thus the eat-
ing/being eaten connotations of consumption introduced in the first chapter
transfer into the economic connotations associated in the second. To
progress with the study of the fate of Emerson's texts in American culture,
the focus in this chapter transfers yet again to a related term, *incorporation,* and to biographies of Emerson. Carrying the sense of *ingesting* ("to
take or absorb into the body") as well as the more current sense of a particular form of business entity, *to incorporate* also denotes "to combine
or unite into one body or uniform substance," "to put (one thing) in or
into another so as to form one body or integral whole," "to furnish with
a body; to give bodily shape to; to embody" (*OED*)—all of which come
to bear on the modes of making sense of Emerson employed by writers of
his life. These modes ensure that Emerson's life and his words will accord
with one another. The following discussion of Emerson's biography assumes, as its operative investigative metaphor, the incorporation of the
Emerson text insofar as Emerson is furnished with a body; Emerson's
writing is made to cohere, to form one body or integral whole; and the
body of Emerson and the body of writings are combined or united to form
another unitary body or uniform substance.

For over a century, the project of making sense of Emerson has been aided
by those capable of remembering Emerson, of looking back on his life and

works from a personal perspective, of again being mindful of Emerson's person.[1] Numerous biographies have told the story of the man behind the writing, each biography staking a claim for a particular version of that man and consequently for the meaning of his writings. The resultant versions function beneath the rubric of the proper name that best contains the reproduction: a reader is introduced, depending on the contact with Emerson experienced by the author, to "Waldo," to "Mr. Emerson," to "the Wisest American," to "our virginal Sir Galahad in America," to "Saint Radalphus."[2] Drawing on personal acquaintance and familiarity with Emerson's journals, other memoirs, and Emerson's published works, numerous versions of the story of Emerson attempt, as in the case of Van Wyck Brooks's *The Life of Emerson,* to give "a coherence, a relevance, a meaning" to Emerson's works "which for most of us they would otherwise lack."[3] And, as in Brooks's work, this has also entailed the "re-membering" of Emerson, revivifying Emerson by piecing together his remains. So remembered, Emerson the man is made to cohere the man's writing. Coherence, relevance, and meaning are effected by the remembrance of Emerson's presence, his person, and his manhood. Remembering Emerson supplements what would otherwise be a lack, gap, or absence of meaning in his works.

In writing the various lives of Emerson, friends and friendly critics sought to bring the figure of Emerson back to life by reviving his living body, which in turn incorporates (gives a body to) Emerson's writing. This body functions to give the writer physical presence and immediacy: he is *here,* right now. To ensure that Emerson's immediate presence registers significantly on readers, biographers often juxtapose his revivified masculine figure with femininity, death, and, hence, absence. Brooks, for example, begins his story with the image of Waldo's necrophilic aunt: "Miss Mary Moody Emerson lived in her shroud. She stitched it all herself, and when death refused to come she had put it on as a nightgown, then as a day-gown. She was even seen on horseback once, in Concord, cantering through the village street, attired for the grave with a scarlet shawl thrown about her shoulders."[4] Commencing with a death-driven, tiny ("a dwarf, four feet three inches tall"), frantic, finger-shaking, gravely attired, Calvinist female guardian of the abyss ("an autocrat and a prophetess and as fiery as the pit"),[5] Brooks relieves Aunt Mary's moribundity with the *life* of Emerson. A tall, life-affirming, male emblem of the modern democratic America of the present, Emerson stands for all that is good, positive, and natural—and he stands out even more so when compared with Aunt Mary, who is posited as the sign of absence and negation, the female gates of hell.[6]

Establishing the presence of the writer accomplishes at least two things:

Emerson's substance is given meaning and an attendant meaning for Emerson's writing is given substance. The figure of Emerson is brought back to life by such works as Brooks's *Life*. Henceforth, that figure substantiates the true meaning of Emerson's text—Emerson is incorporated. An important element of the incorporation process is that the *reader* is brought into Emerson's presence, which will mean further that the reader himself or herself, by enjoying access to the thing itself, finally understands what the thing means.

Switching verb tenses, alternating the objects of address, and recasting bits of Emerson's journal into a narrative of the present, Brooks's biography imaginatively dramatizes Emerson's life, making him live again; for "if one reconstructs in imagination any moment in history one actually lives in that moment."[7] By ushering the reader into the immediate presence of Emerson, Brooks ensures that Emerson's writing will be conflated with the writer's life. The meaning of that writing now inheres in the substance of being; that is, Emerson's meaning, by virtue of being inextricable from Emerson's presence, is *immediate*. Writing is no longer a medium of signification, but rather a natural by-product of the life of the writer; its meaning is to be received or found in nature, as part and parcel of the writer's substantive being. Interpretation, in turn, becomes a much less risky business, for one need only embrace the life of the writer (as represented by the biographer) to comprehend the writing's significance. The biographical incorporation of Emerson makes available for distribution a peculiar and significant version of the writer and his writing.

Waldo, Inc.'s handling of Emerson frees the writer's texts from the vicissitudes of time and the effects of context. Though the body of Emerson might pass away, his Being, the Life of Emerson, will continue: "in several notable cases the voice, the manners, the very smile of Emerson could be recognized moving about in persons to whom he bore no blood-relationship."[8] The end of Emerson, therefore, is not necessarily the end of the body and its significance, for the *Life* peacefully dissolves with a mystical metamorphosis: "Gradually, year by year, the outline had grown indistinct and the halo gayer and brighter, till at last there was left only a sense of presence. And the strong gods pined for his abode; for the universe had become his house in which to live."[9]

Diffused into the universe, Emerson becomes a part of nature. But examining this process carefully, we find a *denaturing* of Emerson's text. Because Emerson himself has been provided an immediate presence through the processes of incorporation, reading Emerson becomes a matter of experiencing that presence. Emerson's writing, now incorporated and subordinated to the life of Emerson, is removed from the field of signification and interpretation. What Emerson means is to be gathered through interaction with his person; his writing is to be seen as but a limb or member of that person. Thus the biographer, removing the biographical subject's writing from textual relations, replaces the textual relations with *personal* relations, even as the subject's personality has been artificially naturalized through incorporation.

Emerson in Concord

> "Concordia its name shall be!" was the sound of Schiller's bell in my ears
> when I began this book about the Sage of Concord.
> —Moncure Conway

The literary incorporation of Emerson began long before Van Wyck Brooks nostalgically smelled the flowers of nineteenth-century New England. In the earliest biographies, Emerson's words and life are made to concur with one another, Concord (Massachusetts) becomes the literal and figurative holy ground of this concurrence, and the resultant concord, or harmony, is established as the true meaning of Emerson. Edward Waldo Emerson (Ralph Waldo's son), in *Emerson in Concord: A Memoir Written for the Social Circle in Concord, Massachusetts,* declares that his purpose "is to show those whom his [father's] writings have helped or moved that his daily life was in accord with his teachings."[10] In the 1890 edition, Edward remembers of Emerson that "his life, brave, serene and happy, was in exact accord with his words."[11] The son brings together the words and the life of the father, establishing a concordance that subsequently signifies bravery, serenity, and happiness.

Even before this, Emerson's life-writers sought to reproduce a harmonious whole under the sign of his name. George Willis Cooke begins *Ralph Waldo Emerson: His Life, Writings, and Philosophy* with prefatory observations on the function of biography: "The following pages are intended as an introduction to the study of the writings of Mr. Emerson. They are biographical only because light may be thrown upon his books by the events of his life. . . . As with all such minds, most of what is truly biographical is in his letters and diaries. Yet the life of Mr. Emerson has been in his thoughts, and these are in his books."[12] Cooke's title clearly lays out the project: on one side of the titular colon, Emerson's life, writings, and philosophy; on the other, the proper and proprietary name. Construe it mathematically as an equation or a ratio (in which the sum is equal to its parts or there exists a fixed relation between two similar entities) or semiotically as a sign (in which the left side is the signifier and the right side the signified) or as a riparian configuration (in which the left bank slopes down to and is united to the right bank with the colonic Concord River)—construe it as we may, we see that name, presence, philosophy, and writing are "in exact accord," tied together in harmony and unity. Cooke's work introduces the writing of Emerson by bringing to light Emerson's life, by which light we can then read Emerson's books in which once again we will find his life.

Similarly, Sarah K. Bolton observes of Emerson that "back of the noble writing was a noble life; beautiful in domestic relations, magnanimous to those who opposed him, strong under most trying circumstances, unselfish, of whom Higginson says, 'Beyond almost all literary men on record, his life has been worthy of his words.'"[13] Here, the life backs the writing, the writing fronts for the life. The being of Emerson and his text's meaning are in Concord, precisely where his son's biography maintains them: "My presentation of my father's life in the pictures here brought together of his daily walk among his own people and the thoughts thereby suggested to him will have been in vain if the agreement of his acts with his words has not everywhere appeared,—the symmetry and harmony of his life."[14] The aptly named town that hosts this symmetry and harmony was, according to Edward, "exactly fitted for his purpose."[15] "Thus when Mr. Emerson moved his household gods to the town which was thereafter to be his home, it was in a sense his home already."[16] Settling in Concord hence signifies settling in concord and presents biographers with the tropic opportunity to fix the purposes (therefore intentions, therefore meanings) of Emerson's writing with accurate and stable coordinates: harmony and symmetry.

Safe and sound in Concord, Emerson's texts are to be heard playing the tune as transcribed by hagiographic incorporation. Whatever else a reader *thinks* Emerson means, what he really meant was optimism, cheerfulness, and a self-satisfaction grand enough to encompass family, town, and country: "Emerson is an optimist who never doubts, who thoroughly believes that all things are good at heart."[17] "He preached a gospel of cheerfulness."[18] "All through his life he was cheerful by temperament and on principle. . . . He took great pleasure in his home. He loved his country, his town, his wife, his family, and constantly rejoiced in the happiness of his lot."[19] Edward further asserts these traits in a passage that helpfully indicates some of the differences between consumption and incorporation:

> His writings are particularly ill adapted for taking out a single quotation as a final statement. Churchman and Agnostic could each find in his writings an armory of weapons against the other, by culling sentences or expressions here and

there. A superficial reading of one essay might mislead, but further study shows certain lines of thought that underlie all: they occur in early writings, wax as the traditional ideas wane with the growth of his mind, and before 1840 he seems to have rested in a security that could never after be disturbed in the main articles of his happy belief, and thereafter all that came to him but illustrated or confirmed or expanded it.[20]

Cautioning against the "superficial," fragmentary reading that would find in "a single quotation" something of a "final statement," Edward instead promotes a reading strategy that ignores the parts on behalf of the whole. This sort of reading dives deep to locate the real meaning of Emerson that "underlie[s] all." Emerson's "happy belief," the facts of his life (from "before 1840" until the end), and his writings are embodied, cohered, secured, and "never after [to] be disturbed."

Before moving on to other aspects of incorporation, I will try another approach to Concord to make clear the consequences of this form of rendering Emerson. Moncure Daniel Conway's *Emerson at Home and Abroad* offers a picture of what Emerson's Concord meant to many of his contemporary followers and indicates what problems this following poses for a textually aware reading of Emerson's writing. Conway's work brings together many of the matters I have been discussing: consumption, transubstantiation, Concord, apotheosis. Immortalizing Emerson by citing the words of Freeman Clarke at Emerson's funeral ("he himself was the best argument for immortality"), Conway connects himself to Emerson's presence with a handshake: "He extended his hand and welcomed me with a smile—his smile, not to be lightly lost by one it has warmed." From the experience of the smile's warmth, the biographer goes on to equate the Concord Sage's presence to that of the Buddha: "This welcoming word and smile was the break of a new day. I could not answer. Many years after I read that one in Paradise was asked how he got there and replied, 'One day as Buddha passed he smiled upon me.'"[21]

Conway continues in this vein in an effort, not only to bring Emerson back to life (this particular biography begins with a vigil after Emerson's death), but also to make of this life something divine and life-giving in itself: "This man in the beginning of that generation had been compelled to leave his pulpit because he could not administer an Eastern sacrament: now did we receive from him the substance of that shadow, and the kneeling heart whispered—Take, eat: it is his body and his blood he gives thee."[22] Emerson's meaning and Emerson's being are brought together, to be received sacredly on the tongue of the public.[23] The biographer's transubstantial offering of Emerson's body and blood constitutes a large portion of the purpose of the biography, which is to record and replay the song of Concord I have described above. Conway cannot get that song out of his head and believes the tune should be piped for the betterment of others: "'Concordia its name shall be!' was the sound . . . in my ears when I began this book about the Sage of Concord."[24] We need only listen, and we can hear the same song.

All of this is quite remarkable enough for what it tells us about the sound of Emerson in the late nineteenth century. But it is made even more remarkable by the founding moment of Conway's presentation—a moment in which the act of reading leads the biographer from South to North, from law book to the Law, from slave master to the feet of the master, from discord to Concord:

> From this vigil beside the grave of Emerson, memory passes over the time of a generation, and across long stretches of sea and land, to a secret nook near my Virginian home, to whose crystal fount and flowers my eighteenth spring carried a wintry heart. . . . Fresh from college, now from every career planned by parent or friend I had recoiled: some indefinable impediment barred each usual path: the last shadow settled around me when the law-book was closed to be opened no more. Utterly miserable, self-accused amid sorrowful faces, with no outlook but to be a fettered master of slaves, I was then wont to shun the world, with gun for apology, and pass the hours in retreat. So came I on a day, and reclined on the grass, reading in a magazine casually brought. The laugh and chatter of negroes pushing their flat-boats loaded with grain, the song of birds, the sound of church-bells across the river, all smote upon a heart discordant with them, at discord with itself. Nature had no meaning, life no promise and no aim. Listlessly turning to the printed page, one sentence caught my eye and held it; one sentence quoted from Emerson, which changed my world and me.
>
> A sentence only! I do not repeat it: it might not bear to others what it bore to me: its searching subtle revelation defies any analysis I can make of its words. All I know is that it was the touch of flame I needed. That day my gun was laid aside to be resumed no more. . . . A human aim had arisen; souls were to be saved; and in that work must begin my small "Wanderjahre." My horse was got ready: my bible, filled with maternal inscriptions holy as its texts, was taken for compass in my wanderings; I only longed to add some book by Emerson. But the Index Expurgatorius of slavery had excluded Northern books so long and so well, that the bookseller in Fredericksburg offered me "Emerson's Arithmetic," and denied the existence of any other Emerson. For a long time I had only my one sentence; but how large it grew![25]

From the resting place of Emerson's corpse, Conway looks back across time and space to a moment of personal crisis, of discord with the world around him. Fatefully, some of Emerson's words seize his attention. (Note that they are quoted *from* Emerson by someone else in a magazine—i.e., an "Emersonism" has laid hold of him, reproduced in an unknown context.) These words mystically defy reproduction and analysis, change the world and the reader, cause a hunger for more of their kind that will not be sated by the bookstores of benighted Virginia, and ultimately transport Conway to Concord. The pilgrim comes to discover that, whether abroad or at home, Emerson is always in Concord, and Conway's biographical incorporation insists that Emerson be found there evermore.

Emerson at Home and Abroad, Emerson in Concord, and *Ralph Waldo Emerson: His Life, Writings, and Philosophy* are examples of the denaturing of Emerson's text. Substituting personal relations for textual relations, these works create a harmony of life and writing that delimits potential signification of the text and restricts possible interpretations. Emerson's words are to be read as being of a piece with his person. Ideas that would interrupt the symmetry, that trouble the harmony, or that simply do not match the image of the benign Concord Sage—even if prompted by Emerson's text itself—are seen as inharmonious, asymmetrical, and hence un-Emersonian. To remember Emerson and his writing in this fashion is to secure the text to the person, the person to a place, and the meaning of Emerson to an authorized version. That version, widely reproduced from the latter half of the nineteenth century and well into the next, stems from and attempts to promote harmony, symmetry, benignity, and stability in the face of the displacing (inharmonious, asymmetrical, malignant, destabilizing) qualities inherent to the increasing incorporation of American culture.

Emerson Remembered

> I have been obliged to dismember and rearrange [the journals] more than I wished, and often to give their general drift in my own words, instead of simply allowing him to tell his own story.
> —James Elliot Cabot

The consequences of confining Emerson to Concord can best be seen in the practice of Emerson's authorized biographer, James Elliot Cabot. Cabot's access to Emerson's life and writings affords him a peculiar status regarding the connection of the two and the propagation of that connection. A family friend who had earned the Emersons' respect and affection, Cabot was, according to Edward, the obvious choice for literary executor: "It was natural for the family to turn to Mr. Cabot. They proposed to

him to begin his task during my father's lifetime and put this book in order. He came, and the tangled skein smoothed itself under his hand."[26]
"This book" refers to *Letters and Social Aims* (1875). Emerson, who "felt
towards Mr. Cabot as to a younger brother," whose "face lighted up" when
this brother visited him on his death bed ("and he exclaimed, 'Elliot Cabot? Praise!'"), "always spoke of Letters and Social Aims to Mr. Cabot as
'your book.'"[27] Through his editing of Emerson's work and remembrance
of Emerson's life, Cabot provides an image of Emerson that still informs
our understanding of the meaning of Emerson.[28]

At the beginning of his *Memoir*, Cabot asserts that he is simply offering
readers

> some details of [Emerson's] outward and inward history that may fill out and
> define more closely the image of him they already have. . . . My aim has been to
> use [unpublished writings and letters] to furnish materials for an estimate of him,
> without undertaking any estimate or interposing any comments beyond what
> seemed necessary for the better understanding of the facts presented. Where I
> may seem to have transgressed this rule, I am in truth for the most part only
> summing up impressions gathered from his journals and correspondence, or from
> the recollections of his contemporaries.[29]

Cabot proposes to begin with a preconceived notion of Emerson, "the
image [we] already have," and substantiate that notion with sources previously unavailable to the reading public. As this section's epigraphs warns,
such a project may require that Emerson be "dismembered" and "rear-
ranged," the "general drift" reformed in Cabot's words.[30] Denying that
such a "summing up" of "impressions" might alter the nature of the text,
the editor insists that, because his data derives directly from the writings
of Emerson or the "recollections of his contemporaries" (including Cabot himself), the impressions as such are unmediated. Rather, the impressions summed in the *Memoir* are imprints of the words of Emerson or the
lived experience of those who knew him; no act of interpretation, therefore, is necessary. Cabot "in truth" is remembering how it was, present-
ing how it is, and representing how it should be.

This dismembering/remembering results in an Emerson who begins life
as a "spiritual-looking boy in blue nankeen," "angelic and remarkable,"[31]
and stays that way, through life's vicissitudes, until the end, when he still
safely rises above it all:

> But what was chiefly remarkable in his conversation, and always new and strik-
> ing, although it belonged to the stuff of which his whole life was made, was its
> uniform and unforced cheerfulness. He did not need to turn away from gloomy

things, from uncomfortable presages in society about him, or from the ever-narrowing line that bound in his own activities on earth; for he saw beyond them, and as clearly now as when, forty years before, he had sounded the notes that told that the lofty soul of Puritanism was not dead in the decay of its body.[32]

The *Memoir* presents an Emerson who is essentially unchanged for forty years. As with Emerson in Concord, this Emerson's meaning and being are tied to one another ("his conversation" is of "the stuff of which his whole life was made"). Although more harmonious with a traditionally Puritan hymn of the loftiness of the soul, Cabot's Emerson still produces the uniform song of cheerfulness.

The keynote of Cabot's presentation is sounded in the preface when he observes that the "portrait prefixed to the first volume is the gift of Dr. William Herbert Rollins, who had it engraved under his supervision after a reduction made by himself from the well-known photograph by Hawes, made, Mr. Hawes thinks, in 1856: the best likeness that we have of Emerson, as it appears to me, and here admirably reproduced."[33] Preface and face signal what is to come from the pages of this "memory" of Emerson: the admirable reproduction of an engraving of a reduction of a representation of Emerson as he placidly looks away from the viewer in 1856. It is indeed the "best likeness" in that it is something like the best image of Emerson, of Emerson at his best, on his best behavior. This is the Emerson that Cabot remembers and the one readers will remember if Cabot's project succeeds.

The little Emersons that orbit around this most central, most true Emerson all yield themselves to the perfect whole in Cabot's account. The angelic boy becomes a self-reliant and contented teenager: "The truth was, the school-boy docility had already given way to a remarkable maturity, which however showed itself as yet only in a feeling of self-reliance and contentedness to wait until his proper course should be made clear to him."[34] And so Emerson will remain his bright, cheerful, self-reliable self: "In manner and disposition he appeared then, in his fourteenth year, just what he was afterwards; kindly, affable, but self-contained."[35] Appearing then as he did ever after, Emerson's various ages are thus incorporated into "the best likeness."

Incorporation of the different stages of the life of Emerson into a uniform whole takes up much of Cabot's effort in his memoir. More importantly, however, this aspect of incorporation makes possible the coherence of Emerson's different writings. In direct contact with the unifying substance of Emerson's being, the executor is qualified to reduce the myriad writings by Emerson and form them into an integral, homogenized, wholesome package. The result is the "real meaning of Emerson"—as espoused by his officially sanctioned literary biographer. Although he does occasionally recognize the difficulties involved in reducing Emerson's writing, Cabot ultimately accomplishes just such a reduction by fusing Emerson's words and his life and representing the latter as preternaturally stable. Hence the reader encounters such phrases as "this house was Emerson's home for the rest of his life"; "Emerson got his study arranged, and settled down to the manner of life from which he never afterwards departed"; "Emerson was now settled in the habits of life to which he ever afterwards adhered"; "Emerson never grew old."[36] Finding the home for the rest of his life, Cabot's "Emerson" settled into orbit around himself—as captured in the image of 1856—and circles there today.

Stuffing Emerson into the same easy chair in which he is to sit for eternity allows Cabot to attempt the more difficult task of securing Emerson's writing, a task accomplished overtly (i.e., before the reader's eyes) in the recounting of Cabot's collaboration with Emerson on *Letters and Social Aims*. Cabot notes that, as Emerson's chosen literary executor, he was selected to assist Emerson in preparing the volume from scattered, often previously unpublished lectures in manuscript. In rounding up the wandering words, Cabot assures his readers that he ever adhered to "Mr. Emerson's wishes" and "what he desired": Emerson's intentions have been saved.[37] As the sage's personal redactor, Cabot enjoys the privity of Emerson's true meaning, and his memoir of Emerson is canonized as volumes 13 and 14 of *The Works of Ralph Waldo Emerson*. (*Letters and Social Aims* is volume 8.) Tidy and tranquilizing, Cabot recovers the order of the disordered and disordering Emerson and fixes limits to Emerson's writing that secure the meaning of Emerson. By ever returning to the religious, the placid Emerson, Cabot ensures that the extravagant Emerson, the Emerson who unsettles all things, the skeptical, questioning Emerson will be safely incorporated into the best likeness.

For as the executor of Emerson's literary estate, Cabot knows truly which tones belong to Emerson and which do not.[38] He feels safe in asserting that the whole of Emerson's work contains essentially five ideas.[39] Cabot's Emerson would not think of writing "Whim" on the lintel (the act of philosophical mischief discussed in "Self-Reliance"), for he is, above all, spiritually pure, deeply religious, always the blue-nankeened boy, the affable, self-contained, good soul. Rejecting the characterization of Emerson as "one who came to unsettle Christian belief" ("Nothing was farther from his intention"),[40] Cabot maintains that "transcendentalism was not a philosophy; it was a religious revival."[41] His Emerson believes that it is "better to remain in the existing forms and uplift and vivify them by faith so long as that was possible."[42] Providing a useful guide to Emerson's thought, page headings in Cabot's memoir encapsulate the chapters' themes. One stretch, which occupies roughly a third of the first volume, summarizes Emerson's life in the 1830s thus: "LECTURES"—"SETTLES IN CON-CORD"—"TRANSCENDENTALISM"—"CONCORD"—"RELI-GION"—"CONCORD." (These headings, which sit atop the right-hand pages, are coupled with each left-hand page heading of "RALPH WALDO EMERSON.") Especially if we consider Cabot's definition of transcenden-talism as a "religious revival," the page headings refer readers to a settled, religious Emerson in harmony with Concord. While it is true that terse words found at the top of a page are decidedly not meant to give an elabo-rate accounting of events, these devices do function as a framework for reading Emerson (and as such are, in miniature, a form of the scholarly-biographic apparatus itself). Because there are no references to Emerson's writings in this briefest (and most reductive) of reductions, the page head-ings have the effect of preserving the writings of the 1830s (which include *Nature*, "The American Scholar," and the address to the Divinity School) in an almost exclusively religious context, which in turn secures the mean-ing of Emerson to the legacy of Puritanism.[43] It is within this context that Cabot makes sense of Emerson; the philosophically excessive and fre-quently shocking texts are contained within the walls of the church the biographer builds.[44]

By employing Religion as the framework for what Emerson meant and inflating the value of Emerson's speech (the effect of which "was immedi-ate and personal, not to be detached from his presence"[45]), Cabot fixes limits and restores order to Emerson's writing. The playfulness of Emerson's writing—a play innate to the multiplicity of possible meanings—is cur-tailed, and the meaning of Emerson is called home. Emerson no longer means; Emerson meant.[46] As I will demonstrate below, there is a remark-able amount of play in the text of Emerson's writing, and it is precisely because this play, by nature, disrupts the process of biographical incorpo-ration that Cabot must close it down.

The operations of Waldo, Inc. and its closing down on the play of Emerson's writing become questionable if we but consider an essay such as "Poetry and Imagination," a work that first appeared in *Letters and Social Aims*—the volume Emerson called "Cabot's book." I find the twist of the possessive most intriguing, indicating a larger question of textual authority. No one would propose that James Elliot Cabot is actually the author of an entire volume of the Ralph Waldo Emerson oeuvre, nor of any particular essay found in that volume. My suggestion is, rather, that the question of authority is made pertinent by the circumstances of production of the eighth volume of the "Standard Library Edition of the Works of Ralph Waldo Emerson with a General Index and a Memoir by James Elliot Cabot *with Steel Portraits and Etchings* in Fourteen Volumes" and further that these circumstances can serve as a metaphor for the composition of the Emerson corpus more generally. These questions and circumstances, when combined with those surrounding the production and reproduction of specific images of Emerson in literary biographies, describe a complex of issues that need be addressed when interpreting the preposterous text of Emerson's writing.[47]

Cabot, alert to some of the permutations of the author question, begins his prefatory note to *Letters and Social Aims* thus: "It seems proper to mention here the circumstances under which this volume was put together, as they may have some bearing upon the estimate to be placed upon it."[48] He reports that Emerson was coerced, more or less, to bring the volume out, and did so with "heavy heart": "Some time perhaps in 1870, Mr. Emerson learned that a London publisher was intending, without consulting him, to make up a volume of his uncollected writings, from the 'Dial' and elsewhere. He was much disturbed by this intelligence, and wrote to his friend, Mr. Moncure Conway, to stop the publication if possible."[49] To accomplish this, Conway arranged for Emerson to prepare such a work for the London publisher in question. The reluctant writer went about his business with a "feeling of repugnance at being forced into an enterprise which he had not intended."[50] This repugnance, coupled with his increasing mental incapacitation, made for "slow progress" in the project, and Emerson "had got ready little more than the first piece, Poetry and Imagination, the proof-sheets of which were in his hands,—indeed had been for some time in his hands,—when on the 24th of July his house was burned and all possibility of work put an end to for the time, not merely by the confusion of his papers and the destruction of his wonted surroundings, but yet more effectually by an illness resulting from the shock."[51] Fire consumes the house of Emerson, causing destruction, confusion, and personal debilitation.[52] According to Cabot, however, the proof-sheets for "Poetry and Imagination" demonstrate an already significant "loss of memory and of mental grasp" by the writer, such that, in regards to bringing out the volume of his writing, "he was quite content to do as little as possible, and desired to leave everything in my hands":[53]

> This will appear to be of the more consequence in view of the fact that with the exception of four, viz., The Comic, Persian Poetry, Quotation and Original-

ity, and Progress of Culture, the essays contained in this volume, though written in great part long before, had never been published: and, further, of the state of the manuscripts, which consisted of loose sheets, laid together in parcels, each marked on the cover with the title under which it was last read as a lecture, but often without any completely recoverable order or fixed limits.[54]

In the production of much of *Letters and Social Aims* fragments written over a considerable period of time are made to cohere beneath a title that describes a general topic to which each fragment more or less relates. Cabot, as authorized biographer and handpicked literary executor, undertakes the construction of the essays by recovering a semblance of order and fixing limits where he can. Such an undertaking, while based on writings accomplished by the man named Emerson, are not precisely done so in his name. The undertaker admits that, regarding the origin of the texts and their relation to the author: "There is nothing here that [Emerson] did not write, and he gave his full approval to whatever was done in the way of selection and arrangement; but I cannot say that he applied his mind very closely to the matter. He was pleased, in a general way, that the work should go on, but it may be a question exactly how far he sanctioned it."[55] If the writer's sanctioning of another's compilation is in dispute; if the writer referred to the book as belonging to another; if the writing consists mainly of stringing together words and phrases loosely related to one another— a stringing brought about by the effort to array disarray—then just who is responsible for "Poetry and Imagination"? If one still insists unequivocably that an admittedly infirm Emerson is that writer, one yet must agree that Cabot has had significant and final say in the construction of the text in question, i.e., in the literary execution of the text.

My own sense is that worries over who constructed "Poetry and Imagination" lead to a dead end. The biographical incorporation of life and text strives to make Emerson cohere and coherent. He is made to be a certain person, whose personality then informs and therefore explains the writing, which ultimately means concord, religion, self-contained happiness, and so forth. The nature of Emerson's text, however, always remains to some extent playful, in the sense of there being a play of meanings in the text itself, which is also frequently concerned with the very nature of this play and its effects on interpretation. The writing, therefore, is always *questionable*: its nature is uncertain and it raises questions, begs questions, insists on questions of reading. Reading the first essay of *Letters and Social Aims* ("Poetry and Imagination"), for example, one finds all sorts of questions regarding texts, nature, and interpretation.

Poetry, Imagination, Gay Science

"Poetry and Imagination" is more or less a collection of various thoughts on the two nouns of the title. These nouns undergo definition and redefinition—are put into play, as it were—and are thus proffered for further thought. Poetry itself is not simply a specific genre of literature originating from the mind of an independent, creative source. For one thing, the poet, according to the essay, is never himself (or herself): "His own body is a fleeting apparition,—his personality as fugitive as the trope he employs."[56] Person and personality are on the wing, in flight from the stasis that would make possible an adequate representation of the poet's identity. The nature of the poet is unsettling, on the move; and this, according to the writer of "Poetry and Imagination," is one of poetry's important lessons: "I think the use or value of poetry to be the suggestion it affords of the flux or fugaciousness of the poet."[57]

The poet is not, then, a fixed thing, hence is not the easily definable source of a particular type of writing. These negative definitions confound traditional modes of construing the poet and are teamed with positive definitions that require further thinking. Instead of the static entity that created a particular work, the poet becomes rather the fugacious employer of tropes and this activity is depicted as thinking: "For the value of a trope is that the hearer is one: and indeed Nature itself is a vast trope, and all particular natures are tropes."[58] Not only a user of tropes, the poet *is* a trope, a figure of speech, say, or a metaphor, a relation, as is everything that the poet observes, Nature writ large. Thus: "All thinking is analogizing, and it is the use of life to learn metonymy. The endless passing of one element into new forms, the incessant metamorphosis, explains the rank which the imagination holds in our catalogue of mental powers. The imagination is the reader of these forms."[59] The poet then becomes a reader as much as a writer, the active interpreter of nature, of "the endless passing of one element into new forms." Interpreting this change involves both the ability to imaginatively analogize and the acknowledgment that the interpreter is as unchangeably changing as that which is to be interpreted.

All of which indicates that fixing on the person of the writer in an attempt to interpret the writer's writing is a distraction at best. According to "Poetry and Imagination," "our overpraise and idealization of famous masters" comes from a mediocre impatience to satisfy ourselves with being in the presence of greatness:

The praise we now give to our heroes we shall unsay when we make larger demands. How fast we outgrow the books of the nursery,—then those that satisfied our youth. What we once admired as poetry has long since come to be a sound of tin pans; and many of our later books we have outgrown. Perhaps Homer and Milton will be tin pans yet. Better not to be easily pleased. The poet should rejoice if he has taught us to despise his song; if he has so moved us as to lift us,—to open the eye of the intellect to see farther and better.[60]

We must not only give up traditional notions of the writer but also change our relation to the writing. Writer and writing are metaphors to be interpreted in such a way as to foster an improved vision; clung to, they contribute to our blindness. This is the reason that "the critic, the philosopher, is a failed poet": critics and philosophers fail to engage the text of nature, to be moved by the text, and to see the text, dwelling as they do on the person of the creator and other limiting notions.[61] It is worth noting that Emerson's speculation on the future of Milton and Homer greatly offended at least one biographer and critic. The often insightful George Woodberry, in his *Ralph Waldo Emerson,* finds this "startling sentence" of Emerson's "foolish," demonstrating his "imperfect hold on the qualities that make for permanence in literature."[62] My argument, Woodberry's judgment and Emerson's foolishness notwithstanding, is that the sentence and its paragraph indicate literature's (and poets' and critics') *impermanence,* thereby insisting on continued thinking of the nature of the literary text and its interpretation.

The nature of the literary text is such that it is analogous to the text of nature. Parts of nature, "like words of a sentence," must be understood in relation to one another—nature is a text, the meaning of which is to be known through engagement of the parts *and* connection of the parts to one another: "Natural objects, if individually described and out of connection, are not yet known, since they are really parts of a symmetrical universe, like words of a sentence; and if their true order is found, the poet can read their divine significance orderly as in a Bible."[63] Hence the text of nature is an immense unity consisting of myriad related parts and characterized by incessant movement or change in these elements and their relations. Everything about this text shifts endlessly, and the poet who would interpret it must acknowledge the shifty relations of the text— including those that comprise the perspective of the interpreter (who, as we have seen, is a trope, a figure of speech, a turning of words). "While the student ponders this immense unity, he observes that all things in Nature, the animals, the mountain, the river, the seasons, wood, iron, stone, vapor, have a mysterious relation to his thoughts and his life."[64]

Such and so do pieces of "Poetry and Imagination" provisionally come together, depicting nature and related texts as never final, stable wholes but as interconnecting elements always on the move. The text of nature teaches that texts require methods of reading that do not settle on particular interpretations for all time. When we as readers arrive at the meaning of a text, we are to do so while acknowledging "that we are not to stay here; that we must be making ready to go"; "that nothing stands still in nature but death; that the creation is on wheels, in transit, always passing into something else."[65] Nature's transitory nature is a "hint, however conveyed, [that] upsets our politics, trade, customs, marriages, nay, the common-sense side of religion and literature, which are all founded on low nature,—on the clearest and most economical mode of administering the material world, considered as final. The admission, never so covertly, that this is a makeshift, sets the dullest brain in ferment: . . . gunpowder is laid under every man's breakfast-table."[66] The acknowledgment that nature is textual and that texts are makeshift and provisional makes possible the explosive situation by which our everyday world might be changeable—if readers will read accordingly. And this decidedly does not involve fixing a final meaning to the very text I am currently engaging. Thus I am not claiming the interpretation of interpretation I have found to emerge from Cabot's/Emerson's essay to be *the* meaning of Emerson or even of "Poetry and Imagination." It is rather *a* meaning of this writing that brings into question certain notions of the author, the work of literature, and traditional methods of interpretation that inform even our most current and theoretically hip approaches to reading; must be seen in relation to other meanings that emerge from the context of the essay; and must lead to further thinking of the meaning emergent, the method that enables the emergence, and what this emergence means for meaning and interpretation more generally.

One element of "Poetry and Imagination" urges the reader to think of poetry as considerably different from versifying. Just as the poet becomes an interpreter, poetry becomes a peculiar type of interpretation involving affirmative versions of vision, movement, and responsible relation to that which is to be interpreted. In the redefining of the poet as trope, the writer consequently redefines imagination as the ability to affirm one's own metaphoricity while engaging in the metaphors that constitute nature or the text one would interpret; "therefore is poetry ever the best reading. The very design of imagination is to domesticate us in another, in a celestial nature."[67] So domesticated in the makeshift metaphorical world, our ability to understand the world becomes connected, not to traditional scientific methods, but to a vastly different sort of science or knowing. Traditional science, like traditional philosophy and criticism, fails because it cannot adequately acknowledge fugaciousness, metaphor, life, the nature of the text, relation, poetry: "Science was false by being unpoetical. It assumed to explain a reptile or mollusk, and isolated it,—which is hunting for life in graveyards. Reptile or mollusk or man or angel only exists in system, in relation."[68]

The reader is challenged to rethink scientific thinking, to move away from the ways of knowing that destructively explain or isolate phenomena. Affirming the system or text that structures the possible relations of all things, the reader can then approximate the poetic, provisional method of interpreting nature and text. Poetry being the best reading, the reader is thus preposterously to become the poet. And this further means engaging in a very different sort of science, for "Poetry," the writer of "Poetry and Imagination" informs the reader, "is the *gai science*."[69] The gay scientist or poet "builds, adds, and affirms," where the "ungay" scientist or philosopher or critic "destroys."

But "the gay science": what does this odd term signify? Where does it lead? To what ways of thinking and interpreting? If we correlate it with the other approaches to interpretation provided in the essay gay science emerges as a reading that travels, that encourages making connections and finding relation, that urges "the benefit of the largest interpretation." It is a thinking that acknowledges thinking to be analogy, metaphor, metonymy, that affirms this acknowledgment and moves on. It is a way of knowing in transit, of making ready to go. One place it might lead is toward the writing of another reader of Emerson's text, another writer of *The Gay Science*. I do not mean to consider, for obvious reasons, the personal relations between Nietzsche and Emerson, but to attempt, rather, a gaily scientific glance down the line of thinking that leads from the "*gai science*" of "Poetry and Imagination" to *die fröliche Wissenschaft* (*la gaya scienza*) of Friedrich Nietzsche.[70]

The gay science of the latter resembles somewhat (and also differs considerably from) that of the former and addresses many of the issues with which I have been concerned in this chapter. That the two gay sciences are connected seems clear. Walter Kaufmann notes that Nietzsche was rereading Emerson's essays while writing *The Gay Science* and that the first edition of the work "actually carried as an epigraph a quotation from Emerson."[71] Although he fails to mention Emerson's use of the precise terminology in "Poetry and Imagination," Kaufmann refers to a similar phrase—"the Joyous Science"—which appears, as he observes, in passages of Emerson's journals, lectures, and essays.[72] Kaufmann quotes from Emerson's "The Scholar" to better establish a relation between the two authors: "'I think the peculiar office of scholars in a careful and gloomy generation is to be (as the poets were called in the Middle Ages) Professors of the Joyous Science, detectors and delineators of occult symmetries'—and so forth, down through 'music and dancing.'"[73] Whether joyous or gay, occult or not, the professing of this science involves, according to Emerson, the office or duty of scholars (call this the sort of reading I have delineated above) as well as "music and dancing." According to Kaufmann, it is a special way of thinking suggestive of "'light feet,' 'dancing,' 'laughter,'—and the ridicule of the 'spirit of gravity.'"[74] And, according to Nietzsche, it is "the saturnalia of the spirit," "a bit of merry-making after long privation and powerlessness, the rejoicing of strength that is returning, of a reawakened faith in a tomorrow," "the *will* henceforth to question further," "a more delicate taste for joy, . . . a tenderer tongue for all good things, . . . merrier senses, . . . a second dangerous innocence in joy, more childlike and yet a hundred times subtler," and a "laughter" that "will then have formed an alliance with wisdom."[75]

This series of interpretations and affirmations of the gay science resounds with the music of movement, relation, thinking, and imagination. In Nietzsche's rendering of the concept, we find complaints (similar to those in "Poetry and Imagination") about prevailing ways of knowing and declarations of the need for different methods of interpretation. Consider, for example, the epigraph that announces the work of this chapter: "To what extent can truth endure incorporation? That is the question; that is the experiment."[76] This question comes after a long description of various modes of incorporation: "The reputation, name, and appearance, the usual measure and weight of a thing, what it counts for . . . all this grows from generation unto generation, merely because people believe in it, until it gradually grows to be part of the thing and turns into its very body."[77] Later the problem of the name, appearance, and reputation being incorporated into a body and taken for the truth of a particular thing is represented as being related to instrumentality, the insistence on a fixed and knowable world, and the failure to acknowledge the changeable nature of things— all of which inform the incorporation of a person with a specific meaning. Under the heading "*A firm reputation*," the critically gay scientist observes (of the one incorporated):

Society is pleased to feel that the virtue of this person, the ambition of that one, and the thoughtfulness and passion of the third provide it with a dependable *instrument* that is always at hand; society honors this *instrumental nature*, this way of remaining faithful to oneself, this unchangeability of views, aspirations, and even faults and lavishes its highest honors upon it. Such esteem, which flourishes and has flourished everywhere alongside the morality of mores, breeds "character" and brings all change, all re-learning, all self-transformation into *ill repute*.[78]

One can see in these words a description of the workings of Waldo, Inc.: the settling of an Emerson (whose name encompasses the being and the writing, the meaning of the two when gathered into a single body), the staking of that Emerson, with an undisturbed nature and a seemingly much-deserved reputation of placid and benign religiosity. One can also discern the makings of a complaint that the writer should not be construed as a static entity but rather as a fugacious metaphor who both reads the world differently and helps other readers do so. This becomes more clear when the later gay scientist challenges us in the following manner: "There is yet another world to be discovered—and more than one. Embark, philosophers!"[79] Note the call for departure, suggestive of a call for moving on in order to better think. To move in this way, one must be willing to question, to keep thinking, to be unsettled: "But to stand in the midst of the *rerum concordia discors* and of this whole marvelous uncertainty and rich ambiguity of existence *without questioning*, without trembling with the craving and the rapture of such questioning, without at least hating the person who questions, perhaps even finding him faintly amusing—that is what I feel to be *contemptible*."[80] The reader warrants the contempt of gay science when he or she stands still in the discordant concord of things and fails to ask questions. Overlooking marvelous uncertainty and rich ambiguity, the consumptive or incorporative reader foregoes the possibility of engaged interpretation of the text (and of nature) and, indeed, "reject[s] the possibility that *it may include infinite interpretations*."[81]

Emerson's *gai science* and Nietzsche's *die frölicbe Wissenschaft* provide a figure for makeshift and mobile reading, a provisional version of ways in which a reader might build from, add to, and affirm the text that is to be read. My hope is that in elucidating some of the problems that have beset the Emerson text, we can initiate a more thoughtful (and hopeful) interpretation of both that text and the larger text of nature. *Hopeful* appears parenthetically here so as to signal an important aspect of this study: I want to see what hope there is for our world, and this is inextricably woven into (according to "Poetry and Imagination") our ways of knowing our world—that is, our ways of reading the text of the world around us. Of the poet, we read that "as everything streams and advances, as every faculty and every desire is procreant, and every perception is a destiny, there is no limit to his hope."[82] Hence one direction this study leads is to our prospects; another is to the role of the scholar in achieving these prospects; a third involves the views that our prospects will afford; yet another regards prospective ways of reading.

A course in the gay science directs the reader to an engaged but creative and open way of reading and teaches that the attempt to see the Emerson text more clearly necessitates challenging the Concord incorporation of Emerson. Students of the gay science learn "that only can we see which we are, and which we make."[83] If we are analogous to nature, if we are *of* nature, and nature is to be known by us through an interpretation of its text, then I must propose another preposterous claim: To read Emerson, to read Nietzsche, to read nature, reading must be naturalized (made natural to or analogous with the nature of the text), but reading can be naturalized only after Nature has been denatured.

4 Foolish Consistencies

Every superior mind will pass through this domain of
equilibration,—I should rather say, will know how to
avail himself of the checks and balances in nature, as a
natural weapon against the exaggeration and formalism
of bigots and blockheads.
  —"Montaigne; or, The Skeptic"

W hat does it mean to see nature as a text, as it is pictured in the essay
"Poetry and Imagination" and more thoroughly elaborated in such
pieces as *Nature* and "The Method of Nature"? How is it that nature's
"checks and balances" can defend us from presumably unnatural "exaggeration and formalism," from bigotry and blockheadedness? What does
reading nature have to do with reading Emerson (or vice versa)? Is reading "naturally" possible? These are the larger questions with which the remainder of the study is concerned, and to address them I will consider
different ways the Emerson text has been affected by critical approaches
to his writings, picking up with biographically oriented versions and moving on from these subject-centered (or "subjective") accounts to putatively
more objective renderings. My hypothesis is that the dominant methods
of making sense of Emerson employed by American critics are analogous
to what Emerson refers to as a "traditionary and limited way" of interpreting texts. I mean the phrase, which comes from "An Address Delivered before the Senior Class in Divinity College, Cambridge, Sunday
Evening, 15 July, 1838," to describe customary usages that neglect the
nature of reading and writing and the contexts of nature in which these
cultural enterprises always occur.

Largely a complaint against "historical Christianity," the Divinity School
address refers to this institution as "the traditionary and limited way of
using the mind of Christ."[1] Two major defects are found in the institutional

method by which the figure of Christ has been read. The second defect, entailing an examination of revelation and the measures by which "the goodliest of institutions" has concealed what would be revealed, is depicted as a "consequence of the first." The primary problem, as the address states quite plainly, is that the contemplation of the figure of Jesus Christ has always involved "an exaggeration of the personal, the positive, the ritual. It has dwelt, it dwells, with noxious exaggeration about the *person* of Jesus."[2] An institutionally sanctioned body of interpreters has been created and ordains that "you must subordinate your nature to Christ's nature; you must accept our interpretations and take his portrait as the vulgar draw it."[3]

Take the last of these passages first. The nature of "your nature" has at once to do with your internal landscape (one might consider this the field of sensorial and intellectual activities that form one's perspective on the world) and with the greater universe in which you and your perspective occur. Your nature—that which makes you "you" *and* the world of phenomena in which you find yourself—is, according to the "traditionary and limited ways" of understanding the nature of things, to be subordinated to a "portrait" or representation of "Christ's nature" (that which made Christ "Christ" and the world of phenomena in which Christ lived). A subordination of our nature *now* to a representation of Christ's nature *then* causes us to overlook the meaning and value of "this refulgent summer" (the description of which opens the address), of "this world, in which our senses converse."[4] Instead, vulgar versions of historic nature are to be accepted, unquestioningly and throughout time.

Moving on to the previous passage, one sees that the problem with the exaggeration of the personal is precisely that it magnifies the features of a figure so much that the figure is taken for something "extra-figural," as it were, or literal—in the address's terms, as something "positive." Taking Jesus literally or positively amplifies unduly an aspect of that figure's significance so as to overrun and lose sight of that figure's very figurality, thereby constructing a definitive and fixed reality—the figure made flesh. I especially have in mind here the *OED*'s denotations of *positive* as "artificially instituted"; "conventional; opp. to *natural*"; "expressed without qualification; admitting no question"; "having no relation to or comparison with other things; free from qualifications, conditions, or reservations; absolute, unconditional; opposed to *relative* and *comparative*." *Ritual* would then refer to the mode by which the person of Jesus is rendered positive, which is to say removed from relations and protected from further consideration. The figure, through ritualized modes of experiencing it, takes on an objective reality as a person, a literalness, and is no longer subject to thinking, which, as we saw in "Poetry and Imagination," always entails analogy, metaphors, and continued figuring.

"Natural" reading, then, emerges as relative and comparative reading, as opposed to conventional or positive ("traditionary" or "limited") reading. Natural reading is not the way we read naturally, but a cultivated method of interpretation; it pertains to the ways in which we interpret nature *and* to the ways in which we interpret the words of human beings (which, by extension, are like nature because they are part of nature). In the example of Jesus, the address proposes that "he spoke of miracles; for he felt that man's life was a miracle, and all that man doth, and he knew that this daily miracle shines, as the character ascends. But the word Miracle, as pronounced by Christian churches, gives a false impression; it is Monster. It is not one with the blowing clover and the falling rain."[5] Because the "idioms of his language, and the figures of his rhetoric" are positively and ritualistically employed as the cornerstone of churches,[6] because his tropes are turned into myths that are taken as truth, "Miracle" (that over which we might wonder, that which is astonishing, strange, wonderful) is made into "Monster"—a warning, "something extraordinary or unnatural" (*OED*). Words that are no longer "one with the blowing clover and the falling rain"—figures removed from the text of nature— lose the life of their meaning and are cemented into cultural foundations. "Truth," when words are treated in this manner, "is foreclosed and monopolized."[7] According to the address, this is what comes from dwelling on the person of the author and building an edifice around the author's words. Tropes are removed from the text, mistaken as positive rather than relational, and perverted into monstrosity (that which is unnatural).

Metaphorically construed, the second paragraph of the address offers an alternative mode of reading along with an admonition about biographical criticism and its role in reading and interpretation. By drawing attention to open-mindedness, the need to understand the world we see as "illustration and fable," persistent questioning, the limits of our "imperfect apprehension," and the acknowledgment of "infinite relations," the address suggests that interpretation must ever be a perpetual process.[8] It must be an act that does not seize monstrously on a fact, person, or single and positive meaning, but openly and assiduously studies in order to know the various relations that make possible the very recognition of any one textual element. Interpretation (of worlds and texts) must engage, wonder, make connections, and proceed, rather than dwell apart on isolated elements monstrously removed.

Part of the problem, then, is the *subject* of criticism, the critical subject or reader who dwells on the subject of the writer. By tending to set up shop around the person of the author, criticism unnaturally severs the text of the writer's words from the falling rain and the blowing clover. Emerson's "Thoughts on Modern Literature" postulates that the direction in which literary matters *tend* is of the utmost import. We are to discern whether a writing's "tendency" "leads us to nature, or to the person of the writer."[9] A tendency toward the latter is always misguided, misguiding. Because reading is inherently caught up in subjective matters, the subjectiveness of a given interpretation must always be a part of what one attempts to read. "Thoughts on Modern Literature" distinguishes between two modes of subjective reading, observing that "there is a pernicious ambiguity in the use of the term *subjective*."[10] On the one hand (and presumably prompted by the Kantian "call to reason, again to undertake the most laborious of all tasks—that of self-examination"[11]), the essay finds that "the poetry and speculation of the age are marked by a certain philosophic turn, which discriminates them from the works of earlier times. . . . And this is called subjectiveness, as the eye is withdrawn from the object and fixed on the subject or mind."[12] On the other hand, the subjective tendency can and frequently does become "intellectual selfishness": "But, in all ages, and now more, the narrow-minded have no interest in anything but in its relation to their personality. What will help them to be delivered from some burden, eased in some circumstance, flattered or pardoned or enriched; what will help to marry or divorce them, to prolong or to sweeten life, is sure of their interest; and nothing else."[13] This, too, is a type of subjective reading, a type that cannot escape the circle of the reading subject's concern for itself. "And this habit of intellectual selfishness has acquired in our day the fine name of subjectiveness."[14] So positively subjective are these intellectually selfish readers that everything they behold, "they behold in this most partial light or darkness of intense selfishness."[15]

Subjective ambiguity is pernicious because one aspect of subjective reading is essential to interpreting a text, while another aspect is destructive of or fatal to the text and consequently to interpretation itself (and hence to nature). Little comes to light when one reads only to serve one's personal interest; like the traveler in "Self-Reliance" who seeks to escape the self but finds always and everywhere the selfsame "sad self, unrelenting, identical, that I fled,"[16] the intellectually selfish reader, interested only in him- or herself, can read only the success or failure of her or his personal interests. A text, to such a reader, *means* only insofar as it affects the reader personally. The ambiguous difference in methods and ends—the difference between attending (poetically, speculatively, after a "certain philosophic turn") to how one sees and attending only to what one wants to see (and for the sake of satisfying one's desires)—ultimately comes down to tenden-cies, namely tendencies toward definition of the subject. One tendency, as I noted above, "leads us to nature," the other to "the person of the writer." That interpretation is marked by (or even founded upon) such ambiguity signals that readers who hope to move beyond intellectual selfishness must always entertain critically self-reflective second (and third and fourth . . .) thoughts—must, that is, accept the necessity of taking part in the most laborious of all tasks. If one's reading does *not* lead to nature, the self-serv-ing side of subjective ambiguity will perniciously undermine or prevent the event of reading.

Neglect of nature, textual destruction, the use of texts merely to prolong or sweeten life, a reading that closes down on the text and closes off fur-ther interpretation—these characteristics acutely resemble those that com-prise the consumptive and palimpsestic practices discussed earlier. As for Emerson's biographers, my argument is that the *tendency* of the biographi-cal work is, by nature, away from the larger text and toward a coherence of writings to the person. The resultant consistency, instead of opening the writer's work to further reading, grounds reading's necessary movement, precludes access to the text, and replaces textual meaning with the writer's being. If reading requires a lively engagement with a text, then biographi-cal criticism can be seen as a failure to read, since personal relations have preempted the infinite relations innate to the nature of textuality. The lives of Emerson consistently spell the death of Emerson's text.

There are, of course, plenty of biographies and apologies for biological criticism that would gainsay this preposterous observation.[17] Gay Wilson Allen, in defense of the methodology that governs his *Waldo Emerson: A Biography* (winner of the MLA's James Russell Lowell Prize in 1981), as-serts that "Emerson's life illustrates his ideas, and a responsible biography can clarify his words, regardless of what the 'new Critics' were saying a few years ago. In fact, I believe the best reasons for writing a literary bi-ography are: (1) to show a creative mind at work and (2) to relate the author's experience and his art in such a way that the biography provides the best critical guide to his writings."[18] Allen's "best critical guide" to Emerson's writings, however, possesses many of the questionable attributes (including those of consumption and incorporation) that characterize the biographical endeavor. Coherence of a writer's life to writing; presenta-tion of this coherence as "natural" ("Emerson's development was as se-quential as the transformation of a tadpole into a frog"[19]); use of this specious coherence to explain the writing (as in such positive formulations as "what [Emerson] meant was . . ."[20]); a severe identification with the perceived person of the writer ("living in imagination through every stage of this man's life and writings was one of the richest experiences of my life"[21]); installation of the subject in Concord ("I had only to state the simple facts of Emerson's death and burial to give my biography a pastoral ending, appropriate for the man who had preferred, of all places he could have chosen for his home, Concord, Massachusetts, a town as peaceful and restful as its name"[22])—these traits do not, I have argued, a best critical guide make. Instead of enabling readers to approach the complex meanings of the Emerson text, works such as Allen's saddle them with excess baggage.

The coherence between life and writing, and the employment of that coherence to explain a text's meaning, revolve around the notion of intention, hence Allen's passing swipe at "the 'new Critics.'" The "Intentional Fallacy" of W. K. Wimsatt Jr. and Monroe Beardsley notwithstanding, biographers generally present knowledge of the writer and the subsequent inferred intention of the writer as the keys to discovering the meaning of the writer's text.[23] The question then becomes, Can readers make sense of a text without recourse to intention? Critics who rely on the notion of intentional fallacy to answer this question inevitably replace dwelling on the subject-who-has-produced-text with dwelling on the text-as-object-in-and-of-itself. As Paul de Man observes, this method results in "a hardening of the text into a sheer surface," which in turn prevents interpretation by failing to approach the profound and extensive relations that "support" the text: "For surfaces also remain concealed when they are being artificially separated from the depth that supports them."[24]

According to Stanley Fish, New Critics as well as those relying on Roland Barthes's argument for the death of the author "have not done away with intention and biography but merely relocated them."[25] Fish fixes the act of construing meaning as "ipso facto the act of assigning intention within a specific set of circumstances" and maintains, "It follows, then, that neither can you read independently of biography, of some specification of what kind of person—and with what abilities, concerns, goals, purposes, and so on—is the source of the words you are reading. And if that follows, it follows too that disputes about meaning are always disputes about biography, whether or not they are explicitly so labeled."[26] While Fish is right that one need attend to the contexts that produce utterances (and, I will add, to the contexts in which they are to be understood) to approach what these utterances mean, he is right about biography only if, as I have claimed above, the tendency of it is toward the life or *bios* of nature rather than toward the person. *Tendency* would thus supersede *intention:* the latter tends toward origins of texts, the former toward engagement of the many contexts in which texts are made, in which they are made sense of, and which consequently produce other significant relations.

The nature of intention is that it is conditioned by a larger context than that contained in a discrete subject. If intention is purpose and therefore meaning, then, as Nietzsche writes in *The Gay Science,* "we still need a critique of the concept of 'purpose.'"[27] If biographical criticism situates meaning and purpose inside of a discrete subject, then its tendencies are misdirected and misguiding. If formalist criticism posits meaning outside of structures and contingencies or relations, then it too misleads. (And one should note that, as de Man argues, structuralist modes of interpretation are not exempt from such a critique: "It could be that, in a legitimate desire to react against reductive ways of thought, the structuralists have bypassed or oversimplified some of these questions."[28]) If, however, intention is seen as "the act of straining or directing the mind or attention to something" (*OED*), then that direction's tendency must be toward the ongoing interpretation of a complex text that may be metaphorized as "nature" and thus considered as a living or moving unstable spatiotemporal field of infinite relations and therefore of infinite meanings. A reading that fails to take into consideration the nature of text and adapt its interpretive methods accordingly will remain a perniciously subjective, self-absorbed, "untextual," "unnatural" way of seeing.

The Nature of the Subject, the Subject of Reading, and the "Best Read Naturalist"

> Of course one must not only see sharply, but read aright what he sees.
> —John Burroughs

To begin to formulate a better idea of what a more "natural" mode of reading would be, I turn now to the relations of text, interpretation, and nature in Emerson's writing—and to another attempt to decipher Emerson's writing through the person of the subject by a reader who positioned himself as both a textual critic and a naturalist. John Burroughs was not only a prominent man of American letters (the first to produce a book-length study of Walt Whitman) but also "the dean of American nature writers,"[29] "one of our most beloved authors."[30] An examination of Burroughs's work on the text of Emerson's writing will assist us in understanding the extent to which Emerson's person obscures his writing even in the interpretive endeavor of one schooled in the complexities of nature and the subtleties of reading.

It is in the text of *Nature* that Emerson offers his observations of what he deemed "the best read naturalist." This early work (1836) describes the writer's preoccupation with vision and the capacity to make sense of what we see. Here we encounter the notorious "transparent eye-ball" as it pauses on the bare wintry common;[31] here we have our ways of looking upon the world called into question by the very first words of the introduction: "Our age is retrospective," the writer laments, the problem being that we do not properly use our eyes: "The foregoing generations beheld God and nature face to face; we, through their eyes. Why should not we also enjoy an original relation to the universe? Why should not we have a poetry and philosophy of insight and not of tradition, and a religion by revelation to us, and not the history of theirs?"[32] From this beginning—with its concern for visual relations, retrospection (backward looking), insight, and revelation—to the concluding chapter ("Prospects," looking forward), *Nature* addresses the various ailments that occlude our sight and dreams of the measures by which we might better see or read Nature.

The problems that beset such reading are many. "To speak truly, few adults can see nature," the writer observes. "At least they have a very superficial seeing."[33] Seeing only the surface, desirously clutching that which we would see (e.g., the moon),[34] succumbing to "empirical science" (which "is apt to cloud the sight"),[35] and other difficulties in our relations with the visible result in a type of blindness: "The ruin or the blank, that we see when we look at nature, is in our own eye."[36] Our prospects, however, are not utterly dim. The essay's closing paragraph envisions a time when we "shall . . . come to look at the world with new eyes" and leaves the reader with the image of "'the blind man . . . who is gradually restored to perfect sight.'"[37] Some of the possibility for clear-sightedness rests with "the best read naturalist," one who reads or sees more clearly by virtue of enjoying different relations with nature. Seeing beyond the surface, abreacting the covetous desire for the object of sight, capable of rethinking and transcending the structural limitations of the empirically scientific, "the best read naturalist" is that person "who lends an entire and devout attention to truth" and sees "that there remains much to learn of his relation to the world."[38]

In light of this interpretive figure and the related notion that nature is a text to be read with care, we can see Burroughs's writings as the attempt to meet the job qualifications of the best read naturalist. The epigraph above indicates that seeing and reading matter significantly to Burroughs. Consequently one might wonder whether this particular naturalist, certainly (at least for a time) best loved, was also best read. If nature is analogous to a book (the trope dates back to the Middle Ages), then an understanding of the methods of interpreting *one* might shed some light on interpreting the *other.* Perhaps we may learn how to read more clearly the text of nature by more fully understanding the way we see texts in general; perhaps we may see more sharply how we might achieve the perfect sight Emerson holds before us. "Of course," as Burroughs reminds us, "one must not only see sharply, but read aright what he sees."[39] In "Criticism and the Man," Burroughs observes that our "tastes and preferences may blind us to the truth," that "what we crave, what our minds literally feed upon, may blind us to the truly excellent."[40] We must, that writer urges us, "be on our guard against our particular predilections, because such predilections may lead us into narrow channels."[41]

That nature might be approached as a text is not a notion peculiar to Emerson, although his writings return to that notion with peculiar frequency: "A life in harmony with nature, the love of truth and of virtue, will purge the eyes to understand her text. By degrees we may come to know the primitive sense of the permanent objects of nature, so that the world shall be to us an open book, and every form significant of its hidden life and final cause."[42] And Burroughs followed Emerson in this troping of nature as a text to be read: "The facts in the life of Nature that are transpiring about us are like written words that the observer is to arrange into sentences. Or the writing is in cipher and he must furnish the key."[43] But what does it mean that Nature is a writing, that its written words are to be gathered? What does it mean that every form is significant, that nature is an open book or a text? What would it mean to approach a text *in harmony* (from the Greek *harmos,* a joining or fitting) with that text? Is such an approach truly possible?

The nature of the text of nature is more fully developed in "The Method of Nature," an essay first delivered as an oration to "the Erosophian Adelphi undergraduate literary society of Waterville (later Colby) College" in 1841.[44] Emerson, once again raising the specter of dulled sight and its consequences, proposes that "where there is no vision, the people perish."[45] To remedy such a situation, he encourages the scholar to "be a bringer of hope," a bringer of prospects of something new and renewing.[46] The scholar is invited to celebrate what Emerson refers to as "this literary anniversary" by "exploring the *method of nature.* Let us see *that,* as nearly as we can, and try how far it is transferable to the literary life."[47] In coming to see "as nearly as we can" the system of nature, we may transfer or carry what we see to a testing of or experiment on the literary life, to a life of literary pursuits *and* to a life that is itself literary or textual.

This transference of the study of nature's text to the understanding of the text of human literary nature has several conditions. First, the scholar or would-be seer must acknowledge the constantly shifting nature of both the seen and the seer: "Nothing solid is secure; every thing tilts and rocks. Even the scholar is not safe; he too is searched and revised."[48] The self-questioning and revision of the scholar is necessary to tune her or his method (as in "way" or "practice") of study to the continuously changing method (as in "system" or "text")[49] of that which is being studied. Neither seen nor seer are to be taken as fixed—*every thing* tilts and rocks. Secondly, because the method of nature ever remains unfixed, fixed methods of analysis will not suffice. The interpreter must forego the radical break between the subject that analyzes and the object that is analyzed: "The method of nature: who could ever analyze it? That rushing stream will not stop to be observed. We can never surprise nature in a corner; never find the end of a thread; never tell where to set the first stone. . . . The wholeness we admire in the order of the world, is the result of infinite distribution. Its smoothness is the smoothness of the pitch of the cataract. Its permanence is a perpetual inchoation."[50] Readers: abandon all hope of systematically taking apart the endlessly relational method of nature; the method itself is too complex to be sufficiently stabilized for the objective dissection of analysis, and you are not sufficiently removed from that complexity to obtain the analyst's necessary (and impossible) objectivity. This method's "infinite distribution" thus points toward the textuality of that method and to what this means for readers of that text.

The textual method of nature is always and everywhere distributing, "emanating," "referring." Its elements are not recognizable in and of themselves, separate from other parts of the text, nor do they seem to issue from one particular and individually identifiable source. Instead the constituent parts of the text are to be known by their relation to one another: "Every natural fact is an emanation, and that from which it emanates is an emanation also, and from every emanation is a new emanation."[51] Potential readers cannot avoid acknowledging this endless emanation— this text ungrounded by a transcendental signified, this unstoppable referentiality—if they are to viably interpret the method's significances: "Away profane philosopher! seekest thou in nature the cause? This refers to that, and that to the next, and the next to the third, and everything refers. Thou must ask in another mood, thou must feel it and love it, *thou must behold it in a spirit as grand as that by which it exists."*[52] I have emphasized this last phrase so that we might begin to connect these textual meditations with the problem of the best read naturalist and the *harmos* that is to inform his or her method of interpretation. To behold the method of nature in a spirit similar to it means to behold it from the perspective of an ever-changing, perpetually emanating, referentially relational *text*. The eye that would see must see itself as always related to the textual landscape or method of nature.

In sum, if seeing the text of nature is to involve an acknowledgment of a certain harmony of relations, what this might mean is that the *harmos* or "fitting" in which we are to engage is neither more nor less than a changing set of textual connections. To understand the significance of nature *as* text, one must think the nature *of* text, and think of oneself as textual by nature. The separation between seer and seen, nature and naturalist is to be thought of as an intersection of two methods. When seer and seen are considered separate entities, their relations are marked by desire, individualizing, a sort of unthinking self-satisfaction and possessiveness. To "ask in another mood," then, is to transcend the desirous optical possession of an object for a relational "love," a love enacted in "a spirit as grand" as what one sees. One then sees with a "poetic spirit," and "when we behold the landscape in a poetic spirit, we do not reckon individuals."[53] Instead, we abandon ourselves to a textual *"ecstasy,"* an "excess of life"[54] that acknowledges connection, love, and textuality, preferring these to disconnection, desire, positivism, and stasis.

"The best read naturalist who lends an entire and devout attention to the truth, will see that there remains much to learn of his relation to the world." Some of this is to be learned through textual ecstasy. "This ecstatical state seems to direct a regard to the whole and not to the parts."[55] "And because all knowledge is assimilation to the object of knowledge, as the power or genius of nature is ecstatic, so must its science or the description of it be."[56] The best read naturalist will come to know nature's text through assimilation *to* it and not by assimilation (or consumption) *of* it. Such a reader does not look at nature or any other text covetously, as something separate to be clutched, but rather as something to which she or he is always already related, requiring a special sort of seeing. "The only way *in*to nature is to *en*act our best *in*sight."[57] The text of nature can be seen only *in* nature and through acknowledgment of the textual relations of seer and seen: "If only he *sees,* the world will be visible enough."[58]

Following the method of "The Method of Nature," we are now prepared to try how far these thoughts on the text of nature are transferable to the literary text and specifically to the nature of Burroughs's reading of Emerson. Was Burroughs truly one of Emerson's best read naturalists? If, using Emerson's and Burroughs's trope, nature is analogous to written copy requiring interpretation, then the method of reading nature is perhaps transferable to the method of reading other texts (and vice versa). Hence Burroughs's method of reading literary texts may tell us something about his reading of nature.

Strikingly, for Burroughs reading is something of a dating game. "Literary Values" proposes that authors "are not to be analyzed, they are to be enjoyed; they are not to be studied, but to be loved."[59] We are not to "*study* a great poet*" but "rather seek to make the acquaintance of his living soul and to feel its power."[60] The end of such relations is a form of intercourse, a measure of intimacy demonstrating just how personal reader and author have become: "The end here indicated cannot be reached by analysis, or by a course in rhetoric and sentence-structure, or by a microscopical examination of the writer's vocabulary, but by direct sympathetic intercourse with the best literature, through the living voice, or through your own silent perusal of it."[61] Although elsewhere Burroughs describes the aims of reading to include "judgment, interpretation, analysis, and description,"[62] in the above metaphorical courtship between reader and author we find a note that sounds throughout Burroughs's writings and reminiscences: the author's duty is to "give us himself";[63] the reader's work entails accepting the gift.

Establishing a personal connection in our literary relations means, for Burroughs, penetrating all barriers so that "there is nothing secondary or artificial" between writer and reader.[64] Reading is undertaken to gain intimacy with or an *immediacy* to the (consequently extratextual) Real. It is an act designed to result in pleasurable access to the essence of things in themselves. "We read it [a work of literature] for the pleasure and the stimulus it affords us, apart from any other consideration." "In all good literature we have a sense of touching something alive and real." "The true writer always establishes intimate and personal relations with his reader. He comes forth, he is not concealed; he is immanent in his words, we feel him, our spirits touch his spirit." Hence, "studying an author from the outside by bringing the light of rhetoric to bear upon him is of little profit. We must get inside of him through sympathy and appreciation"; that is, by reading we are to get to "the living thing itself."[65]

The results of the drive for intimacy and essence should be apparent. Burroughs the reader is ever on the prowl for "the man behind the book,"[66] for "a certain genuineness . . . like the validity of real things,"[67] and for reality itself: "Reality, reality—nothing can make up for a want of reality."[68] The preferences and predilections that Burroughs warns against in interpretation thus come to bear on his own methods of reading. He desires access to the essence of things; he wants the pleasure of personal contact, the fulfilling feeling of his own coming to him (as he writes in his most famous poem);[69] he yearns for a return to the Old Home—a yearning that, as he noted himself, became an incurable sickness. The burning desire for the real manifests itself in the hunger for the being of the author, which makes reading less like the interpretation of a written text and "more like a transfusion of blood from [the author's] veins to yours."[70] Do not these tastes and preferences, as the writer himself observed of others, blind one to the truth?

Indeed they do. Reading for the person prevents encounters with texts from leading to the sort of textual acknowledgment called for in Emerson's writings. "Let me confess that I am too conscious of persons,—feel them too much, defer to them too much, and try too hard to adapt myself to them," Burroughs admits in "An Egotistical Chapter."[71] He also describes his first case of authorial adoration, in which as a young man, "I saw my first author; and I distinctly remember with what emotion I gazed upon him, and followed him in the twilight, keeping on the other side of the street."[72] What this means for reading is that the text is always to be read through the filter of one's impressions of "the man" who wrote the text; text is not considered as text but as "the man" himself, and is understood in light of his perceived person and personality. By a strange twist, a book is judged by neither its cover nor its contents but by the perceived cover and contents of its author. Consequently, the meaning of Burroughs's Emerson is intimately connected to the latter's divine looks, his detached bearing, his benign dignity: "Everything about a man like Emerson is important. I find his phrenology and physiognomy more than ordinarily typical and suggestive."[73] "When I think of Emerson, I think of him as a man, not as an author; it was his rare and charming personality that healed us and kindled our love."[74]

In Burroughs's interpretation, the text of Emerson's writing comes to mean what Burroughs believes the person of Emerson means, and this in turn is nothing other than what Burroughs longs for in the man. Again, it is a set of desires that become evident in Burroughs's writing on Emerson: the desire for something essential, for proof of existence, for healing, and for wholeness. Accordingly, the Emerson that Burroughs sees possesses the qualities necessary for the fulfillment of his longing search: "In fact, Emerson is an essence, a condensation; more so, perhaps, than any other man who has appeared in literature." "Where he is at all, he is entirely." He goes "beyond the symbol to the thing signified." Although Burroughs's Emerson is not above criticism, nevertheless "after we have made all possible deductions from Emerson, there remains the fact that he is a living force, and, tried by home standards, a master."[75]

The effect of this type of reading is that the complexities of the text of Emerson's writing are eliminated or bottled up in the narrow channel of the reader's perception of the person of Emerson. And these narrow channels, recall, are, in Burroughs's terms, the product of the very sort of "predilections" we are always to be "on our guard against."[76] We are to be on our toes because "a broad culture demands wide reading." The opposite— narrow reading—serves the needs of a narrow culture and leads to a narrow version of the world. When Burroughs describes the difficulties encountered when he first picked up a book of Emerson's essays and the subsequent "seeing of the light of Emerson," what he more accurately sees is what he has hungered for all along. The following comes from a conversation with Burroughs recorded by Clifton Johnson:

> "When I was studying at Cooperstown, I one day took from the Seminary library a book by Emerson, and read his essay on 'The Poet.' I couldn't make anything of it, and I tried others of the essays; but they were all the same sort of thing, and I carried the book back.
>
> "A year later I went out to Illinois to teach, and while browsing in a Chicago bookstore happened on Emerson's books again. I looked into them and said to myself: 'Why, this is good! *This is what I want.*' And I bought the whole set.
>
> "For a long time afterward I lived, moved, and had my being in those books. I was like Jonah in the whale's belly—completely swallowed by them. They were almost my whole intellectual diet for two or three years. . . . For years all that I wrote was Emersonian. It was as if I was dipped in Emerson."[77]

Finally finding what he wants, Burroughs both eats and is eaten by the Emerson text. We must surmise, however, that what he finally finds, purchases, consumes, and is consumed by is exactly what he has wanted all along: an idealized essence, a living force, the man behind the book, the reassuring presence, the promise of return to the real, the person of Emerson. The text of Emerson's writing comes to mean precisely what Burroughs craves it to mean.

That meaning, of course, has been seemingly arrived at "naturally," through the simple act of reading. That act, however, is not as simple as Burroughs appears to believe. A complicated mind made up of myriad cultural warps and woofs, of desires and creeds and fears and facts is at work deciphering a complex text of multiple significances; the reader is working through the electrifying, explosive pages of an elusive, exotic, experimental writer. To be the *best read* naturalist, then, to *read naturally,* one would therefore need to read with an eye toward the magnificent and unfathomable natures of the text and oneself.

Burroughs noted time and time again, and particularly in his essay "Reading the Book of Nature," that the text of nature requires more than just a keen and discriminating eye: "In studying Nature, the important thing is not so much what we see as how we interpret what we see."[78] Reading the book of nature concerned his sharp eyes perhaps even more than his reading of Emerson's books, and much of his writing offers "intensive observations" regarding how such reading is to be accomplished: "The casual glances or admiring glances that we cast upon nature do not go very far in making us acquainted with her real ways. Only long and close scrutiny can reveal these to us. The look of appreciation is not enough; the eye must become critical and analytical if we would know the exact truth."[79] Neither the admiring look nor the casual look nor the appreciative look—neither the look of longing, the look of desire, the hunter's hunting, the hungry seeker's search—are adequate if we would truly "see nature." For such methods of looking mean that the one who would see projects a distance, a separateness between seer and seen, neglecting the nature of the textual relations that inform seer and seen *and* the act of seeing itself.

What often occurs, Burroughs warns us in "Reading the Book of Nature," is that we see precisely what we want to see: a mother crow disciplining her delinquent son, a loon chivalrously assisting a grebe in need, gophers cooperating conspiratorially to commandeer a miner's bread-loaves. These "interpretations" are produced by "the sentimental 'School of Nature Study'" scholars, those who are "possessed of" certain "notions."[80] Is this not true for literary texts as well? Is this not "intellectual selfishness," subjective reading of a pernicious sort? But objective reading is not a realizable remedy. Regarding the qualities of his own best read naturalist, Burroughs asserts, "The power to see straight is the rarest of gifts; to see no more and no less than is actually before you; to be able to detach yourself and see the thing as it actually is, uncolored or unmodified by your own sentiments or prepossessions. In short, to see with your reason as well as with your perceptions, that is to be an observer and to read the book of nature aright."[81] If, as it appears in the passage, reason and perception represent a freeing of oneself from sentiment and prepossession, then a way of seeing that could detach itself from subjectivity and view the book of nature objectively would offer the promise of becoming the best read naturalist. But such objectivity (considered more fully in the next chapter) is itself suspect and carries its own pernicious effects. Perhaps, following *Nature* and "The Method of Nature," rather than pretend to disinterested objectivity in visual and interpretive relations, the reader of texts (both natural and literary) would do better to seriously and perpetually question the conditions of his or her attachments. To ever investigate and revise the nature of our relation to the text we would come to know: there lies the hope of becoming "best read"—which, as a consequence, means not only the reader who reads best but also the reader whose perspective is best read or understood.

The Conquest of Emerson: Mastering the Subject's Contradictory Nature

> Therefore all that befals me in the way of criticism & extreme blame & praise drawing me out of equilibrium,—putting me for a time in false position to people, & disallowing the spontaneous sentiments, wastes my time, bereaves me of thoughts, & shuts me up within poor personal considerations.
>
> —Emerson's journal, 8 September 1838

The pernicious textual destruction caused by biographical reading (even by a reader schooled in the complexity of nature) can be seen as an extension of the other modes of reading Emerson described above. Subjective reading resembles these practices of reading that foreclose on meaning and delimit or denature the text. Texts, I have suggested (somewhat archly), are lively, unstable, contradictory, and thus comparable to the text of nature or the world we survey. Hence a method of reading that results in a conquest of a text's nature is perhaps analogous to our understanding and use ("wise" or otherwise) of nature itself. A closer look at some of the ways this conquest proceeds might enable a critical method of interpretation that treats text (and nature) differently. Instead of promoting a practice of reading that masters the subject, consumes the text, and tends toward the end of interpretation, an alternative, "natural" reading would attempt a lively, responsible, continued consideration of the nature of a text in such a manner as to propagate that nature.

The subject-centered approach to Emerson's writing entails remembering Emerson's presence, securing the presence of his being to his writing, and thereby containing the writing's movement. This, I am suggesting, amounts to a foolish consistency. Inconsistencies and contradictions that abound in Emerson's writing are quietly covered over by, for example, a pervasive religious context. Indeed, contradictions that exist among poems, essays, sermons, personality, lifestyle—and especially the contradictory elements of a spiritual idealism and a capitalistic pragmatism—are often encapsulated in the image of Emerson as a two-faced "Plotinus-Montaigne."[82] How a biographer addresses Emerson's contradictoriness, then, depends upon the figure of Emerson that is to be reproduced in the biography: Cabot admits (albeit infrequently) some of Emerson's contradictions, but these admissions are taken up within a prevailing religious discourse that renders them no longer contradictory.[83] Aporetic moments in Emerson's writing are dissolved, the resulting mist glistening in the light of the sage's halo. To close this chapter, I will briefly consider three similar instances in the history of Emerson criticism, examples of taming the nature of Emerson's text through making the inconsistent consistent.

Oliver Wendell Holmes, another prominent early biographer who knew Emerson personally, attempts to explain Emerson's inconsistencies by employing an encompassing discourse of American practicality. Holmes admits that Emerson contradictorily "unites many characteristics of Berkeley and of Franklin";[84] while reckoning Emerson's idealistic side, however, Holmes clearly favors the Franklinian streak. With often sardonic hyperbole, he depicts Emerson as "Saint Radulphus" and *Nature* as his "Book of Revelation."[85] Emerson becomes a visitor to our earth bearing "the message with which he came commissioned from the Infinite source of Life,"[86] and Concord "the place which the advent of Emerson made the Delphi of New England and the resort of many pilgrims from far-off regions."[87] Furthermore, the philosophy of this extraterrestrial oracle is trinitized, so that the "ever-blessed ONE," the "Over-Soul," and "Representative Men" "correspond" to the Father, the Holy Spirit, and Jesus.[88] Holmes maintains that "Emerson's reflections in the 'transcendental' mood do beyond question sometimes irresistibly suggest the close neighborhood of the sublime to the ridiculous"[89] and fears that the "oriental side of Emerson's nature delighted itself in these narcotic dreams, born in the land of the poppy and of hashish."[90]

To counter the hookah of transcendentalism, Holmes holds to the tenet that "too much has been made of Emerson's mysticism. He was an intellectual rather than an emotional mystic, and withal a cautious one. He never let go the string of his balloon."[91] This Emerson, then, is mystically idealistic, but he is *practically* so. That transcendental stream running through Emerson's text and seemingly leading him away from the world ultimately runs into the more productively riparian Emerson, the one that generates pragmatic power. To accomplish this early example of the detranscendentalization of Emerson, Holmes ties the sometimes dreamy sage securely to that most useful of Americans, Benjamin Franklin. He notes in the first chapter that his subject's "birthplace and that of our other illustrious Bostonian, Benjamin Franklin, were within a kite-string's distance of each other."[92] United by Franklin's legendary twine, the two illustrious Bostonians work together to carry out the business of America: "The common-sense side of Emerson's mind has so much in common with the plain practical intelligence of Franklin."[93] Indeed, this Emerson "lays down some good, plain, practical rules which 'Poor Richard' would have cheerfully approved.[94] He might have accepted also the Essay on 'Wealth' as having a good sense so like his own that he could hardly tell the difference between them."[95] The effect of this coupling is Montaigne's triumph over Plotinus. Pragmatism becomes Emerson's better half, the dominant trait and prevailing discourse amid apparent inconsistencies.

As do other biographers, Holmes believes that the life of Emerson and the work of Emerson are consistent: Emerson's "life is in exact accord with his words." "His life corresponded to the ideal we form of him from his writings."[96] The writing causes an ideal to form of the person of Emerson, which then accounts for or explains the vagaries of the text. The resultant "meaning of Emerson," formulated through the combination of person and writing, can be rewritten into "larger formulae" that we may apply to particular problems: "Once accustomed to Emerson's larger formulae we can to a certain extent project from our own minds his treatment of special subjects."[97] As in the methods employed by Napoleon Hill, the Emerson text is transformed and consumed, undergoing extraction, introjection, and projection in Holmes's work. The reason for explaining Emerson to Americans through acquainting us with the larger formulae is that "the plain and wholesome language of Emerson is on the whole more needed now than when it was spoken." The sage's words are "in a high degree tonic, bracing, strengthening to the American, who requires to be reminded of his privileges that he may know and find himself equal to his duties."[98]

To enhance the capability of accomplishing our chores, Holmes posits Emerson as the model American, a formula for better living: "Emerson was American in aspect, temperament, way of thinking, and feeling; American, with an atmosphere of Oriental idealism; American, so far as he belonged to any limited part of the universe. He believed in American institutions, he trusted the future of the American race."[99] Holmes's Emerson is American through and through, a firm believer in and staunch upholder of

American institutions. America itself is what boiling down Emerson yields—a peculiar concoction indeed, composed of three parts Franklinian practicality and one part "Oriental idealism," or one part Plotinus and three parts Montaigne. Stirred together, these ingredients constitute a dose of Emerson to be administered to the populace, a tonic that will brace and strengthen.

Holmes intends that such a medicine will instill in patients a condition of *practical idealism;* where Cabot emphasizes the pure and lofty idealism of Emerson, Holmes dilutes idealism with a pragmatic, Franklinian common sense that will ameliorate sickly Americans and enable them to get their jobs done. Where Cabot dismisses the practical side or the worldly aspect for the ideal and universal, Holmes plays up the combination (albeit with emphasis on the practical and American). Cabot ignores inconsistencies; Holmes compromises, finding a larger formula to make the seemingly disparate elements coalesce. The phrase that best represents the resultant consistency is a divine injunction gracing the pages of Emerson's "Civilization":

> This Essay of Emerson's is irradiated by a single precept that is worthy to stand by the side of that which Juvenal says came from heaven. How could the man in whose thought such a meteoric expression suddenly announced itself fail to recognize it as divine? It is not strange that he repeats it on the page next the one where we first see it. Not having any golden letters to print it in, I will underscore it for italics, and doubly underscore it in the second extract for small capitals:—
>
> "Now that is the wisdom of a man, in every instance of his labor, to *hitch his wagon to a star,* and see his chore done by the gods themselves."—
>
> "'It was a great instruction,' said a saint in Cromwell's war, 'that the best courages are but beams of the Almighty.' HITCH YOUR WAGON TO A STAR."—[100]

For Holmes, this slogan brings together the inconsistent strains of Emerson's thought as well as the double duty required of every American. Power must be harnessed and put to use, but in heavenly matters as well as mundane ones. Thus will the American be made "equal to his duties."

By removing this excerpt from Emerson's essay, further reducing the excerpt so as to call attention to a single phrase, and further emphasizing that phrase with two different graphic devices, Holmes concentrates Emerson into a new golden rule. The extract then becomes something of an inoculation; Holmes introduces into the reader a vagary in Emerson's writing that will henceforth enable the reader to withstand other vagaries: "The habitual readers of Emerson do not mind an occasional over-statement, extravagance, paradox, eccentricity; they find them amusing and not misleading."[101] All of Emerson's "amusing" contradictions and excesses thus conform to the nature of "hitch your wagon to a star." For Holmes, being a healthy, wealthy, and wise American means pulling your own weight, doing your work, but also working with your eyes on the pie in the sky. Holmes's Emerson is that most American of Americans because, on the one hand, he believes in practicalities, hard work, individualism, self-involvement, and concentrating our energies on the task before us and, on the other hand, he believes in a heavenly guiding influence that should make us be kind to our neighbors and concentrate our energies on the universal good. Two inconsistent modes of operation are made consistent by Emerson himself—his very person promotes simultaneously the wagon and the star, the practical and the idealistic, society and solitude. This Emerson stands for the living synthesis of oppositions, which itself accounts for contradictions in Emerson's writing.

And I do not want to lose sight of the fact that the consistency of practical idealism is founded in a special attachment to the subject of writing: "His books are so full of his life to their last syllable that we might letter every volume *Emersoniana*, by Ralph Waldo Emerson."[102] The books are so full of the man that the writing must mean what the man meant. This not only reduces the possible interpretations of Emerson, tying meaning to the person and therefore to those who knew the person, but also relegates writing to the status of an artifact of the person. Replaced, reduced, relegated, rendered motionless, the nature of Emerson's text is conquered, made consistent, made sense of once and for all. Where the writing wanders away from the person, where it produces ruptures, where it reveals openings in the supposed consistency of meaning, it is reined in by the force of the subject's personal gravity.

A later critic who yet felt the pull of Emerson's personal magnetism—in Jonathan Bishop's words, "one of the last of the Emersonians whose response was conditioned by the afterglow of Emerson's personal authority"—contributed portentously to the tradition of consistency and conquest.[103] "The dean of all teachers and scholars of Emerson," Bliss Perry, "was perhaps the first to emphasize the actual embodiment of [the Plotinus-Montaigne] dualism in the physical lines of Emerson's face."[104] Perry continues the subjugation of Emerson's writing to his life by returning to and emphasizing his journals. Covering over fifty years of a life in writing, the journals are seen as more life-like than writing-like, as if Emerson whispered into the pages, his breath condensing there and depositing meaning.[105] Because the journals are more life than writing, they need to be witnessed rather than read.

For Perry, willing witnesses will encounter Emerson's presence, which is the manifestation of an unmediated truth radiating from a mystical source, but taking on the shape of a middle-class American male. It is pure truth, and as such it need only be received. Truth itself, that is, could be experienced in the past by simply being in Emerson's presence, by looking upon Emerson and hearing him speak. A half century after his death, the truth of Emerson can be experienced by looking upon the image of the man as it is reconstituted either by those who knew him or by the man himself in his journals. Perry, the editor of *The Heart of Emerson's Journals*, insists that Emerson's heart yet beats. He begins his *Emerson Today* by remembering Emerson's visage, where he saw that familiar contradictoriness: "His features were slightly asymmetrical. Seen from one side, it was the face of a Yankee of the old school, shrewd, serious, practical; the sort of face that may still be observed in the quiet country churches of New England or at the village store. Seen from the other side, it was the face of a dreamer, a seer, a soul brooding on things to come, things as yet far away."[106] The two inconsistent constituents—the practical doer and the dreaming seer—appear once again, but this time they will be coalesced by an underlying ontological wholeness. Beneath the Janus-faced physiognomy, up from the burning core below, as it were, bubbles the truth of Emerson: "Emerson's character, it is true, possessed a singular unity; few men in history about whom we know as much as we may know of him, had such a flawless integrity of nature."[107] Emerson's nature is flawless integrity, wholeness itself. Accordingly, the journals, wherein we find the singular unity of the person of Emerson, afford access to the real meaning of Emerson.

In the those journals resides the good, the true, the beautiful Emerson, with neither inconsistency nor paradox; only the public or published Emersons contradict one another. Hence the journals form a necessary guide to the published writing. The published writing bears reading, in Perry's book, but one must look beyond the actual text of Emerson's writing to the man's face and heart to get the truth. When Perry admonishes that "in our overspecialized and distracted and generally be-deviled generation there is some virtue in simply sitting down and looking at Ralph Waldo Emerson,"[108] he urges us not to read Emerson's writing but rather to gaze upon the fellow's presence (as presented in the heart of his journals). Therein stands the benevolent "master of parable," whose visage is itself a lesson.[109]

To look upon Perry's Emerson is to view an Emerson similar to Holmes's. A figure designed to "de-bedevil" this generation, his Emerson is the conglomeration of practical idealism. In Perry's version, however, the subject tilts toward the Plotinus side. Emerson was "a man of many gifts, and of manifold intellectual interests and practical activities, but his mystical tendencies were innate."[110] One truth of Emerson rests in his face: he was practical and idealistic. But the deeper truth—mystic, canny, and content—rests within. Perry demonstrates Emerson's practical activities and mystical tendencies by having him don the metaphoric apparel of an innocent but wise sportsman, playing cards and golfing his way to a happy self-containment that will get the devil behind him. Other critics of Emerson "feel that they have been fooled. Like Truthful James and his friend William Nye, who, according to Bret Harte's poem, once played a disastrous game of euchre against a pensive and inexperienced Chinaman with long sleeves, they perceive that there is something wrong somewhere. And the trouble lies, they are sure, with Emerson, the 'childlike and bland' Oriental, who 'did not understand' the game of life, but managed somehow to cheat them."[111] Here, Perry's Emerson is a lucky and resourceful card player who, at the end of the game, "draw[s] out this trump card of his, and lay[s] it quietly, benignly on the table!"[112]

This "trump card," according to Perry, "which he plays at the end of every close game," is the key to Emerson's meaning: the concept of "the moral sentiment."[113] An intuitive, extrasensorial perception, the moral sentiment "became Emerson's life-long creed."[114] Perry deploys the phrase as the cohering thread underlying the split visage and unifying Emerson's often paradoxical inconsistencies. Depicting such a gambit as the necessary fulfillment of the critic's duty, Perry summarizes the situation thus: "To most of us, in most hours, it seems as if Emerson the pupil and lover of Montaigne were one kind of man, and Emerson the lover of Plato and Plotinus were another. And yet we are perfectly aware that such a dichotomy is absurd, and that criticism should at least attempt that problem of unification."[115] Moral sentiment is Perry's answer to the problem of the seeming discontinuity of Emerson's thought and visage and Perry's Emerson is the answer to every difficult issue. Rising from the card table, Emerson slips into golf slacks, exercising himself on the links. There, he is "a golfer with naturally beautiful form, but with a tendency to pull or slice his drive, so that he is frequently in the rough. Yet it is precisely here that he shows his true quality. He pulls out of his bag an old iron club stamped 'M. S.' [Moral Sentiment], and no matter how bad the lie or how great the distance he pitches his second shot dead to the pin."[116] Whether pulling to the left-hand rough (call this Plotinus) or slicing to the right (Montaigne), Emerson's moral sentiment always puts him back in the game.

Readers can thus rely on it to ground and understand the vicissitudes of the meaning of the "great gentleman," who, after all, is of greater import than the text of his writing. "As I reflect upon Emerson's life in Concord as he earned and shared his daily bread, I confess that I sometimes forget that he was a thinker and writer at all. I see only the great gentleman."[117]

A more recent example of the inconsistent being made consistent occurs in Stephen E. Whicher's *Freedom and Fate,* a cornerstone of contemporary Emersonian criticism.[118] In the manner of other biographical criticism, *Freedom and Fate* brings about a conquest of the nature of Emerson's writing, a conquering of the territory of the possible meanings of that text. Arguing for switching attention from the exterior life of the man to the "inner life" of the mind, Whicher intensifies the consistency of writer and writing, locating the rationale for such consistency (as was the case in Perry's version) in the dramatic tale told by the journals. Once again, this most private form of writing provides the key for understanding Emerson. *Freedom and Fate* asserts that "as we move from his uneventful outward life to the inner life recorded in his journals, we approach the fire under the Andes of his reserve."[119] Turning his back on the outer life of Emerson and the benign duality of the sage's visage, as well as on the middle-class figure sportily exercising the moral sentiment, Whicher recasts his subject as a volcanic process: a perpetual churning, burning, eruption, receding, churning . . .

What distinguishes *Freedom and Fate* from other forms of consistency and conquest is that Whicher's story does not posit a central point that grounds the movement of Emerson's writing. By suggesting that Emerson's inconsistency bespeaks a process, Whicher calls for an entirely different approach to contradictory meanings. Rather than a spot to be pinpointed, Emerson becomes a "surprisingly eventful voyage," an evolutionary trajectory that requires charting.[120] As such, *Freedom and Fate* painstakingly maps out the contradictions of Emerson—the Plotinus-Montaigne elements of Emerson that cause critics such consternation—as evidencing the ultimate truth about Emerson: an unfolding, a more or less logical progression necessitating a cartographical overview. By charting the subject's voyage, one will be better prepared to make the journey to the core of the truth. Accordingly, Whicher deploys two poles, two axes, on which to plot the meaning of Emerson:

> I propose, as a rude scaffolding for this analysis, the sufficiently difficult image of two crossed polarities. The north and south poles, the major axis, are the conceptual poles of the One and the Many, the Universal and the Individual, faith

and the rest of experience, Reason and Understanding, between which Emerson saw man suspended. And across this lies a minor axis, whose poles, shifting and blending into each other, are harder to define, the temperamental west and east poles of pride and humility, egoism and pantheism, activity and passivity, power and Law, between which, again, Emerson's nature was divided. Most of his central convictions can be plotted in some manner in relation to such coördinates. At the top of the chart belong the quasi-mystical moments in which, as he put it, he is dissolved in the Mind; self-reliance is a northwest idea; the moral law lies northeast; what Santayana called "normal madness," and Emerson "exaggeration," is southwest in quality; the idea of fate, perhaps, southeast.[121]

While this "game," as Whicher calls it, is undertaken "not too seriously," it is nevertheless indicative of the project of *Freedom and Fate*, which is the conquest of "Emerson's divided nature," the mapping of the "total *truth of experience* larger than the opposing *truths of statement* of which it is composed."[122]

To make the inconsistent consistent, Whicher replaces the point of Emerson with a line to be plotted that describes the real meaning of Emerson, which itself entails a drive to conquer nature. Significantly, the desire for territorial conquest evident in Whicher's half-joke is displaced onto his subject. *Freedom and Fate* tells the story "of what [Emerson] found—his first exploration of his new world of thought, his gradual discovery of its hazards, and his eventual mapping and settlement of a home there."[123] Whicher characterizes *Nature* as an "effort" that "took two directions: one, toward the conquest of nature intellectually, by achieving her Idea or theory; the other, toward a practical conquest, a kingdom of man, by learning the lesson of power."[124] Ultimately, this permits Emerson to navigate the treacherous course to truth, to the point where "he can chart his relative position—orient himself, that is, for practical purposes."[125] The voyage thus ends after both a practical and an ideal conquest, a practical idealism similar to that of Holmes and Perry in which "we are subject to necessity; yet, practically, a man must look on freedom as if he were free, whatever the intellectual difficulties."[126]

Making Emerson consistent in this manner means several things: the "total truth" or *nature* of Emerson is chartable—the public and private writing and the inner and outer life can be mapped by the competent cartographer; Emerson's nature has been made safe and navigable—the terrain has been subdued by the efforts of the concerned scientist and explorer; by following the map provided, the reader too can negotiate the twists and turns, the polar effects of freedom and fate, and arrive at the projected destination; the charted truth about Emerson is practical idealism, which is itself a map for the conquest of nature and knowledge. Whicher, by charting Emerson, maps out a place for himself and for future tourists to the Land of Emerson. The text of the writing, made consistent with the inner life of the subject, is mastered once and for all. Emerson's nature is conquered.

5   American Scholars and the Objects of Criticism

But to what purpose did they read?
—"The Man of Letters"

Biographical or subject-centered criticism, in conquering the nature of a text, limits textual movement, curtails interpretive vision, and impedes a participatory, engaged reading—all in the name of the author and by virtue of the perceived meaning of his or her person. Reading is always preposterous when it puts the subject before the object or fails to see the object for the subject. But to shift the focus of inquiry from the subject to the object—that is, from the writer to the text—is to enter the uncertain territory of objective criticism. In this chapter, I try to elucidate the nature of criticism's object, the ends to which that object is put (i.e., criticism's objectives), and the methods employed to attain these ends. The result, I hope, will be the possibility of more clearly seeing the *relations* between object, end, and method. What objects or "Emersons" do American critics produce? For precisely what objectives are these objects produced? The connection of object to objective, which I will deem "objectification," manifests a visual economy in which the object is understood to enjoy a self-contained, self-evident status, radically separate from the critic who can then cast a cold eye upon it—objectively, as it were. In other words, to obtain its objective, criticism struggles to *disentangle* the object from the reader.

This separation or disentangling results in foregoing the "good" aspect of subjective reading as enunciated in "Thoughts on Modern Literature"; the interpretation of interpretation is rendered unnecessary in the positing of objective truth. But the question of objectivity is raised frequently in Emerson's writing, and nowhere as entanglingly as in *Nature*. Reading it by a method that illuminates the problem of reading itself—a method that involves entangling rather than disentangling—leads to a reconsideration of the truth claims of objectification and its practitioners. As Charles Feidelson Jr. has observed, *Nature* serves as an attempt to confront the problem of the division between the seer and the seen.[1] *Nature*'s writer, finding such a division to extend from and perpetuate "mean egotism," strives to transform the dichotomy by becoming the "transparent eye-ball."[2] Not only does such a transformation alter the relation between seer and seen but it also reworks the relation of being and seeing. The nouns of the first relation give way to the verbs of the second, so that "I am nothing. I see all."[3] The dissolution of object into event leaves only vision—the act of seeing—which itself is the recognition of the circulation of "Universal Being."

Picking up on this, Feidelson understands Emerson to be proposing that "nature is a network of significant relations."[4] Emerson "move[d] the focus of study from the seer to the act of seeing; and from the act of seeing he worked back to the thing seen, which he reinstated as one aspect of the perceptual event."[5] Worrying over the relation of seer and seen, *Nature* attends to the act that connects the two, hoping that such attention will transform the dichotomy into unity. If objectification means seeing that opposes seer and seen, and this oppositional vision has resulted in the (mis)placing of subjects and the (mis)taking of objects, then its alternative should undo that opposition. *Nature*'s Emerson, as he is described by Feidelson (and as he appears as the interpretive and communicative figure of the essay) can be seen as promoting a different mode of seeing. His "transparent eye-ball" means the dissolution of the seer-seen split into the act of seeing. In what way, though, does this dissolution transfer to the literary act? To answer this question, one needs to further consider the difficulties involved in vision.

Those difficulties become readily apparent in *Nature*. The particular visual problems with which the essay is concerned, however, do not seem to extend from the nature of vision. Rather, a culturally instituted worldview befogs our sight in several aspects. For example, as I noted in the previous chapter, the opening sentence of *Nature* declares, "Our age is retrospective." We look backward, through the eyes of "the foregoing generations," and consequently cannot "enjoy an original relation to the universe."[6] Along with looking the wrong way directionally, we look the wrong way methodologically by looking scientifically, for "empirical science is apt to cloud the sight."[7] All this results in the prevailing dualistic approach to the world: "Philosophically considered, the universe is composed of Nature and the Soul. Strictly speaking, therefore, all that is separate from us, all which Philosophy distinguishes as the NOT ME, that is, both nature and art, all other men and my own body, must be ranked under this name, NATURE. In enumerating the values of nature and casting up their sum, I shall use the word in both senses;—in its common and in its philosophical import."[8] A difficulty confronts the writer of *Nature* at the outset. Working here in philosophy, in words, in writing, the writer is forced into a discourse that, by its very existence, must undo that which it would do over. Philosophical consideration must occur within words; words, by their nature, "are finite organs of the infinite mind. They cannot cover the dimensions of what is in truth. They break, chop, and impoverish it."[9] Discourse can never accomplish the integration of the ME and the NOT-ME. When we consider philosophically, we are alienated from what we would be a part of; "strictly speaking," a writer can only "enumerate values" and "cast up sums." The philosopher, that is, can only further enrich the impoverishment of the world, even as she or he attempts to better the world by describing an original relation with it. Nature "must be" named and considered under the rank of that name. The problem for the writer of *Nature* is not an incapacity to see nature, but that he must see nature as something separate.

As remarked above, the solution to this problem appears to come in the form of dissolution. The radically separated seer dissolves into a transparent eye-ball, into sight itself. This is what is involved in "the greatest delight which the fields and woods minister": the eye-ball, sauntering through the woods, overcoming a gladness that has brought it to the brink of fear, experiences "an occult relation between man and the vegetable. I am not alone and unacknowledged. . . . Its effect is like that of a higher thought or a better emotion coming over me, when I deemed I was thinking justly or doing right."[10] Something *like* the sublime, this greatest delight that comes over the seer nearly overcomes him, *almost* immerses him into the landscape through which he walks and on which he looks. The failure indicated by the approximations, a failure with which Emerson's writing wrestles, is a problem of recognition. The sentences elided in the above quotation describe the writer's inability to move out of the retrospection of the age and the philosophy of ME/NOT-ME. Both the me and the not-me (pluralized in the ensuing quotation) recognize me, peg me for what I am: "They nod to me, and I to them. The waving of the boughs in the storm is new to me and old. It takes me by surprise, and yet is not unknown. Its effect is like that. . . ."

Attempting to move through the not-me and, in and through that movement, to see its way out of the old separation and into its place as part of the new, exhilarating, fearful landscape, the me is yet caught in a standstill between new and old, between itself and everything else.

Movement and vision are to rescue the me from its radical separation from the not-me. The me, transcending self-involvement (i.e., pernicious subjectivity) as well as the reification of the not-me (i.e., objectification or pernicious objectivity), involves itself in nature and is thereby "delighted" (which, from its Latin root, carries the sense of being lured away from, enticed away). "Yet it is certain that the power to produce this delight, does not reside in nature, but in man, or in a harmony of both."[11] The resultant tension between the desire to be lured away and the desire to be the one who "takes up the world into himself" further divides the me of *Nature,* even as that me preoccupies itself with the conditions of division.[12] "It is necessary," the writer sees, "to use these pleasures with great temperance" because the writer's eye must finally stand its ground.[13] It ceases to move, that is, and therefore ceases to see. The writer who encourages the reader of *Nature* to "look at the world with new eyes" first characterizes this new looking as contingent on the double movement of the I into the eye and the eye through the world.[14] The eye becomes part of that which it sees and through which it moves. The writer, however, leery of taking too great a pleasure from this movement, returns to the me by way of arguing that it is the landscape, the not-me, that must be put into movement, thereby reinstating the common separation:

> In these cases ["small alterations" in our "local position"], by mechanical means [whether "seeing the shore from a moving ship" or "looking at the landscape through your legs"], is suggested the difference between the observer and the spectacle,—between man and nature. Hence arises a pleasure mixed with awe; I may say, a low degree of the sublime is felt, from the fact, probably, that man is hereby apprized that whilst the world is a spectacle, something in himself is stable.[15]

Here, something in the I remains stable, while the field of objects of vision is put into motion, detaching that field from the stabilized observer. Seeing the world from this remove makes it agreeably unreal. Thus is a low version of the sublime attained.

"In a higher manner," continues the writer, "the poet communicates the same pleasure. By a few strokes he delineates, as on air, the sun, the mountain, the camp, the city, the hero, the maiden, not different from what we know them, but only lifted from the ground and afloat before the eye. He unfixes the land and the sea, makes them revolve around the axis of his primary thought, and disposes them anew."[16] The change in emphasis from a moving eye to a fixed I marks a turn in the discussion of vision that undoes the possibilities for "looking with new eyes." *Nature*, which works in places against fixity of viewpoint and the parceling out of the visual world into radically separate elements, also and with equal interest fixes that within the viewer which must be stable, falling back on the depiction of vision as the apprehension of things.

Such difficulties cast a shadow over our prospects for seeing. One can gather from the problematic for reading nature as adduced in *Nature*, however, some clues that might help negotiate the problems for reading *Nature*. The writer of *Nature*, in detailing one aspect of the problematic, remarks that the philosophical split between seer and seen causes us to look badly, and, as a consequence, to not truly see: "Go out of the house to see the moon, and 't is mere tinsel; it will not please as when its light shines upon your necessary journey. The beauty that shimmers in the yellow afternoons of October, who could ever clutch it? Go forth to find it, and it is gone; 't is only a mirage as you look from the windows of diligence."[17] According to this passage, one seems capable of seeing only if one does not look. By making the "necessary journey," by seeing the moon as part of the textual landscape that includes the traveler, the seer dismantles the frame constructed by diligence and a type of desire that would make of the moon an object. (From its Latin root, *diligence* carries the sense of "gathering apart," setting off, preferring.) Objects of vision, "if too eagerly hunted, become shows merely, and mock us with their unreality."[18] The reality of what is to be seen must be conditioned by "your necessary journey" and not your eager hunt. Of course, some sort of looking must occur for the moon to be recognized, for its beauty and/or existence to be registered by the seer. What appears to mark the difference in this passage is the acknowledgment that seer and seen enjoy a relationality different from the radical separation between the hunter and the hunted. They are mediated—as Feidelson has shown, nature is a network of significant relations, a textual series of mediations that require interpretation. The interpreter, however, no longer appears as either radically other than or identical to the interpreted. Seer and seen come to make meaning as the seer recognizes (on "the necessary journey") that both the moon and the seer of the moon are inextricable from a textually conditioned relation.

If, in Feidelson's terms, American literary criticism has always hunted (and here I am substituting "Emerson" for "the moon" as the prey), such a predatory approach to the literary object would not result necessarily from the failure to treat the literary object qua literary object. *Symbolism and American Literature* commences with the complaint that the critic's "account has been given over to bibliography, anecdote, sociology, and the history of social, economic, and political ideas."[19] While success writers and biographers have set their sights on Emerson for various reasons (social, economic, political, philosophical), we must ask now to what extent Feidelson's assertion that criticism has always done this might mean also that it always will. But we must ask as well whether criticism has note done exactly what Feidelson would have it do: investigate the literary object as literary object.

The introduction to *Symbolism and American Literature* closes with a concise statement of method and purpose: "I have tried to let the materials speak for themselves as much as possible; and my end is not pure theory but practical criticism."[20] In this formulation, practical criticism is that which permits the literary object to speak for itself. Even if we take the phrase *practical criticism* in its traditional sense (the application of aesthetic principles to specific works), we can see that, for Feidelson, the literary object enjoys an unquestionable status, both as literature and as object. Practical criticism would then tend to be objective (in the sense that it originates from the object itself) and "pure theory" would be subjective or gauzy historical-sociological-political accounts that dress up the object and make it more or less presentable. In letting the object speak for itself, however—in letting the object be itself and letting that being present itself—objective criticism would seem to commit the di-vision described in *Nature*. Think of Feidelson, for example, rushing out of his cottage to see the moon; finding instead a string of clouds (produced by vapors: historical, economic, and so forth), he waits for the night sky to clear. Behold! The moon! But is it? For, as the writer of *Nature* observes, in the very act of clutching at the moon, in that covetous sprint from doorway to vantage point, other vapors (e.g., the sweat of the diligently objective brow) have arisen. In his quest to see the moon and nothing but the moon, Feidelson has still found "the moon."

Scare quotes again—clouds covering a full moon. They signify in this instance the objectification of the seen (or that which would be seen), the removal of the object from its textual relations and the refusal to admit the relationality (and its effects) of the would-be seer. The seer is not seeing Emerson (which is what the seer claims) but "Emerson." The objective critic's reliance on the facticity of its object, the "object-ness" of Emerson, constitutes a hunt for Emerson. The very hunt puts in place the quotation marks that surround the name of Emerson, a name that stands for the person and his writing. These are marks, however, that the hunter refuses to or cannot see. Practical criticism's unquestioning belief in the facticity of its object is (at least in part) responsible for the factitiousness of the object. As a mode of reading, then, objective criticism constitutes a way of taking the literary object away from its various networks of significant relations, be those relations and networks economic, political, social, ontological, historical, cultural, epistemological. Approaches to the "literary object" that close it off as exclusively a historical matter, an epistemological matter denature the literary object in their very approach. For literary objects are always textual objects, elements of relational networks, and must be approached as such. Objective criticism, consequently, supposes a termination of relations, marking another end of reading.

Made in and Making America

> There is to be a new religion, and it is to come from America; a new and
> better type of man, and he is to be an American.
>
> —John Jay Chapman

Consider further the notion that it is the very race to view the moon that produces "the moon." To understand the nature of the object, it would be helpful to investigate the nature of the race. Why do American critics diligently hustle to know or value Emerson? To what extent does that effort produce "Emerson"? What Emersons have American critical practice produced and why might that practice have done so? In reviewing the history of American criticism, it becomes evident that the making of different Emersons connects significantly with the making of different Americas. Questions necessary for such a review have less to do with whether a particular critic is either right or wrong about Emerson than with what sort of "Emerson" emerges from the critic's interpretation and what sort of America the critic desires. What are the characteristics of Emerson that are accorded privileged stature? What language informs the interpretation? To what use is Emerson put? Such questions should help us see more clearly the objectives of American critical practice and the objects it constructs.

A contemporary American reader of no little critical acumen, Harold Bloom, has written that Emerson's "peculiar relevance now is that we seem to read him merely by living here, in this place still somehow his, and not our own."[21] "This place" is America—in this case, Bloom's anxious, influenced, poetic America. What it means that this place is "still somehow Emerson's" takes on great importance: the definition of America is tied to the definition of Emerson. Such a tie no doubt has serious political and philosophical ramifications. Perhaps most remarkable is Bloom's suggestion that we read Emerson simply by residing in America. Emerson permeates the nation's atmosphere. What does such a startling concept mean for Emerson? America? Reading? What are the figures by which an Emersonian object is manufactured, and how does that object figure in the manufacturer's apparent objectives?

The three major forms of producing "Emerson" that develop in American literary criticism revolve around questions regarding the various meanings of the literary object. The first substitutes the subject for the object. In the examples of Holmes and Perry, the substitution was conditioned by the biographers' own program for America—a program frequently organized around a principle of practical idealism. That principle accounts for two contradictory positions within "Emerson himself" (the Plotinus-Montaigne), and makes the resultant "Emerson" into a good American (the one who hitches his wagon to a star, the morally sentimental sportsman, the conqueror of nature). Objective critics draw on practical idealism to answer their own questions: one worries most over what Emerson means for America, the other over what Emerson means for art. All three of these ways of approaching Emerson operate in the domain of practical idealism, and all three produce various algebraic equations composed of the terms "Emerson," "Literature" (or "Art"), and "America."

In *The American Mind,* Henry Steele Commager compares the career of Emerson to that of William James. "Both," Commager finds, "expressed the optimism and practical idealism of the American character; both were individualistic and democratic."[22] The historian leaves us here to work out any contradictions for ourselves, but his remark is nonetheless helpful in that it succinctly frames the arguments proffered in the sundry constructions of the American traits of Emerson. Practical or idealistic, individualistic or democratic, the Concord Sage is made by critics to stand for either one or the other or both—as if each critic builds a little park called America and deposits in its center a statue of Emerson, posed according to the critic's preference: perhaps smilingly hitching the wagon or benignly eyeing the star. Regardless of the statue's attitude, it is *here,* standing in and for America. As Mencken puts it, "One discerns, in all right-thinking American criticism, the doctrine that Ralph Waldo Emerson was a great man, but the specifications supporting that doctrine are seldom displayed with any clarity."[23] Mencken goes on to disparage the two primary methods of obscuring Emerson's works: the "lavender buncombe" of New Thought and "Nietzscheism." The latter is dismissed summarily for its "headlong attack upon egalitarianism, the corner-stone of American politics";[24] the former, however, Mencken opposes to pragmatism, the prevailing philosophy of the day, and finds both guilty of claiming Emerson as an ancestor, even as they both neglect his "truths." The linking of New Thought to pragmatism thus affords us another perspective of that paradox most characteristic of "the American Mind."

Disclaiming against the failure of Americans to heed the words of "this prophet of Man Thinking,"[25] Mencken asserts that it is the absurdity of a practical idealism and its grip on American culture that closes minds and precludes the possibility of intelligently reading Emerson (who "remains to be worked out critically").[26] New Thought, complains Mencken, "substitutes mysticism, which is the notion that the true realities are all concealed, for the prevailing American notion that the only true realities lie upon the surface, and are easily discerned by Congressmen, newspaper editorial writers and members of the Junior Order of United American Mechanics."[27] This, however, is only one side of the problem; for "the circle of Emersonian adulation," the "Emerson cult," also includes "chautauqua orators" and "literary professors," among whom Mencken includes William James.[28] Although Emerson's program (in Mencken's interpretation) insists upon inquiring for "facts amidst appearances" and never deferring to decorum and respectability, "the philosophy that actually prevails among his countrymen—a philosophy put into caressing terms by William James— teaches an almost exactly contrary doctrine: its central idea is that whatever satisfies the immediate need is substantially true, that appearance is the only form of fact worthy the consideration of a man with money in the bank, and the old flag floating over him, and the hair on his chest."[29] Practical idealism, then, becomes both an idealism made practical (or applicable or useful) and a practicality nothing if not idealistic (based on a middle-class "ideal" of a financial nest egg, showy patriotism, and hirsute virility). Caught between these two possibilities, Emerson disappears; "his manner has vanished with his matter. There is, in the true sense, no Emersonian school of American writers."[30] "He had admirers and even worshippers, but no apprentices."[31]

It is perhaps this disappearance of Emerson that his critics and commentators rush to fill. Mencken, although railing against reductive misreadings of Emerson, appears comfortable with his own minimalist packaging: "His whole metaphysic revolved around a doctrine of transcendental first causes, a conception of interior and immutable realities, distinct from and superior to mere transient phenomena."[32] Mencken does, nevertheless, gesture toward the prevention of reductions, or at least he cautions against one-sided accounts of Emerson's writing, finding that "he was dualism ambulant. What he actually *was* was seldom identical with what he represented himself to be or what his admirers thought him to be."[33] Representations of Emerson abound, but what the man was—dualism ambulant, a walking contradiction (instead of a stalking eye-ball)—remains to be worked out critically. Mencken has some clues to the true identity: "imitative and cautious"; the "theoretical spokesman, all his life long, of bold and forthright thinking"; a man of "mellifluous obscurity."[34] But those clues, he fears, are insufficient for the project of rescuing the Emerson object from the "monopolization" it has suffered at the hands of New Thought and "American superficiality." Even though the dualisms that animate Emerson and ambulate through Emerson's writing have thwarted thorough criticism of that work, practical idealism has hastily and simplistically resolved any contradictions, tendering up by turns a preposterously pragmatic or impossibly mystical "Emerson."

Mencken's own production of Emerson, as we can see, tends toward the transcendentalist while resisting the mystical. Applying his "Unheeded Law-Giver" to the problems of the "country in which every sort of dissent from the current pishposh is combated most ferociously," Mencken holds that a transcendental Emerson presents the possibility of resistance to "American superficiality."[35] Such a belief ties into a discourse of American history that would firm up Emerson's transcendentalism in the name of Democracy. An attempt to save Emerson from the hands of the villains described by Mencken emerged in the sweeping accounts of American literature and thought that proliferated in the first half of the twentieth century. The Emerson of the Beards' *The Rise of American Civilization* strides forth from "among the dissenters" as "first in penetration and high expression."[36] A politically radical prophet of apocalypse, this Emerson is no gentle sage but an anticipator of Marx and Engels, Darwin and Spencer.[37] Similarly, Vernon Louis Parrington complains that America ignored the anarchic side of Emerson, preferring instead "to dwell on pleasanter aspects of his teaching."[38] What is so radical about Emerson, for Parrington, is his idealism. Opposing Emerson to Daniel Webster, he portrays the former as "idealistic," "ethical," "the intellectual revolutionary, ready to turn the world upside down in theory, planting at the base of the established order the dynamite of ideas," while Webster stands for "the practical," "the rationalistic," "the soberly conservative."[39] Emerson's radical idealism, however, is also a practical program for "meddling with the real . . . with institutions, laws, society, with the state itself."[40] Such idealism is neither mystical nor impractical.

It was, nevertheless, transcendental—or, more accurately, "transcenden-tal individualism."[41] In this discourse of American history, individualism comes to be the body of practical idealism and democracy its spirit, con-stituting a duality that explains away the apparent contradictions in Emerson's philosophy. Emerson is made safe for America by a strip show that reveals the shining truth of practical idealism. Hence Lewis Mumford claims an Emersonian nudity as the possibility for America's future: "Emerson achieved nakedness: his central doctrine is the virtue of this intellectual, or cultural, nakedness: the virtue of getting beyond the insti-tution, the habit, the ritual, and finding out what it means afresh in one's own consciousness."[42] Bare Emerson, standing there in the light of Mumford's Golden Day, is "the central figure," "an original," a "glacier" that "must be climbed, and there is so much of him that people become satisfied with a brief glimpse";[43] he is "a sort of living essence,"[44] and, "strong or weak, Emerson was complete: in his thought the potentialities of New England were finally expressed."[45] Weak or strong, erect or flaccid, Emerson's manliness stands for America, expresses its essence. (Or, as Lowell puts it, Emerson had the "masculine faculty of fecundating other minds."[46]) From his potentialities, "an imaginative New World came to birth during this period, a new hemisphere in the geography of the mind. That world was the climax of American experience. What preceded led up to it: what followed, dwindled away from it."[47]

The spirit that Emerson seemingly possesses and for which his manli-ness stands is that of the "Transcendental Critic," a term Parrington em-ploys to explain the Emersonian program: "In the midst of a boastful materialism, shot through with cant and hypocrisy and every insincerity, fat and slothful in all higher things, the critic proposed to try the magic of sincerity, to apply the test of spiritual values to the material forces and mechanical philosophies of the times. His very life must embody criti-cism."[48] Although Emerson embodies criticism, however, his own body is ephemeral; for Parrington, Emerson's nakedness reveals "an extreme unfleshliness":[49] this Emerson, "with his serene intelligence" is "almost disencumbered of the flesh."[50] Thus the critic's take on Emerson depends in part on the layers one is capable of removing from him. An unclothed Emerson, standing at attention, is the Emerson of individualism, Ameri-can manliness, a sire of better days. A skinned Emerson unveils he who "was the conscience of America," the democratic spirit: "By every com-pulsion of his transcendental philosophy Emerson was driven to accept the abstract principle of democracy."[51]

These two Emersons, the body and the spirit, generated by the "original Emerson's" ambulatory dualism, generate further binaries in critical works, as in Parrington's remark that "Emerson was the apotheosis of two centuries of decentralization that destroyed the pessimism brought to the new world by refugees from the old, and found its inevitable expression in the exaltation of the individual, free and excellent, the child of beneficent order."[52] Pessimism versus optimism, Old World versus New World, refugee versus citizen, other versus self, chaos versus order: Parrington's practically ideal, individualistically democratic, truly American Emerson occupies a position superior to the masses, here represented by the refugees. The spirit of democracy must be realized in the body of the Central Man, who in turn is to ameliorate the masses by imbuing them with his individuality. The individual embodies the spirit, manifests it, represents it; individualism stands for democracy.[53]

Or does it? What appears to be a tidy packaging of complementary traits becomes, in other critical reworkings of Emerson's contradictions, a war of opposites that tears apart such packaging from the inside. John Jay Chapman's oft-lauded essay on Emerson commences with a lengthy excerpt from *The Conduct of Life* in which the author comes down hard on the "masses" ("The calamity is the masses"). Chapman deploys Emerson's passage as the opening salvo in a war against the masses and the political system that defends them: "Emerson represents a protest against the tyranny of democracy."[54] In so doing, Chapman provides us with a casebook example of objective criticism. Reducing Emerson's writing and unabashedly employing the reduction in the name of Emerson, Chapman eliminates the contradictory bulk of that writing and tempers what remains into a sharp-edged knife with which to slice up the world around him. The excerpt the critic chooses, as with Holmes's "hitch a wagon," is posited as the central tenet of Emersonian philosophy: "This extract from The Conduct of Life gives fairly enough the leading thought of Emerson's life."[55] So armed with "Emerson," Chapman joins the "unending warfare between the individual and society."[56]

Indeed, Chapman is ready for battle *because* of Emerson; the latter carries the banner for Chapman because "he has probably succeeded in leaving a body of work which cannot be made to operate to any other end than that for which he designed it."[57] That design, according to Chapman, is the crusade for the "new religion" of the American. As with the biographers, the true meaning of Emerson is plain to Chapman and comes to him objectively in a heightened act of reception needless of interpretation. Emerson "writes as he speaks. . . . It is impossible to name his style without naming his character: they are one thing." "His style is American."[58]

The man's writing is the man—know him and you know what he means: "You cannot always see Emerson clearly; he is hidden by a high wall; but you always know exactly on what spot he is standing."[59] Therefore, Chapman assures us, "it is unnecessary to go, one by one, through the familiar essays and lectures which Emerson published between 1838 and 1875."[60] We do not have to read Emerson any longer. He was here. He spoke to us. We know what he meant.

And what he meant, of course, is neither more nor less than what Chapman offers us: "Philosophical exaltation of the individual," as first perceived and expressed by Plato, is "the corner stone of [Emerson's] thought."[61] The result of this form of objective criticism is the deification of the ideal American, which Chapman defines as an individualistic, commonsensical, practical Man. "As a man, Emerson is as plain as Ben Franklin."[62] He is a man and not a thinker; "he is a patriot" and "no cosmopolitan"; "but he is much more than a theorist: he is a practitioner."[63] Dismissing the accusations of contradictoriness, Chapman utilizes binaries to insist that the real Emerson is as plain as the nose on Franklin's face: manly, patriotic, and, above all, practical: "his interest centred in the practical man,—even his ideal scholar is a practical man."[64] "Emerson was divided from the Transcendentalists by his common sense."[65] In Chapman's version of Emerson as "a fighting animal,"[66] the "transcendental individualist" of Parrington is converted into a heavyweight individualist wrestling with the masses.

With repeated use of weaponry tropes, Chapman and his "Emerson" wage war against soul-crushing democracy on behalf of individualism. Chapman's "Emerson" is made possible by a practice of interpretation narrowed by individualism and aimed at the destruction of democracy, the primary threat to the individual. The objective critic here, refusing any truck with a line by line reading, bases his interpretive effort on a prior knowledge of his object. Knowing *that*—a knowledge inseparable from the objectives of his practice—Chapman knows all he need know of Emerson. He writes to his wife, "You know I've never known the literature of the subjects I wrote on. I never knew the Emerson literature—except Emerson himself."[67] Even though this confession of ignorance most likely refers to literature *about* Emerson, the wording is provocative. Chapman need not bother with reading Emerson; the object is what it is, means what it means. Emerson himself proves the divinity of the individual; critics need only accept that proof to "get Emerson." Indeed, actually reading Emerson may only confuse us: we are unable to *see* logical connections, yet we may *feel* that "they are germane."[68] In this way our "tired" and "apathetic" spirits can get a rise out of Emerson, enabling each of us to fend off the other.

Taking Chapman's interpretation as an example of objective criticism, we can readily discern some of the ways in which this critical practice operates. The sight of the literary object is shaped by a division, by a way of seeing marked by radical separation of the viewer and the viewed. Divisive vision, evident in the rabid individualism that views the other as an enemy to be defeated, cuts up the world into binaries. The terms of the binaries, which together (as a binary) are in opposition to the viewer who constitutes them as a binary, are employed in the war of self versus other according to their status in the binary: the "good" is taken into the self, enlisted in the fight; the "bad" is attacked. This way of seeing conditions a methodology of interpretation that destroys the "literary object," either by an introjection (as with Chapman) or by a distancing rejection (as with, say, Yvor Winters).[69] The former, which is more often the case with Emerson as literary object, applies what remains from the initial objectification in pursuit of its objectives (such as, from the examples above, the fight against democracy, the fight for democracy, the fight for an American literature and/or an American criticism, the maintenance of a particular sexual economy, and so forth). Any surplus, any aspect of the object that might contradict the critical objective disappears.

Aesthetic Objectives: Raising the Standard

In another prominent strain of American criticism, the Emerson object merits a more dubious value in light of that criticism's objective: higher standards for art that will check Western man's dizzying plunge into disorder. Due to the contradictory nature of Emerson's writing, his figure can be seen as both contributing to the raising of standards and causing the condition that warrants such raising. As espoused in the works of the New Humanists, this form of objective criticism, distraught over the state of things, calls for an improved Emerson, one who "aids criticism in its search for inner standards to take the place of the outer standards it has lost; he helps it to see in the present anarchy the potentialities of a higher order."[70] Such an Emerson, incapable of being a standard himself, is to be remade into a standard around which American criticism can rally and culture can be revived.

Irving Babbitt's *The Masters of Modern French Criticism* manufactures an Emerson that will assist the critic in the shoring up of "inner standards" necessary for the amelioration of a civilization tending toward chaos and caprice. For Babbitt, culture is suffering ruin, literature is being vulgarized, and we are losing "the struggle between our lower and higher selves."[71] It is noteworthy that Babbitt finds Emerson a possible contributor to both sides of that struggle. Among the characteristics of the "bad" Emerson is his inability to see evil, his inconsistency and general feebleness of thought. He has, following Rousseau, given "undue encouragement to the ordinary man, to the man who is undisciplined and unselective and untraditional."[72] "The Rousseauist," Babbitt explains, "would eliminate from the norm the humanistic or aristocratic element. He would value a book, not by its appeal to the keen-sighted few, but by its immediate effect on the average man."[73] Positing a sharp distinction between the humanistic and the humanitarian, Babbitt portrays the latter as participating in the tyranny of the "average man," while the former represents aristocratic standards, classicism, and universal good. Unfortunately, Emerson is found to entertain "humanitarian illusions of his own."[74] This has led to Emersonianism, "a sort of emotional intoxication," and to such offshoots as Christian Science.[75]

Nevertheless, Babbitt also finds Emerson greatly useful in establishing "a standard that is in the individual and yet is felt by him to transcend his personal self and lay hold of that part of his nature that he possesses in common with other men."[76] "That part of his nature" is something eternally, internally, objectively true, known to the best people since the beginning of time, but apparently inaccessible to the "average man." The "average man" must be governed by the humanists, or aristocrats, who are capable of critically knowing and applying the standard. Accordingly, the "good" Emerson is so by virtue of his doctrine of the Over-Soul, that overarching unity both in us and beyond us: "The oversoul that Emerson perceives in his best moments is the true oversoul and not the undersoul that the Rousseauist sets up as a substitute. He can therefore supply elements that will help us in forming our critical standard."[77] Babbitt's Emerson is a mixed bag, a compound object of positive and negative attributes. To derive the good elements, Babbitt's objective criticism opens the Emerson bag and sorts through the contents, according value to the traits that stand for tradition, elitism, and the establishment of norms.[78] The objectives—to reverse and control the anarchy of "equalitarianism," to establish standards for and thereby institute higher order—mandate a remade object.

While this program of objectification is most clearly articulated in a treatise on French criticism, Babbitt and other New Humanists—e.g., Paul Elmer More and Norman Foerster—have a controlled and ordered America in their sights. The New Humanists' America "suffers not only from a lack of standards, but also not infrequently from a confusion or an inversion of standards."[79] For More, a critical ally of Babbitt,[80] the inconsistencies inherent to the Emerson object are responsible for the Emersonianism that imperils right thinking, as it did even in Emerson's own day: "And if Emersonianism was mischievous to weak minds then, what shall we say of its influence in New England to-day—nay, throughout the whole country? For it is rampant in our life; it has wrought in our religion, our politics, and our literature a perilous dizziness of the brain."[81] The Emerson that permeates the American atmosphere is a dangerous pollutant threatening to undermine American culture. Unrefined Emersonianism leads to unrefined culture, to infected religious, political, and literary scenes. In religion, it begets Christian Science. Even more dangerously, "in politics the unreflecting optimism of transcendental Boston has given birth to that unformed creature called Anti-imperialism."[82] This is what results when "men and women with no mental training" are exposed to Emerson's inconsistencies.

The problem, as More sees it, is that the Emerson object only *looks* inconsistent; viewed more carefully, however, the parts cohere, and the result is unsatisfactory. Emerson's "essays ripple and recoil on the surface, but underneath there is a current setting steadily to one point."[83] Contradictions abound "on the surface" of Emerson's writing, but an "inner logic" (unrecognizable to people of weak or untrained minds), comprised of "one or two master ideas," yields the true nature of this particular literary object. Thus More describes Emersonianism as a failure to read well *and* the failure to read something good. Aggrieved that readers lack the intelligence, insight, and standards to see what Emerson really means, More collapses the contradictions that thrive in Emerson's writing in an aggressively reductive critical practice: "The apparent contradictions in his pages need but a moment's reflection and a modicum of understanding to reduce them to essential harmony."[84]

No average person, More believes himself to possess the "modicum of understanding" necessary for comprehending the objective truth. Despite Emerson's "jaunty optimism," his "lack of system," his innumerable inconsistencies, the objective critic sees that "all the manifold applications of his genius may . . . be summed up in this single paragraph from his later essay on Fate."[85] Once again, the diversity and bulk of Emerson's writing is pillaged, leaving a reconfigured object that the critic dubs "Emerson." In this case, More has chosen from *The Conduct of Life* a passage that describes the "propounding . . . of the double consciousness."[86] That this would be the summation of More's "Emerson" does not speak highly for that literary object; in a later essay, More finds double consciousness indicative of the insufficiency of Emerson's philosophy.[87] Ultimately, Emerson is only the "poet of religion and philosophy for the young; whereas men as they grow older are inclined to turn from him, in their more serious needs, to those sages who have supplemented insight with a firmer grasp of the whole of human nature."[88] More's "Emerson" fails to be a firm upholder of the standard in the war for higher culture.

Norman Foerster ("a disciple of Babbitt and More"[89]) takes up the standard as described by his predecessors and carries it further into the culture war. Distressed by criticism that "more and more became (to use its own big words) impressionistic, expressionistic, sociological, and psychological,"[90] he calls for a return to "the central aim of criticism, which is the determination and the application of standards of value."[91] *American Criticism* argues for a more objective (in the traditional sense of the term) criticism and reiterates the need for standards that will objectively combat creeping cultural chaos. The objects of criticism—that on which criticism practices—are separable from those practices; the literary object must be isolated and then evaluated according to the value system instantiated by objective standards. This summarizes *American Criticism*'s objectives: the creation of a new order of literary objects. "Before a new order of creative literature can arrive, however, the way must be prepared by criticism."[92]

Criticism makes literature possible; even more importantly for Foerster, however, right criticism makes right living possible—that is, living according to (classical) norms.[93] Listing the basic characteristics of the humanist standard—completeness, proportion, normality, reason, intuition or imagination, restraint or control, centrism[94]—Foerster enumerates a standard of value with which one is to evaluate any work of art. Judged by such criteria, the Emerson object is clearly deficient. In his scrutiny of the object, Foerster finds it to possess all of the limits of flighty mysticism as descried and decried by Holmes, but nothing else: "Beneath [Emerson's] mysticism there is little articulated thought—such thought as Plato's or even Plotinus's—to sustain and direct it." In other words, Emerson is "dominantly priestly rather than poetic, mystical rather than aesthetic."[95] Hence this particular literary object is not literary enough, and in its priestly and mystical workings, it gives "palpably false advice" to the "ordinary man."[96] Thus judges Foerster by the humanist standard, which, due to its "extraordinary," highly evolved objectivity, does not shape or misshape the objects of its critique: "If Emerson nowhere states his meaning quite so definitely, it is nevertheless plain that this distinction exists implicitly in his text. We are clarifying his sense, not distorting it."[97] This brand of American criticism, in search of objective standards, sees the Emerson object for what it is and finds it wanting.

Objective criticism operates as a mode of preemptively reformative reading that alters the nature of its object to conform with its objectives. There are two primary sets of objectives: one, more pointedly political or historical, entails the making of America; the other, more aesthetic, regards the institution of high standards. The objects (or Emersons) that these objectives bring forth are legion and range in nature from the practical to the idealistic, the pragmatic to the mystic, often consisting of volatile combinations of sundry elements. But they always *do* consist—Emerson is made into a consistent whole, for American good and American ill or for the improvement and impoverishment of aesthetic standards. Although the history of the interpretation of Emerson by American scholars describes an entangling of object and objective, the methods adopted by those scholars rely on a distancing of reading subject from the object read. When the nature of the object and the nature of the interpretive method proceed without question, the tangle obtains, but its effects are neglected.

"Our Perpetually Emersonian America"

The consequences of a disentangling that entangles, of an objective approach to Emerson's writing that distorts the nature of that writing, become apparent in the aesthetic theories of the influential critic Harold Bloom. Bloom provides a clear example of the interpretive problems resulting from objective criticism. A close look at his remaking of Emerson—the object his criticism manufactures (the "Emerson," to use Bloom's phrase, that "we want and need"[98]), the objectives to which that object is put (the realization of "our perpetually Emersonian America"[99]), and his particular modes of objectification—elucidates the problems of a reading style that radically separates subject from object, closing off the natural movement of the text and constraining the process of interpretation.

Bloom relies on a distinctly formulated version of Emerson's writing, a definitive encircling of the object that removes it from complex relations and maintains it as a readily knowable thing. Thus defined, the nature of the Emerson object, self-evident and stable, can serve the ends to which it is put. The objective critic does admit (infrequently) the difficulties involved in coming to a conclusive definition of "*the* Emerson." In *Agon,* for example, Bloom observes that "Emerson and Nietzsche and James and Pater and Wilde all teach us that *the* Emerson and *the* Nietzsche and so on do not exist, except as critical fictions."[100] Earlier, in *Figures of Capable Imagi-*

nation, the story is that "there are six or seven Emersons in Emerson's prose, and three or four more in his verse, and he would have delighted at our total inability to reconcile all of them."[101] The bulk of Bloom's work, however, accomplishes just such a reconciliation and amounts to a reduction of the multiple meanings emerging from the Emerson text that yields the "real meaning of Emerson," readied for service in Bloom's program.

The definition of this Emerson bears several notable traits: a cultural paternity, a combination of disparate elements (in the manner of practical idealism), and, most importantly, the quintessence of American individuality. Bloom's criticism establishes Emerson as "the starting-point, the defining element, the vexatious father."[102] Emerson is the "founder of *the* American religion, fountain of our literary and spiritual elite."[103] The vexatiousness of this founding father stems from the now-familiar ambulatory duality that marks the father's figure—Emerson is at once "the shadow and the despair, liberating angel and blocking agent, perpetual irritant and solacing glory."[104] Despite his crotchety contradictoriness, this "American Moses"[105] begets Americanness itself; "the unsurpassable prophet of the American Sublime"[106] prophesies the sublimity of American individualism. In *A Map of Misreading* Emerson appears simply and enormously as the "father of the American Romantic Selfhood,"[107] which role expands in *Agon* to "the quintessential American."[108]

An Emerson thus objectified embodies two central characteristics: individuality and the essence of America. As the quintessential American, the Emerson object stands for what Americans truly are and for how we should behave. In *Agon,* Bloom takes up the problem of the seer and the seen in Emerson's *Nature.* Instead of tending toward a rethinking of the nature of the relations that are alive in the act of seeing or interpreting, Bloom suggests that the text's "optics prod us towards a pragmatic difference . . . , because Emerson as American seer is always the shrewd Yankee, interested in what he called 'commodity.'"[109] By favoring the pragmatic Yankee side of Emerson, Bloom negates the complex nature of interpretive vision and grounds his Emerson in a commodifying subject-object division purportedly American in essence. This divisiveness subsequently necessitates a religious strain of self-reliance: "The mind of Emerson is the mind of America, for worse and glory, and the central concern of that mind was the American religion, which most memorably was named 'self-reliance.'"[110]

Standing at the center of self-helping American individuality, Bloom's Emerson "insists upon the necessity of the single self achieving a total autonomy."[111] The object is intensely isolated, removed from any network of significant relations and instantiated as its own little world unto itself.

Pictured as "the more perfect solipsist,"[112] Emerson embodies "triumphant solipsism," "isolate Selfhood,"[113] and his "purpose is to present . . . an American individuality."[114] (As such, this particular Emerson object closely resembles the naked, autonomous self configured by Chapman and Mumford, whose work Bloom values highly.[115]) A circle has been drawn around the meaning of Emerson, defining the object once and for all. Having thus girded his object, and having equated the Emerson circle with a circle that represents a particular version of America, Bloom uses both objects to argue for a peculiar method of reading, which in turn will help maintain the circles he has defined.

The primary objective in this series of objectifying circles is to create a truly American criticism, which will perpetuate a truly American literature. This last provides the best hope for maintaining our perpetually Emersonian America. Emerson is converted by Bloom into a godlike teacher of American scholarship, an avenging angel to smite the "younger rabblement celebrating itself as having repudiated the very idea of the individual reader or an individual critic."[116] The "rabblement" is constituted in part by "those academic covens akin to what Emerson, in his 1838 journal, called 'philanthropic meetings and holy hurrahs,' for which read now 'Marxist literary groups' and 'Lacanian theory circles,'"[117] but consists also of makers of the "'literature of Women's Liberation,'" African-American poets, and any other group that writes outside the lineage stemming from Emerson the Father.[118] The line Emerson founded leads to a "prophecy," which more closely approximates a prayer for the perpetuation of Bloom's Emersonian America:

> I prophesy that [Emerson], rather than Marx or Heidegger, will be the guiding spirit of our imaginative literature and our criticism for some time to come. In that prophecy, "Emerson" stands for not only the theoretical stance and wisdom of the historical Ralph Waldo, but for Nietzsche, Walter Pater and Oscar Wilde, and much of Freud as well, since Emerson's elitist vision of the higher individual is so consonant with theirs. Individualism, whatever damages its American ruggedness continues to inflict on our politics and social economy, is more than ever the only hope for our imaginative lives. Emerson, who knew that the only literary and critical method was oneself, is again a necessary resource in a time beginning to weary of Gallic scientism in what are still called the Humanities.[119]

This astonishing bit of prophetic objectification calls into being an Emersonian horseman of the Apocalypse, an interpretive and imaginative roughrider capable of trampling out the vintage where meaning is stored, all in the name of America, the Individual, and the humanities. Whatever the dangers of so-called Emersonian individualism, they pale in comparison to the real dangers confronting the autonomous self. Such a self is faced with changes in the world that make its central status precarious at best. "The rabblement" that threatens Emerson's centrally located self—consisting of blacks, feminists, "Gallic scientists" or deconstructionists, disciples of Artaud, "the tides of aggressive ignorance, or the counter-culture"[120]—surrounds the circle, terrorizing the interior and menacing the very lines of circumscription.

Hence the need for "*the* American religion" to fortify the wagon train and unite the besieged. Combat metaphors are apt, for they thoroughly inform the Bloomian project. The threatened Self must defend itself. Whether it is a "battle between strong equals, father and son as mighty opposites,"[121] or a "contest," an "unending match," a "hidden civil war,"[122] whether it is "the way poets war against one another" or "a triumphant wrestling with the greatest of the dead,"[123] Bloom's belletristic criticism is bellicose, agonistic, under fire. The nature of nature, in this reading, is always adversarial: writer versus writer, father versus son, self versus other, subject versus object. Bloom's American religion, called variously individualism or self-reliance or pragmatism, encompasses both a poetic tradition and a style of reading seen to stem from and be accountable to that tradition. An Emersonian aesthetic is created that will serve Emersonian America. That aesthetic, in service to such objectives, perpetuates a divisiveness that separates true America from the invading rabblement, objects from subjects, readers from texts.

The aesthetic is practiced under different names (e.g., strong reading, misreading, misprision), but always its purpose is to defend America and the aesthetic principle itself. In Bloom's view, criticism is both a tactic and a battlefield, part of the ground to be won and the method for winning it. Just as Emersonian America is threatened by sundry subversive elements, so is its critical aesthetic: "Criticism is in danger of being over-spiritualized by the heirs of Auerbach and by Northrop Frye, and of being excessively despiritualized by the followers of the school of Deconstruction, the heirs of Nietzsche."[124] Strong reading, a "critical theory and *praxis* that teaches the defensive necessity of 'misprision' or strong 'misreading,'"[125] is the necessary protector against these threats, for it alone can help maintain the pragmatic middle ground of spirituality that criticism must occupy.

Strong reading accomplishes nothing less than a reworking of the critical object, according to the desires of the self and the objectives it must meet to satisfy those desires. "We read to usurp, just as the poet writes to usurp. Usurp what? A place, a stance, a fullness, an illusion of identification or possession; something we can call our own or even ourselves."[126] Strong readers or revisionists remake the meaning of the object in their own images, making it their own. Usurping the power to define the nature and meaning of literary objects, strong readers willfully misread texts, processing them into new, improved works that will strengthen the circle against such enemies as the "Franco-Heideggerians" and other purveyors of the "gorgeous nonsense," which is "at worst only another residuum of the now wearisome perpetual crusade of intellectual Paris against its own upper middle class, and this just has no relevance to, or in, our perpetually Emersonian America."[127]

The operations of strong reading entail first the making of the Emerson that will be most applicable, even if that making requires mistaking, and then the conservation of that object. A methodology of misprision is, for Bloom, "a new and starker way";[128] as we have seen, however, Bloom's objective misreading, in which "*you forget something in order to present something else,*"[129] has long marked American criticism's practice on the Emerson object. Strong readers from Cabot to Babbitt have appropriated the portions of Emerson best suited to the constitution of their Emersons, discarding the refuse. The Emerson that remains is carefully preserved, in turn preserving America, Art, the Individual. In Bloom's program, "Emerson's single aim was to awaken his auditors to a sense of their own potential *power of making*. To serve his tradition now, we need to counsel a *power of conserving*."[130] Strong reading reduces Emerson to a single aim and, to properly serve the reduction, insists upon conservative measures.

Maintenance of the Emersonian America circle is aided by the service of a true made-in-America tool: pragmatism. Because of its pure Americanness, and especially because "poetry and criticism (by which I do continue to mean a single entity) have always been pragmatic events,"[131] pragmatism thoroughly informs Bloom's aesthetic, his America, and his Emerson.[132] Pragmatism is at once the process of making the circle, the conservation of circularity and that which it contains, and the reinforced necessity of working within the contained space. As such, it is the refusal of "alien" methodologies, the utter denial of the complex nature of texts, and the rejection of transcendence. Pragmatically configured, "Emerson is an experiential critic and essayist, and not a Transcendental philosopher."[133] A "pragmatics of interpretation"[134] results from Bloom's misprision of Emerson, in which the latter is positioned as the founder of an aesthetic of misreading that will offset the threats to the circle by the unpragmatic, un-American critical rabble.

Pragmatic interpreters are deployed in the war against other readers in an effort to win back the real meaning of poetry and criticism (and Emerson and America). Another of Bloom's revelations ominously asserts that "the final pragmatists of agon have been and will be the Americans of Emerson's tradition."[135] The finality of this prophecy carries us further toward an interpretive armageddon when Bloom ordains defiantly that "Bertrand Russell warned that pragmatism could lead only to warfare. So be it."[136] Not to be solved through diplomatic means, this struggle must yield a victor, a Central Man, the Strongest Reader: "on a pragmatic view there is no language *of criticism* but only of an individual critic, because again I agree with Rorty that a theory of strong misreading denies that there is or should be any common vocabulary in terms of which critics can argue with one another. Gnostic and elitist, a strong reading, like Emerson's, champions the literary culture of the isolate individual, the solitary construer."[137] Invoking the latter-day pragmatist Richard Rorty, Bloom asserts that the strongest individual reading will prevail and become *the* reading. Pragmatic interpretation, the usurpation not only of particular meanings but also of the possible grounds of meaning, converts texts into objects that have significance only insofar as they have a use-value commensurate with the value system of pragmatic interpreters. "American pragmatism, as Rorty advises, always asks of a text: what is it good for, what can I do with it, what can it do for me, what can I make it mean? I confess that I like these questions, and they are what I think strong reading is all about."[138]

Bloom's confession of faith in Rorty's reading practice brings together several of the modes of American criticism's diligent objectification. What is Emerson good for? What can I do with Emerson? What can Emerson do for me? Such are the questions American scholars have asked, fabricating particular Emersons to answer their questions. Objective criticism has always produced its Emersons by appropriating pieces of the extensive and complex text of his writings and forgetting the rest, according to the ends to which Emerson is to be put. (Not surprisingly, the forgotten Emersons are often the very ones that most trouble the circles that objective criticism would establish and maintain.) Bloom's "perpetually Emersonian America" closes down the complicated, contradictory body of writings Emerson produced, removing fragments from their context and piecing them together into a version of a text that refuses its textual nature, that claims, in other words, to be unquestionably The Truth—whether it is the truth about Emerson or America or reading.

In this way, objective criticism limits approaches to the literary object to matters of use-value operative within an unquestionable truth system, dismissing matters of epistemology, economics, politics, metaphysics, textuality, nature—approaches, in short, that challenge the structure of the truth system and the facticity of objects that come into being within that system. By maintaining the primacy of individuality and the autonomy of the single self, objective criticism sustains an oppositional view of the world, a view that insists on the radical separation of the self from everything around it. But this neglect of the relations between subject and object speciously separates readers from the texts we consider and the meanings we glean. Circles are drawn at the cost of myriad other figures of interpretation, and consequently the nature of texts is destroyed. Bloom's Emerson has "come to prophesy not a de-centering, as Nietzsche had, and as Derrida and de Man are brilliantly accomplishing, but a peculiarly American re-centering, and with it an American mode of interpretation."[139] That mode recenters around the object its practitioners want and need: in Bloom's case, an Emerson always pragmatic, patriotic, patriarchal.

"Emerson," according to the strong reader, "who said he unsettled all questions, first put literature into question for us, and now survives to question our questioners."[140] The Emerson text, however, does not only question "our" questioners—it questions us, too, exactly by putting literature and reading into question. And I am suggesting that we should respond by taking those questions on. It is in the essay "Circles" that the Emerson text claims, "I unsettle all things."[141] Where Bloom's misprision has Emerson unsettle questions, the text unsettles things, which I take to mean "objects," facts, answers: "No facts are to me sacred; none are profane; I simply experiment, an endless seeker with no Past at my back."[142] A securely sacred or securely profane Emerson is off-limits. A practically ideal Emerson is but a limited, diluted, reconciled, no-longer-questioning object. But "the only sin is limitation," "Circles" tells us.[143] Objective criticism wishes to settle on the Emerson. "Circles" observes that "people wish to be settled: only as far as they are unsettled, is there any hope for them."[144] Preposterously, then, the text of "Circles" would have readers persistently ask questions of the answers that institute and maintain the circles in which they find themselves—especially the literary or interpretive circles in which readers entangle with texts.

What hope is there in these entanglings? Bloom holds that "Emerson opposed the party of Memory to the party of Hope, but that was in a very different America. Now the party of Memory is the party of Hope, though the hope is diminished."[145] It is a preposterous, conservative move to tie hope inextricably to memory. Looking forward differs from looking backward. Perhaps we should consider George Woodberry's pronouncement that the hopefulness of the Emerson text is ever for "a distant posterity."[146]

We cannot remember this distant posterity, for it has not yet arrived—we must reckon ourselves "pre-posterity," unsettlingly so. And this involves, in part, seeing our seeing as always before the object, as what constitutes the object, and therefore as always pre-Emerson. And it leaves us with more questions to ask: To what purpose do *we* read? How do these purposes condition *our* readings? The objects of our readings? Our Emersons? Further, a related question turns on us even more provocatively: Might the Emerson text be said to read us and our methods of reading?

6 Toward a Natural Philosophy of Reading

Gladly we would anchor, but the anchorage is quicksand.
This onward trick of nature is too strong for us: *Pero si muove.*
— "Experience"

The multifarious distortions of the nature of Emerson's writing may well cause us to wonder what hope there is for reading that text. To redress the situation, we need to inquire further into the nature of hope, of reading, and of the text in question. Accordingly, I shall attempt to make the "certain philosophic turn" that "Thoughts on Modern Literature" posits as the sort of interpretive movement that will render reading (as a certain mode of relational, self-reflexive seeing) possible. Such a turn requires that I question the nature of philosophy and its pertinence to matters of interpretation. What will come of this is not philosophy per se and not *not* philosophy, but a method of textual thinking—a natural philosophy of reading. To begin, let us return to hope.

As the last chapter concluded, hope emerged in relation to unsettlement, which had something to do with the use of literature. The ways in which Emerson's writing have been used result in a condition of textual hopelessness. The prospects for the text that would be read are severely limited, due in part to a condition of reading I have termed "preposterousness." If the scholar is to be a bringer of hope, and if this bringing would involve an unsettling method of using books, then it remains for us to figure out what is being brought, how we might transport it, and how it pertains to literary endeavors.

What is hope? In Emerson's writing, the answer often lies in different methods of thinking and reading. Essays such as "Circles" call for the cul-

tivation of an ideational power that will transform tomorrow, supersed-
ing the maintenance of a limited cognition that holds us in check today:
"In the thought of to-morrow there is a power to upheave all thy creed,
all the creeds, all the literatures of the nations, and marshal thee to a heaven
which no epic dream has yet depicted."[1] Reading is to play an important
role in these new ways of thinking, and the text suggests how texts themselves might be used to best cultivate the necessary upheaval. "Literature,"
it says, "is a point outside of our hodiernal circle, through which a new
one may be described. The use of literature is to afford us a platform
whence we may command a view of our present life, a purchase by which
we may move it."[2] The use of literature is an act by which we can come to
see where and who we are, what we have become, and what we have done
(to ourselves and our world); but it is also the means by which we might
change our condition.

Change is necessary because of the continuous flux and refiguring of
nature and because we can no longer see "our present life" in nature very
well. Our perspective has become only retrospective, our eyes harden to
the light of the day, the day's obligations harden us to tomorrow's changes.
Nevertheless, "Circles" tells us, "there is no sleep, no pause, no preserva-
tion, but all things renew, germinate, and spring. Why should we import
rags and relics into the new hour? Nature abhors the old, and old age seems
the only disease: all others run into this one. We call it by many names . . . ;
they are all forms of old age; they are rest, conservatism, appropriation,
inertia, not newness, not the way onward. We grizzle every day. I see no
need of it."[3] In the grizzling of every day, even the young are grown old.
Old age is an age in which everything is old, a cultural, rather than a human, senescence. Consistency, rest, conservatism, appropriation, inertia
infect us all, even—or especially—scholars. In another essay, one is met
with the lament that "public and private avarice make the air we breathe
thick and fat. The scholar is decent, indolent, complaisant. See already the
tragic consequence. The mind of this country taught to aim at low objects,
eats upon itself."[4] Scholars are caught in a system of institutional practices
that construe the merely hodiernal to be eternal and immutable, thereby
perpetuating greed, laziness, and the self-satisfying status quo. In the essay "Education," Emerson writes, "I call our system a system of despair,
and I find all the correction, all the revolution that is needed and that the
best spirits of this age promise, in one word, Hope."[5]

The revolutionary word denotes an attitude and connotes a way of seeing or expecting, from the Latin *expectare*:[6] to look out, look forward, to
see what might be ahead, what might be possible. To be able to look for-

ward, affirming "newness" and "the way onward," we must be able to look beyond ourselves. As bringers of hope, scholars must convey the ability to *expect* a world, a vision, a truth outside of the circle in which we presently find ourselves. Hoping is seeing or, better, reading—a "creative reading" that acknowledges the multiplicitous nature of meaning and participates in the contingent, continual recreation of our worldviews. The scholar, then, must encourage inventive interpretations, for "one must be an inventor to read well." In a frequently quoted passage from "The American Scholar," prospective interpreters are notified that "there is then creative reading, as well as creative writing. When the mind is braced by labor and invention, the page of whatever book we read becomes luminous with manifold allusion. Every sentence is doubly significant, and the sense of our author is as broad as the world."[7]

This form of creative reading differs radically from the manufacture of new literary objects in important ways. Instead of remaking texts according to the objectives one desires to attain through reading, readers and their reading practices undergo transformation. That is, creative reading creates new reading instead of fabricating a new Emerson or even a new version of "The American Scholar." The work of the scholar is the opening up of meaning and not the pinning down of truth, the conveyance of the notion that texts are multisignificant and not the purveyance of the single sense that a book must give and readers must get. The scholar's labor must always entail the unsettling of literature and especially the scholar's own unsettling, which means being willing to think again, differently, to envision newness and the way onward. "The American Scholar" announces that American scholars must be always prospective, always becoming, always alive in nature.

In accepting this charge, scholars will need to understand themselves as textual thinkers or natural philosophers. Such philosophers, however, would not subscribe to institutionalized schools of thought that partialize objects of knowledge, nor would they exempt themselves from connection to the larger circles wherein thinking transpires. Philosophical thinking, in the textual, relational, "natural" sense, cannot cut itself off from thinking politically, say, or economically: the scholar must be open to thinking about thinking and its foundations, about cultures and their philosophical and political systems, and about the larger environment in which thinking occurs—which is perhaps why the writer of "Intellect" claims thinking is "the hardest task in the world."[8] Thinking is always thinking within the circle of a world(view). Natural scholars or textual philosophers would essay to think the conditions of their thinking in nature and the consequences of their thinking on texts.

As "The American Scholar" has it, "Fear always springs from ignorance. It is a shame to [the scholar] . . . if he seek a temporary peace by the diversion of his thoughts from politics or vexed questions, hiding his head like an ostrich in the flowering bushes, peeping into microscopes, and turning rhymes, as a boy whistles to keep his courage up."[9] Natural philosophies would then have everything to do with thinking the textual relations that structure one's knowledge of and actions in the circles of the world. Thinking differently is thinking up different worlds and thinking our way into (and out of) such texts or networks of significant relations.

Perhaps this rather subtle definition of philosophical thinking explains why the figure of Emerson has not loomed larger in the traditional discipline of philosophy. Merton Sealts observes that "as Arnold recognized, the essays aren't exactly *philosophy*; indeed, few professional philosophers later than William James and George Santayana have looked in a kindly way on Emerson." (Sealts goes on to note that "like Teufelsdröckh in his friend Carlyle's *Sartor Resartus,* Emerson was a 'Professor of things in General'—*Allerley Wissenschaft*—and was rightly suspicious of all compartmentalization and departmentalizing."[10]) There are, of course, exceptions to Emerson's negative reception in philosophical circles.[11] As we can see in the work of Bloom, some strains of pragmatism, for example, cite Emerson as an important ancestor. And Stanley Cavell, also responding to Arnold's criticism, has written that "we ought no longer to be as sure as Arnold was that the great philosophical writer is one who builds a system; hence that Emerson is not such a writer on the ground that he was not such a builder."[12] Defining philosophy as a method of reading or thinking textually, instead of as disciplinary system-building, may afford us a position from which we may better view the significant relations obtaining in the interconnections of reading, nature, philosophy, and Emerson.

Reading Emerson and Learning to Read

Reading Emerson becomes an important issue for Cavell, a way of doing philosophy, and the provocative attention he gives Emerson's text merits careful consideration. Promisingly, Cavell reads Emerson in a way that attends closely to the text of the writing and to writing's texture, thereby enabling a reading that avoids many of the pitfalls of predominantly subjective or objective renderings:

> In my way of reading Emerson, his passage naming the unattained but attainable self[13] suggests two ways of reading (reading him, to begin with), in one of which we are brought to recognize our own idea in his text (reading with our

unattained self), in the other not (reading with our attained self, appreciating our given opinions, learning nothing new). To recognize the unattained self is, I gather, a step in attaining it. . . . I do not read Emerson as saying (I assume this is my unattained self asserting itself) that there is one unattained/attainable self we repetitively never arrive at, but rather that "having" "a" self is a process of moving to, and from, nexts. It is, using a romantic term, the "work" of (Emerson's) writing to present nextness, a city of words to participate in.[14]

One way of reading Emerson suggests two ways of reading. In one, "reading with our unattained self," we are led to see something new about ourselves in the text of Emerson; in the other, "reading with the attained self," we merely increase the value of opinions that have been given to us, thus "learning nothing new." The layers of reading Cavell invokes, including the play on the underlying legibility of "I gather" (from the Latin *legere*) and the rhyming of text and next (so that the "process of moving to, and from, nexts" involves a process of moving to and from texts), signify the extent to which the way we read makes us the way we are. How we gather meaning from texts informs how well we will participate in the worlds of our words; how well we do our readerly work directly affects (and is affected by) our ability to go on toward nextness and out of prefabricated notions of who we have become.[15]

Reading, then, is nothing other than a method of thinking, of gathering the world. In the foreword to the expanded version of *The World Viewed*, Cavell proposes that "reading is not an alternative to seeing but (as its root in a word for advising suggests) an effort to detail a way of seeing something more clearly, an interpretation of how things look and why they appear as, and in the order, they do."[16] Linking reading with reding, Cavell includes interpretation among the tasks facing readers; but we are also to consider why we have come up with particular interpretations. What is it about that which we interpret and what is it about us as interpreters that have yielded just these interpretations? How have we come to see what we see, to read what we read? (I suppose these questions are variations of Thoreau's question that serves *The World Viewed* as an epigraph: "'Why do precisely these objects which we behold make a world?'"[17]) An integral part of reading is taking our own roles as readers under advisement.

This, however, does not call for mere introspection, a point made clear in a chapter titled "The Philosopher in American Life." Recalling the reading/seeing/advising observation in *The World Viewed* (and a similar one in *The Claim of Reason*[18]) while discussing a fragment from *Walden*, Cavell questions the validity of a reading that construes the nature of literary objects based on the reader's own objectives. Instead, reading itself becomes the objective and starting point, the end and beginning of seeing one's way more clearly. "That reading is a way, or a goal, of seeing, is something attested . . . by the history of the word *reading* in a word for advising, which in turn contains a word for seeing."[19] The passage Cavell is thinking about regards the writer of *Walden* looking up from his book but continuing to read (in this case, a passing train).[20] Reading, therefore, does not simply mean running one's eyes over pages of writing, but seeing "more clearly" the relations between one's reading of books and one's reading of landscape. Reading is not something we do all the time but something we could (and should) do more often, if we would learn to see differently.

In "The Philosopher in American Life," Cavell posits reading as his preferred form of philosophy (preferred, that is, to "argument"). Reading, according to Cavell, leads us back to Emerson and Thoreau, against the objections of the discipline of American philosophy:

> There has been no serious move, as far as I know, within the ensuing discipline of American philosophy, to take up Emerson philosophically. The moral to draw here may of course be the one Kuklick[21] draws, that Emerson and Thoreau are to be comprehended as philosophical amateurs, toward whom, it would be implied, there is no professional obligation. But suppose the better moral is that Emerson and Thoreau are as much threats, or say embarrassments, to what we have learned to call philosophy as they are to what we call religion, as though philosophy had, and has, an interest, I think I may say, in repressing them. This would imply that they propose, and embody, a mode of thinking, a mode of conceptual accuracy, as thorough as anything imagined within established philosophy, but invisible to that philosophy because based on an idea of rigor foreign to its establishment.[22]

Addressing the refusal to consider Emerson and Thoreau "real" philosophers, Cavell attempts a reinterpretation of their writings *for* philosophy. In that reinterpretation, Emersonian and Thoreauvian "modes of thinking" become modes of reading. New reading and new thinking are understood as the promise of philosophy, a promise that few American scholars have kept, even when (or especially when) those scholars claimed to be reading or philosophizing. To read Emerson (and Thoreau), in the manner proposed by Cavell, is to suffer embarrassment.

And such embarrassment comes when readers suddenly find that what we have been doing when we have claimed to be reading is not actually reading. With connotations of perusing, seeing, advising or counseling, lecturing or lectoring one's own poetic response to the world, narrating, interpreting, and taking readings, reading begins to resemble an attitude, a tendency or set of tendencies brought about by the affirmation of changes in consciousness and self-consciousness. To read, we must tune our senses, attune ourselves differently to the world. Becoming a reader, for Cavell, entails seeing differently, listening carefully, catching the smell of prose, and feeling the claims that a textual encounter may produce. We have shut our senses to that which we would read, have lost the sense or the meaning of our words and hence of ourselves. This is what prompts Cavell to follow Wittgenstein in the attempt to "bring words back home," an effort also operating in Emerson's work: "Wittgenstein's return of words to their everyday use may be said to return words to the actual language of life in a life momentarily freed of an illusion; Emerson's return of words may be said to return them to the life of language, to language and life transfigured, as an eventual everyday."[23]

For Cavell, then, reading Emerson's writing in a certain way is to accept a new relation to the life of language, which could in turn lead to new life and new language. There springs reading's hope, in the prospect of the eventual everyday that can be created through different textual relations. The difficulty in realizing these expectations lies in the proposal that we must read in Emerson's writing Emerson's own theory of reading in order to learn how to read: "'Self-Reliance' as a whole presents a theory—I wish we knew how to call it an aesthetics—of reading. Its opening words are 'I read the other day,' and four paragraphs before Emerson cites the cogito he remarks, 'Our reading is mendicant and sycophantic,' which is to say that he finds us reading the way he finds us doing everything else. How can we read his theory of reading in order to learn how to read him?"[24] The question raised at the end of the passage brings us to the brink of preposterousness. We cannot be said to read Emerson's writing until we have been led by that writing to learn to read; but being led to learn to read only occurs through reading. How, then, can we read in order to read?

Cavell's answer to the question rests mainly in the realm of philosophy, particularly the philosophy of language. Returning words to the actual or ordinary language of life holds the key for remaking the subject of philosophy, hence the "therapeutic" side of Cavell's philosophical endeavors.[25] The goal of these lessons in philosophical literacy is to change the subject; the method requires a certain form of mastery: "On the reading side, the idea of mastering Emerson is not that of controlling him, exactly (though it will be related to monitoring him), but rather that of coming into command of him, as of a difficult text, or instrument, or practice."[26] Mastery, however, not only comes short of curing us of our preposterous use of books but also effectively guarantees such use. The "difficult text" of Emerson's writing can only be commanded, controlled, or mastered if that text is denatured.

For if texts, as Emerson's theories of reading frequently propose, are analogous to nature, if texts are *of* nature, then the necessary excess of relations cannot be subdued by limiting a text to a single discursive area. Cavell's philosophizing on ordinary language continues the work of bringing words back home, which I assume means, at least to some extent, being on the way to returning language to nature. But unless the return attends to the larger relations to which philosophy and language belong, unless the tendency, as suggested in "Thoughts on Modern Literature," is toward nature, even the philosophically bent reader will not have learned to read.

Thus my own response to Cavell's excellent and most pertinent question is, as Beckett's Estragon proposes to Vladimir, to "turn resolutely toward Nature."[27] (Vladimir's rejoinder is equally noteworthy: "We've tried that." As their creator says elsewhere, though, one must "Try again. Fail again. Fail better."[28]) Where Cavell wants to read Emerson in order to learn how to read Emerson, which reading will then rework (American) philosophy as a form of therapy, my hope is that persistence in learning how to read Emerson's text will provide us the means to improve our perspective of texts and our relations to them, as well as our perspective of nature and our relations to it. That is, we are never just in language (however ordinary) or just in philosophy; we are in these realms, yes, but these are in nature, and we continually have to try to think the conditions of the consequent interconnectedness if we are to learn to read. The transfer between the method of nature and literary life works both ways.

The very process of this transfer would enact a *natural* philosophy—a method of interpretation that better attends to the entanglements of nature, thinking, reading, and texts. In other words, I am suggesting that Cavell capably assists us in making that "certain philosophic turn," but the turn is only partial because it does not lead readers to the larger relations in which philosophy and reading, Emerson and writing, we and our interpretations occur. *Representative Men* asks of readers a wary approach to "the effort of Plato or any Philosopher to dispose of Nature,—which will not be disposed of."[29] The tendency of non- or unnatural philosophy to dispose of nature coincides with a tendency to master texts, which means controlling texts by positioning interpreters and the objects of interpretation in "purely philosophical" situations, removed from larger interpretive relations. Consider Cavell: "[Emerson's] difference from other philosophical writing is, I think, that it asks the philosophical mood so purely, so incessantly, giving one little other intellectual amusement or eloquence or information, little other argument or narrative, and no other source of companionship or importance, either political or religious or moral, save the importance of philosophy, of thinking itself."[30] By characterizing the mood or disposition of Emerson's writing as *purely* philosophical, Cavell disposes of the natural connections (which include the political, religious, and moral as well as the biological, historical, ecological, semiotic) in which texts mean.

If the cost of thinking philosophy so purely in reading Emerson is that the text is made unnaturally clean, the advantages of Cavell's approach nevertheless outweigh the disadvantages. The benefits of his philosophical entangling with Emerson's text include reopening the problem of the figure of Emerson (your ability to learn from Emerson how to read "will depend on who you think Emerson is, something I am trying to leave, or to get, open"[31]) and the sounding of terms (e.g., "aversion," "whim," "abandonment") that have largely been neglected in the history of American scholars' renderings of Emerson's writing. More significant to my study, readers are encouraged by this form of philosophy to question the reading subject, to allow Emerson's text to question the reader. Cavell depicts Emerson's writing as "turning the picture of interpreting a text into one of being interpreted by it,"[32] indicating that interpretation is interactive or that reading a text requires being read by a text. Readers move between making readings of a piece of writing to allowing what they read to take the measure of their own thinking. Writings, in this theory, are living, almost conscious, perceptible and perceptive, actual and prospective events, and we come to them so as to somehow reenter or even retake our own lives. Reading such writing involves an unpredictable series of reflections in which one moves between attending to the possible meanings of a text and attending to the contexts in which those lines are construed, perpetually forth and back and forth.

Thinking Nature, between Texts

> Thou art the unanswered question;
>   Couldst see thy proper eye,
> Alway it asketh, asketh;
>   And each answer is a lie.
> So take thy quest through nature,
>   It through thousand natures ply;
> Ask on, thou clothed eternity;
>   Time is the false reply.
>   —"The Sphinx"

This passage from Emerson's poem brings together several of the circles in which and between which I have been trafficking: the notion of the reader as both questioner and question; problems in the acts of seeing and knowing (literal and metaphorical vision); the preference of questions to answers, of a skepticism that reckons the inability of partial answers to settle complex questions; nature as a text to be interpreted, a text in which we find ourselves finding ourselves (and find our findings to demand further questioning); time—especially the time of reading, the timing of readings that put answers before questions and that consequently enter the process of interpretation with the end to be achieved already achieved; hope (that our questing will result in a responsible reply); and Emerson, the Poet—about whose position in American culture much has already been written, so much that the text of his writings may be said to have been obscured, undermining the possibility for further reading.

The undermining and obscuring agencies are many and various; looking back over this study, one could construct an alternative to the "Lords of Life" that amble through the occasional poem heading the essay "Experience": "The Rules of Reading, The Rules of Reading, / We see them pass . . ." The slow and spectral muster that follows consists of portly consumption and grim palimpsest, like and unlike subjective and objective rules that mark out a place for and measure the value of Emerson's text. As these modes of using writing become entrenched, they isolate that which would be read from broader methods of study. Each rule of reading, each firm form of figuring Emerson, each divisive or disciplinary device (or school, theory, discourse, institution) conditions the object being read. The object being read, removed from relations (which relations *involve* a text in nature), is made unnatural. The work of each rule is to make the object of knowledge knowable within and because of the rule, separate from other relations. The drive to rule the object of reading strictly measures the object and ultimately defines the approach to it by partial and partializing boundaries. What is written in Emerson's "History" may be said in the case of reading: "What the former age has epitomized into a formula or rule for manipular convenience, [every mind] will lose all the good of verifying for itself, by means of the wall of that rule."[33]

If an alternative mode of reading is possible, it would approximate a broader, messier, more textually aware engagement remodeled on an ongoing interpretation of texts out of materials provided by unending speculation on the method of nature. And this would entail a critical acknowledgment of an unsolvable set of problematic relations between reader and what is being read. Although not solvable or resolvable, the complexity of this set, the contradictoriness of the problematic is open to continued questioning, persistent intellectual venturing forth, and informed reformation. But this can come only from an engaged traversing that in *Nature* is called going the "necessary journey." Such traversing would be a movement or, rather, an endless series of expeditionary moves and removes undertaken by the reader between the ever-fugacious nature of the text being read (be it nature or *Nature*) and the equally fugacious nature of the text that reads (the textual or significantly relational nature of the reader's culturally, bioregionally, physiologically, and psychically conditioned perception process).

A natural philosophy of reading involves thinking between texts and beyond contexts while thinking of nature. Methods of reading that do not undertake the necessary movements of interpretation lock themselves into one particular circle, cutting off means of communication with other circles and foregoing the possibility of seeing beyond their own. This I have called a preposterous form of reading in which the meaning of the text takes the shape provided by the precepts dictated by its preception (or pretextual circle of reception)—that is, "with the first last and the last first." But when the last comes first, the first does not last. What is lost in this way of taking texts, besides the texts themselves, is the possibility of being led by one's reading, and this in turn inhibits the possibility of others being led by their readings. Such a use of literature, instead of drawing a new circle or being drawn into a new circle, simply follows the old course and confirms its layout. Emerson suggests as much in "The Comic": the "classification or nomenclature used by the scholar" is to serve "only as a memorandum of his last lesson in the laws of nature, and confessedly makeshift, a bivouac for a night." Failure to operate in a makeshift modality causes the terminology employed to "[become] through indolence a barrack and a prison, in which the man sits down immovably and wishes to detain others."[34]

Makeshift reading—thinking between texts—requires becoming mindful of the circle from which one's reading proceeds, the circle in which the text resides, and the methods one employs to traverse the interval between those circles. Such a reader will need to consider the consequences of traversing in a particular way and to speculate on other prospective circles. To read well, to be led by one's reading one must be willing and able to move on. But the objects one would read must be capable, at the very least, of moving on also. If scholars' classifications "detain" a text, that text cannot accompany readers, let alone lead us. Some of the difficulties that readers with naturally philosophical tendencies face may best be illustrated in a parable, comprising an anecdote from the writings of that most excellent makeshift backpacker, bivouacker, naturalist, and Emersonian, John Muir.

The aged Concord Sage visits Muir in Yosemite. Muir, a longtime admirer of Emerson (who was not unimpressed by Muir),[35] writes that he "had read [Emerson's] essays, and felt sure that of all men he would best interpret the sayings of these noble mountains and trees."[36] Although Muir had, in his copy of Emerson's prose, argued with some of Emerson's interpretations of nature, he looks forward to taking Emerson into the wild groves of sequoia, which he deems to be Emerson's "brethren."[37] Indeed, Muir, "forgetting [Emerson's] age, plans, duties, ties of every sort . . . proposed an immeasurable camping trip back into the heart of the mountains." Emerson appears game for such an expedition, but "his party, full of indoor philosophy, failed to see the natural beauty and fullness of promise of my wild plan, and laughed at it in good-natured ignorance. . . . Anyhow, they would have none of it, and held Mr. Emerson to the hotels and trails."[38] Somewhat crestfallen, Muir gets only a "poor bit of measured time" with Emerson and, before wandering off to interpret the mountains and trees by himself, comments that Emerson "was now as a child in the hands of his affectionate but sadly civilized friends, who seemed as full of old-fashioned conformity as of bold intellectual independence."[39]

I am suggesting that what Muir wishes to do with Emerson, the natural philosopher of reading should want to do with Emerson's text—free the writing from its well-meaning handlers, forget its obligations, and return it to nature, thereby relating one wildly fluctuating, contradictorily provocative method or text to another. The natural philosopher seeks such an "immeasurable camping trip" thanks to the hunch that the Emerson text might, by its nature, have something to teach us about our nature and to the hunch that nature provides an excellent, educational context in which to read and learn from, say, *Nature* or "The Method of Nature." Let us enact insight and read Emerson's writing in nature, as related to other texts, moving as we read, getting different angles on the text being read, the text reading, and the contexts in which reading happens. Makeshift reading, moving away from hotels and well-trod trails, goes forward by wandering off, by virtue of the bivouac, a sense of adventure, and the hope for potential illumination. Extravagant progress of this kind requires that we not settle beforehand what the Emerson text will mean, how it will affect the context in which it is read, or how we will respond to the questions posed by the textual encounter.

The natural philosopher can expect resistance, though, from the party of "indoor philosophers," the keepers of the Emerson text, scholars who fail to acknowledge or sufficiently value the "natural beauty" outdoors, the "fullness of promise" of a "wild plan." In his story, Muir calls Emerson's fate in the hands of handlers "sad commentary on culture and the glorious transcendentalism."[40] In my metaphorical rendering, the sad commentary is on approaches to Emerson's writing that, however affectionate, confine the writing to a circle of "old-fashioned conformity" from which it is forbidden to stray. The Emerson text, wild by nature, is unfortunately civilized by the good intentions òf the scholars looking after it. To overcome the limited and limiting management of indoor philosophy, natural philosophers of reading will have to gently insist that to experience the complex nature of texts, one need reckon the complex text of nature.

But why think nature, how think nature, and what nature are we to think in order to read Emerson's text? Keeping in mind the warning in "The Comic" against detaining classifications and imprisoning nomenclature, I will define nature provisionally as a multiform complex, a web of biotic, historical, cultural weaves in which we live and of which we continually proffer makeshift meanings based on psychosensorial impressions and the ongoing processing of those impressions. In other words, nature is not a single thing or place as much as it is an ever-onward process or event. Hence this nature is very much alive and changing, a *physis*—or, better yet, a constantly fluctuating spatiotemporal cosmos to which our understanding of nature and all of our thinking belong. Thinking in a way that acknowledges the complexity of nature (which means becoming aware of as many sides, dimensions, and signifying elements as possible, as well as regarding the naturalness of thinking itself) is, in Whitehead's term, thinking "heterogeneously": "We are thinking 'homogeneously' about nature when we are thinking about it without thinking about thought or about sense-awareness, and we are thinking 'heterogeneously' about nature when we are thinking about it in conjunction with thinking either about thought or about sense-awareness or about both."[41] Nature's nature is such that our thinking of it needs to be thought when we come to understand why nature means what we think it does.

Texts, too, are *of* nature. Indeed, they are little natures, minicomplexes, microcosms. As such, they warrant a heterogeneous approach, one that considers their multirelational makeup; the approach itself, which comprises a significant portion of that makeup; and nature, of which and in which microcosmic texts are made and mean. Perhaps this more clearly explains why an early Emerson work summons literary scholars to an exploration of "the *method of nature*. Let us see *that*, as nearly as we can, and try how far it is transferable to the literary life."[42] Method, again, signifies both a way of doing something (a "going after" or pursuit [from the Greek *méthodos*]) and a system, structure, or text. Nature's method is something like a biotext, the inquiry into which can shed light on lesser texts. Transferring the method of nature to literary life means first seeing nature as *nearly* as we can, which requires the heterogeneous method of thinking about thinking while thinking about nature. Next, it means imagining what nature's text tells us about analogous literary texts. Transfer from biotext to text (and back) comprises the "necessary journey" of reading—a movement made necessary precisely because, as nature demonstrates, texts are always changing. "There is no holding nature still and looking at it," notes Whitehead.[43]

Led by these observations of the relations between text and biotext, I propose three primary elements of a natural philosophy of reading: *Movement*—in and through the biotext, foregoing settlement for the necessary journey from bivouac to bivouac; transfer between these bivouacs or perspectives and literary texts, which opens up a better view of the perspectives themselves, the texts to be perceived, and the intervals traversed by the interpreter. *Vision*—of the vistas afforded by movement, making shift, and transfer; of ways of seeing as well as visible phenomena, of the directions in which we might move next and of the actions necessary to go that way, of the time and space of our movement and the results. *Participation* (or "participance," to distinguish it from mere "taking part in")—actively moving and seeing, taking part in reading, but also acknowledging one's part in reading; "the action of partaking" in text and biotext; "having or forming part *of*" the text and biotext; "partaking of the substance, quality, or nature *of*" biotext and text and acknowledging that partaking (*OED*). Given these elements, reading becomes a thoroughly textual, contextual, and intertextual experience, a thinking of and in the biotext, a thinking between text and biotext, between perspective and text, and a thinking onward from the contexts in which meaning occurs.

"Our Preposterous Use of Books"

What, then, would a natural philosophy of reading hope for? What might a theory of thinking between texts achieve? In the earliest moments of my study, I imagined its prospective conclusion would mark out an interpretive territory that might be said to exist in the wake of Emerson. Consequently, investigation of this territory would involve "reading (after) Emerson"—the parentheses signaling the *provisional* nature of the enterprise. The unsteadiness and inconsistency of Emerson's writing demand no less. Responsible "provisional criticism," then, should *provide* a reading of a text and *provide for* further reading of that text. That is, it must supply a reading and prepare for more reading. It must also look forward (*providere*), by means of a reading that is good for only a while, until we necessarily move on.

I found myself, in the beginning, reading (after) Emerson, which meant reading in the aftermath of Emerson's writing, being led by Emerson's writing and in search of Emerson's writing—all of which occurred in the process of reading Emerson's writing. But the very nature of that writing led me to consider the *preposterousness* of reading, the other-than-chronological state of textual encounters, and the absurdity of placing the last first and the first last. It then became necessary to think the promise of reading, the *before* of reading instead of simply resting in the familiar territory *after* reading. Finding that Emerson's readers frequently take reading's end as reading's beginning, I saw my hope for countering such practices in the call for reading's beginning to be taken as its unending end.

Part of what I mean by a phrasing itself so archly preposterous is that when the end (outcome, result, upshot, finish, completion) of a reading is brought to bear on the outset of a reading, it very well may be that reading never begins, never goes anywhere, never happens. The meaning of the text, rather than found in an interpretive engagement, instead is preconceived, then brought within the boundaries of the previously settled idea or pretext. The pretext, established before the text is encountered, makes possible what will be construed as the nature of the text itself. The ends ordain the means: fragments are combined, contexts overlooked, texture ignored, and meaning predestined by the expert or scholar. Preposterously enough, to remedy such a practice, readers need something along the lines of the Buddhist notion of "beginner's mind." In the words of Shunryu Suzuki, "in the beginner's mind there are many possibilities; in the expert's mind there are few." "Even though you read much Zen literature, you must read each sentence with a fresh mind."[44] A reader of much *Emerson* literature, informed by the notion of beginner's mindfulness, would acknowledge the condition of reading after *and* before Emerson. I mean *before* to signify a reading that unfolds "previous to" the establishment or settling of a meaning for Emerson's text; provocatively, Cavell employs a "before" that stands the reader *in front of* the Emerson text, facing it.[45] Both "befores" may be necessary to challenge the prevalent "after." "After/ Before" readers would come to terms with the historical contexts in which Emerson's writing traffics, but would nevertheless envision the necessity of creative reading, all the while attending to the present moment.

To see this more clearly, consider the searcher of "Circles": "No facts are to me sacred; none are profane; I simply experiment, an endless seeker, with no Past at my back."[46] The writer of "Circles"—who, in the course of that essay, depicts himself as a particular kind of reader as well, one who cannot remember writing what he has written[47]—refuses to admit that facts exist in an either-or, sacred-profane opposition. Instead, an *experiment* is conducted on so-called facts, which has more to do with cultivating experience than with establishing expertise (both forms stemming from the root *experiri*, "to try out," "to test"). This particular seeker imagines himself as without ends that would taint the search. And, while the circle in which the seeker currently travels may be said to front something like a *past*, this is distinguished from having the *Past* at or on one's back. The "past" (lowercase *p*) designates the not-altogether-knowable history of the seeker's experiences—and especially the energies and powers derived from those experiences. "The new position of the advancing man has all the powers of the old, yet has them all new. It carries in its bosom all the energies of the past, yet it is itself an exhalation of the morning."[48] The "Past" (capital *p*) alludes to the conventional, the traditional, the expert, the linear, "rest, conservatism, appropriation, inertia," which have the capacity to sit on the shoulders of the writer/reader and impose consistency on a "Life" that is nothing if not "a series of surprises."[49] Breathing in the morning's exhalation relates to reading from the attitude of beginner's mind in that both involve the acknowledgment and affirmation of the "new moment": "I cast away in this new moment all my once hoarded knowledge as vacant and vain. Now, for the first time, seem I to know anything rightly."[50]

The reader proposed in "Circles" may not be the same reader proposed in "Spiritual Laws" (given the foolishness of consistency, moods that do not believe in one another, a writer who turns reader and disremembers what he has written), but both essays indicate that our methods of interpretation are preposterous and in need of revision. "Let us unlearn our wisdom of the world," we read in "Spiritual Laws,"[51] a call made imperative by the prevalence of unwise wisdom. The mode of reading that presently obtains could be characterized as having finished a book before starting it or (in the manner of Johnny Carson's Carnak) putting the closed book to one's forehead, divining the meaning of the book, and finding only that meaning when the book is finally cracked. To use books in this manner is, according to "Spiritual Laws," to shirk the duties of the reader or scholar, either for escape from responsibilities, voyeurism, or other forms of neglected relations. "Is not that a just objection to much of our reading? It is a pusillanimous desertion of our work to gaze after our neighbors. It is peeping." End and means combine in "our preposterous use of books," and Emerson's essay urges as a counterpractice the rethinking of "time," "facts," the "net of relations," and the "texture" of life.[52]

The term *preposterous* describes the conditions of our engagements with texts. Denoting an absurdity or unnaturalness due in part to temporal unsteadiness, *preposterous* connotes a bizarre but widespread mode of disconnective seeing. Knower is disconnected from known, objects from relations, subject from participance, and vision from movement. As we read in "The Comic," "Separate any object, as a particular bodily man, a horse, a turnip, a flour-barrel, an umbrella, from the connection of things, and contemplate it alone, standing there in absolute nature, it becomes at once comic; no useful, no respectable qualities can rescue it from the ludicrous."[53] What is most preposterous about such a visual economy is that the viewer fails to recognize the absurdity of disconnection or that everchanging nature is never absolute. The supposition that underlies the scene holds that there is a coherent viewer (separable from space and time relations or the biotext) standing before an object (also separable from the biotext), and that the seemingly "absolutely natural" visibility produces a seemingly untroubled knowledge of what is viewed. Applied to reading literature specifically, the logic or chronology would run thus: I am who I am; the text is what it is; I read the book from front to back; then I know the book and what it means. Such logic, however, ignores the fugacious natures of text, reader, "time," "facts," the "net of relations," and "texture." The obtaining chronology limits interpretive movement to a settled, linear succession.

I have termed this chronic denaturing *preposterous* and have suggested that something of an inverse preposterousness—preposterous preposterousness or acknowledged, affirmed, and redoubled preposterousness—might well serve a natural philosophy of reading. One aspect of this proposed method involves rethinking our relations with nature's time, the time of writing, and reading's time. Emerson's writing encourages a reconsideration of time itself, as has been remarked by others. Cavell observes obliquely that "Emerson loves playing with time, that is, making time vanish where truth is concerned."[54] Instead of making time vanish, though, Emerson's writing frequently questions our existing notions of time and refers the reader to alternative versions. Further, these alternatives, by their nature, cannot help but be preposterous or *untimely*. In *Twilight of the Idols*, Nietzsche writes, "Emerson has that gracious and clever cheerfulness which discourages all seriousness; he simply does not know how old he is already and how young he is still going to be; he could say of himself, quoting Lope de Vega: '*Yo me sucedo a mi mismo.*'"[55] A writer who succeeds himself and contravenes seriousness—what could be more promising for a preposterous approach to preposterousness?

Writing that pointedly challenges its readers' prevailing preposterousness can be expected to cause interpretive confusion and will most likely
unsettle its interpreters. Instead of ignoring or explaining or resolving the
disturbing issue of timeliness, a natural philosophy of reading attempts to
engage its own preposterousness and think the temporal experience of
interpretation differently. This amounts to continual, thoughtful recovery
of the *hic et nunc* of reading, a heterogeneous reading that considers its
conditions, attends to the complex and transitory present, and envisions
its consequences. The natural philosopher of reading, aware of the temporal and spatial richness of a multiverse of textual relations, neither
mendicant nor sycophantic of the Past or the Future, approaches texts with
beginner's mind, which means overcoming the attitudes that generally rule
our literary efforts. Perhaps such acknowledgment of temporality informs
the complaint in "Self-Reliance" that "man postpones or remembers; he
does not live in the present, but with reverted eye laments the past, or,
heedless of the riches that surround him, stands on tiptoe to foresee the
future. He cannot be happy and strong until he too lives with nature in
the present, above time."[56] "Above time" would mean transcending the
predominant, conventional *chronologos;* "in the present": mindful of the
messy, mingling now; "with nature": interconnected, mutually textual, and
on the move.

Principles, Methods, Ends:
Of a Natural Philosophy of Reading

To try my theory of a natural philosophy of reading, I will turn to Emerson's
"Experience" to see what that essay can teach us about nature, texts, and
readers. The principles from which one would proceed in enacting a natural
philosophy of reading are several. First, one must consider one's interpretive ends and methods. To forego questioning the objectives for which one
reads and the practice one employs to attain them cannot but lead to denaturing reading. The natural philosopher must cultivate the willingness
to restart the reading process, which will mean rethinking nature and one's
relations to nature, one's place between and among the biotext. Restart-
ing my own study with "Experience," it becomes clear that neither text
nor biotext are readily definable, even provisionally. Nothing sits still long
enough for the reader to satisfactorily get her or his bearings. "Experience"
represents this uncertainty by reference to Galileo: "Gladly we would
anchor, but the anchorage is quicksand. This onward trick of nature is too
strong for us: *Pero si muove.*"[57] The solar system clips along at 12 miles

per second with respect to surrounding stars, the center of the solar system revolves about its galactic center at the rate of 155 miles per second, and the earth orbits the sun at 18.6 miles per second (which is not to mention, on one extreme, the earth's rate of revolution or, on the other, the universe's projected speed).[58] However stable the world may sometimes seem, however stable we may want it to be, nevertheless, *it moves*. Partly because of nature's onward tendencies, we must perpetually take readings of our world's spatiotemporal dimensions and location; and these readings are well served by the text's opening question.

"Where do we find ourselves?" "Experience" is more or less a series of responses to this question, readings that attempt to piece together who or what we think we are. The first of these responses is the question itself, meaning that we find ourselves to be something of a question mark, "the unanswered question," questioner, question, and questioned. Next (in the succession that the essay ultimately calls into question) comes temporal uncertainty ("in a series of which we do not know the extremes"), then spatial uncertainty (poised, just after waking, unpredictably and vertiginously on "a stair"). If this were not disconcerting enough, we then find ourselves in a world where "all things swim and glimmer. Our life is not so much threatened as our perception." Finding ourselves in the first paragraph of "Experience," everything around us swimming and glimmering, we too swimming and glimmering, we seem to "lack the affirmative principle" and must then discern how we are to go on from this most dizzying, precarious, oneiric sense of being lost. "Experience" shows us our insubstantial and unsubstantiatable standing: "Ghostlike we glide through nature, and should not know our place again."[59]

The condition of not knowing our place returns us to a questionable aspect of reading—as if we had lost our place in a book and cannot, for the life of us, return to it. "Experience," in confronting nature's technical difficulties, teaches us that we are alienated from ourselves even in those instants of the present in which we feel most present or most ourselves. "If any of us knew what we were doing, or where we are going, then when we think we best know!" the writer exclaims, as if none of us who makes up the essay's "we" (i.e., neither the reader nor the writer of "Experience") truly knew what we were doing at any given moment, even (or especially) in the activity of experiencing "Experience." The quality of being lost, of losing one's place, proves a problem of time in general and of the present in specific. "So much of our time is preparation, so much is routine, and so much retrospect, that the pith of each man's genius contracts itself to a very few hours."[60] Time construed as succession requires that we prepare for the future, look back to the past, and connect these two with a passive, habitual present. Little wonder, then, that we can no longer make sense of our experience and find our place in the world.

This complaint of temporal alienation precedes, in "Experience," the equally plaintive observation that we find ourselves in an unbecoming state of missed connections, in relations "oblique and casual": "I take this evanescence and lubricity of all objects, which lets them slip through our fingers then when we clutch hardest, to be the most unhandsome part of our condition."[61] Cavell, who names one of his own books after this condition, first commands readers' attention to the matter in an earlier work: "Look first at the connection between the hand in unhandsome and the impotently clutching fingers. What is unhandsome is I think not that objects for us, to which we seek attachment, are as it were in themselves evanescent and lubricious; the unhandsome is rather what happens when we conceive thinking, say the application of concepts in judgments, as grasping something, say synthesizing."[62] After tying this to Heidegger and the "relation between thinking and the hand," Cavell suggests that "clutching's opposite, which would be the most handsome part of our condition, is I suppose the specifically human form of attractiveness." His rendering of the text describes a condition in which our attempt to know things falls short—not because things are, in themselves, unknowable, but because we have gone about knowing in a manner that assumes things are to be known in their totality or that we can totally know things by grasping them. Such a condition, for Cavell and Cavell's Emerson, always leaves us grieving.

But a different sort of unhandsomeness arises if we consider evanescence and lubricity in the context of the problems with time that surface in "Experience." Add the condition of time's fugitivity to the difficulty we have spending a moment *in* the moment, and finding ourselves at all becomes wonderful indeed. *Evanescence* carries with its "vanishing" or "fading" a sense of "quickly passing away," of a *transitory* nature; *lubricity*, along with its oily slipperiness (and a sense of the lewd), conveys figurative slips, "shiftiness," "unsteadiness," "instability" (*OED*). Our unhandsome condition indicates the inability to put a finger on where we are at any given moment; we find ourselves in a perpetual state of transitory temporality, delivered from dream to dream,[63] incomplete and radically fragmented.[64] The very lords of life are "threads on the loom of time," and as such necessitate that we change our temporal perspective. Instead of operating within the temporal framework or loom of time that presides over us, "Experience" suggests affirming the transitory nature of life: "Thy sickness, they say, and thy puny habit, require that thou do this or avoid that, but know that thy life is a flitting state, a tent for a night, and do thou, sick or well, finish that stint."[65] Acknowledging transitoriness leads to a willingness to make transitions from one moment to the next, across the "astronomical interspaces betwixt atom and atom,"[66] as opposed to clinging to an extended duration connected seamlessly to the temporal expanses that precede and follow it.

What this means for experiencing nature or the experience of reading becomes more clear in a passage from "Inspiration" that calls readers to an affirmation of the act of reading as a form of being in transit. Here the writer asserts that "the experience of poetic creativeness . . . is not found in staying home nor yet in traveling, but in transitions from one to the other, which must therefore be adroitly managed to present as much transitional surface as possible."[67] Emphasizing neither traveling nor staying home, "Inspiration" advises attending to the "transitions from one to the other," to movement or even to the movement between moving and being stationary. Transitory reading—reading that occurs in transit, in moments of transition or transfer between the reader's textual means of knowing and the textual nature of what is being read—of course requires patience and persistence. It involves being neither here nor there, but *between* here and there so that you can get a look at where you are/were/are going momentarily. Transition as such is the possibility of reading, a condition we must meet in order to read. Reading involves making transitions between our own moments of experience, between these moments and "Experience" (for example), from one occasion in which we find ourselves to the next: not anchored but adrift, fleeting; not in situ but in transit.[68]

Transitional movement answers for the first of the three primary elements (movement, vision, and participance) of a natural philosophy of reading; readers' transitions are of a special form of movement, one that is not necessarily spatial or temporal, but relative. A movement that includes sitting, standing, walking, and shifting between these positions (and others), a movement that is not in the past, present, or future but between them—this sort of movement is suspicious of conventional or "classical" rules of time and space. Werner Heisenberg writes that, under these rules, "one was led to the tacit assumption that there existed an objective course of events in space and time, independent of observation; further, that space and time were categories of classification of all events, completely independent of each other, and thus represented an objective reality, which was the same to all men."[69] After the special theory of relativity, it became evident that the interval "we call [the] 'present'" "is determined by the position of the observer who is deciding on 'past' or 'future' and by the location of the events whose course in time is being investigated."[70] Being in transition is more than moving in space and time, it is movement that allows one to get one's bearings in various relations: spatiotemporal, sociocultural, and psychophilosophical, among others.

The aggregate of these relations comprises the biotext. Being in transition is then something along the lines of becoming biotextual, becoming aware of the different relations that occasion one's betweenness. Coming into (or perhaps owning up to) relations with the biotext is the only way to know it. To know the text of nature, one must move with it. The natural philosopher of reading must attempt to find him- or herself in nature, to cultivate an awareness of being in nature or "becoming in nature," which would mean acknowledging that one is in the process of nature and that one is contemporaneously in the process of becoming something else all the time.

Nature, nature's movement, and interpretation's necessary transitions are among the principles from which natural philosophy begins. "Experience" presents a curious version of persistence as pertaining to the method that proceeds from those principles. Persistence has something to do with moments, which have everything to do with "Experience." The essay calls readers to "finish the moment, to find the journey's end in every step of the road, to live the greatest number of good hours"; to "respect . . . the present hour," to "not postpone and refer and wish, but do broad justice where we are."[71] Responding to these calls constitutes the responsible fulfillment of what the essay has just referred to as our office: "Since our office is with moments, let us husband them." Husbanding our moments is necessary because time as we know it merits suspicion: "We must be very suspicious of the deceptions of the element of time."[72] Whether cultivating, making the most of, or marrying our moments, *these* moments—those that "Experience" describes and those that make up experience—comprise our responsibilities.

If, in our methods of reading experience or "Experience" or any other text, we ignore moments and continue to wish, refer, and postpone, we abdicate our office and remove our lives from the light—it takes "a very little time to entertain a hope and an insight which becomes the light of our life."[73] To interpret our experiences, we need the light of insight and hope, and this light comes to us precisely in moments, in little, indefinite intervals—in the very present that we are currently experiencing. The method of reading by that light entails seeing moments as enormously momentous and standing in relation to moments in a particular way. The sort of persistence announced by the text is a reading or thinking that proceeds moment by moment: "By persisting to read or think, this region gives further sign of itself, as it were in flashes of light, in sudden discoveries of its profound beauty and repose, as if the clouds that covered it parted at intervals."[74] "This region" ("a new and excellent region of life") can mean both that of the experience of the "I" in the text and that of the reader of "Experience" (and hence the reader's broader experience, if the reader is responsibly finishing the moment).

To persist to read or think "Experience" is to continue to address the questions that arise from this region. The word *persist* grows from a root of "standing (through)." Different standing postures might be said to constitute the persistent practice of reading or thinking. One could "stand a text" in the sense of tolerating the challenges or questions a text poses, which would first require being provoked by the text. This entails letting (for example) "Experience" question you about the conditions of your reading, your methods, and the ends you are after and then responding to these provocations while keeping an eye on the multiplying relations that go into and emerge from the moments of textual encounter. The moment itself must be reckoned; readers must stand the moment of reading in such a way as to acknowledge the numerous relations that comprise that moment, which again involves more than simply sussing out or sitting in judgment of a text from a safe (critical, scholarly, objective) remove. One need find oneself standing in the tangles of the moment of reading.

And persistence would then require "hanging in there" in one's encounters with texts. Persistent readers would not quit the text, would not run from the encounter, would not stop their relations with the text, but continue to read or to think or to question their own experiences, time, findings. Another aspect of persistence relates to endurance or tolerance of suffering, as in exercising patience ("patience and patience," "Experience" asks of us).[75] The reader must not hasten to determine the meaning of reading's moment or allow that moment to be overdetermined by set objectives, ill-considered conditions, or narrow methods. Persisting to read or think would mean patiently refusing determinate measures and making rather a deliberate and unrelenting effort to see what forces and conditions are at work in the processes of determination. Readers of "Experience" must not only stand the initial question—Where *do* we find ourselves?—but stand it responsibly, even perpetually, as the rest of the text and its questions and findings (and thus our relations to them) unfold.

Without thinking the nature of the moment of reading, the momentous effects of one's approach to the moment, and the potential effects of the moment on one's approach, one will not persist in reading or thinking. Perhaps this means that neither reading nor thinking can have a past tense, in which case persisting in the moment of reading or thinking would seem to mean I "finish the moment" by never being finished with it. This, in turn, could be said to approximate Emersonian "onwardness." The end, then, of persistent reading is endless reading. Onwardness becomes participating in the birth of ever new moments. Consider a related passage from "Education":

> We have our theory of life, our religion, our philosophy; and the event of each moment, the shower, the steamboat disaster, the passing of a beautiful face, the apoplexy of our neighbor, are all tests to try our theory, the approximate result we call truth, and reveal its defects. If I have renounced the search of truth, if I have come into the port of some pretending dogmatism, some new church or old church, some Schelling or Cousin, I have died to all use of these new events that are born out of prolific time into multitude of life every hour. I am as a bankrupt to whom brilliant opportunities offer in vain. He has just foreclosed his freedom, tied his hands, locked himself up and given the key to another to keep.[76]

This passage rues renouncing the "search *of* truth," not the search *for* truth. Truth is something the searcher is *in*, not something she or he is *after*. A series of events or moments, truth is both eventful and eventual, momentary and of diffuse momentum. It comes *out of* the testing of our theories with our experience of "the event of each moment" rather than preexisting the conditions of our search. We produce truth by being alive to the new events of our experience or our movement in the biotext (the "multitude of life every hour").

We neglect our relations to the biotext when we renounce thinking or reading and repose in dogmatism. To do so is to die, to absent oneself from the world, from new events or moments, and to let one's reading or thinking expire. Resting in this state of dogmatic repose follows from, among other things, succumbing to institutions (new and old churches) of interpretation. To counter this, the paragraph on "Education" calls us to open ourselves to biotextual relations, to stand being questioned by the texts we read, and to let our theories be tested by those texts. The opposite of being dead to texts, persisting to read involves "announcing" the search of truth, departing from port, becoming alive "to all use of these new events that are born out of prolific time into multitude of life every hour"—beginnings that mark persistence as a form of being born and persisting to read as "continuing to begin to read." This would entail questioning the theories of interpretation that we have and that have us, that constitute who we are and how we treat the "event of each moment."

To find the journey's end in every step of the way is always and never to find the journey's end. But to have innumerable or no ends need not indicate a lack of direction, nor does it terminate onwardness. If interpreting texts requires that we attend to the connections between us, the texts we would interpret, and the biotext to which all these belong, then interpretive attention needs to be directed toward biotextual complexity. This means that interpretation involves reconnecting the intellect with nature, and I want to close with speculations that emerge from reading between the essays "Intellect" and *Nature*. The end of the natural philosophy of reading is, as I have suggested, to begin again. "Intellect" represents this as persistent interrogation (as in "the inquisitiveness of a child"[77]), rejections of convention, and reflections on observations. The essay informs us that "the first questions are always to be asked,"[78] the hope being that through taking on these questions, we cultivate the possibility of overcoming the conventional "considerations of time and place, of you and me, of profit and hurt [that] tyrannize over most men's minds."[79] Think of these "considerations" as the facts or forces or tendencies that cause us to see things in just the way we do. If we do not let the texts we read question us and thereby shed light on our considerations, we yield to their tyranny, close our minds, and terminate the journey (of thinking, of reading, of learning) before it ever begins.

Directing our attention to the conditions from which we near the texts we read, undergoing scrutiny of these conditions by virtue of the texts we read and our engagement with them, and intellectually persisting, we perhaps may find that "at last comes the era of reflection, when we not only observe, but take pains to observe; when we of set purpose sit down to consider an abstract truth; when we keep the mind's eye open, whilst we converse, whilst we read, whilst we act, intent to learn the secret law of some class of facts."[80] Reflecting, painfully observing, keeping the mind's eye ever open for business—"Intellect," considering what it asks of its readers in this passage, asks rhetorically, "What is the hardest task in the world?" and answers, "To think." I understand this question and answer to indicate that to read, we have to continually attempt to think the conditions, consequences, and methods of our reading. Reading must always involve thinking about what, how, and why we read. Reading, then, is probably the second hardest task, after thinking. Thinking is the hardest task precisely because it is a way of making sense of the world while being inextricable from it. Could one exempt oneself from relations with the biotext and thereby obtain a purely subjective or purely objective view of the world, thinking would be quite easy and easy reading would follow. But persisting to read or think means accepting our intellectual responsibilities and undertaking these arduous tasks without surcease, which means, according to "Intellect," keeping oneself "aloof from all moorings."[81]

The scholar persists in unmoored movement by assiduously asking the "first questions," as opposed to "accept[ing] the first creed, the first philosophy, the first political party he meets,—most likely his father's." The opposite—the poor moored fellow—"gets rest, commodity, and reputation; but he shuts the door of truth."[82] Always asking the first questions—letting the world we think and the texts we read ask questions of our reading and thinking—is persisting that opens the door of truth and ushers us through it, out of our seats. To remain seated is to use literature preposterously, to be foolishly consistent, whether from unnatural philosophies or consumption or objectification or textually deleterious subjective tendencies: "How wearisome the grammarian, the phrenologist, the political or religious fanatic, or indeed any possessed mortal whose balance is lost by the exaggeration of a single topic. It is incipient insanity. Every thought is a prison also."[83] "Intellect," in proposing a remedy for these maladies, asks neither more nor less than that we perpetually question ourselves on what we bring to and take from the texts we think or read.

Textually aware persistence connotes several different means by which one occupies one's moments and participates in these events intellectually. Included among such means are *thinking a text through, thoroughly*—that is, considering the multifarious threads that make up the weave, the multifarious contexts that frame it, the multifarious signs that constitute it; *using texts to think*—about reading, about thinking, about the responsibilities associated with different methods of making meaning; *reflecting on the textual nature of our thinking,* on the extent to which a certain notion of "text" might condition the possibilities for thought, possibilities for cultivating responsible understanding of and participation in the world; *continuing to read or think* and reread or rethink, to examine (from the Latin for "to weigh, ponder," to look at or into critically or methodically), to explicate (from the Latin for "to unfold," to make clear or explicit, carrying the French concept of extensive scrutiny of a text), and to extrapolate (to speculate as to consequences on the basis of observation or what we might see as the counter to interpolating, i.e., altering or enlarging or falsifying a book or writing by inserting new matter) the complex texts of our knowing.

All this, I fear, must seem a bit vague. And vague it must be, given that the reading I am proposing suggests endless beginnings, calls for readings of Emerson's (and other) texts that are not yet (are not ever) done, and insists on individual readers attending to each one's own particular position in relation to the text/biotext. Finally, I can only speculate how we might get started with reading Emerson to unlearn ways of reading, provide hope to other readers, and inspire. And my perspective on where and how to get started comes from what I see when I "read for the lustres,"[84] or when I read in such a way as to let a text's elements illuminate my current position in relation to the biotext in which I read and in relation to the text I read. To think or read in this manner, I need to acknowledge, as nearly as I can, the nature of the world in which reading occurs. "Intellect" suggests that "neither by detachment, neither by aggregation, is the integrity of the intellect transmitted to its works, but by a vigilance which brings the intellect in its greatness and best state to operate every moment. It must have the same wholeness which nature has."[85] To think *naturally* one would have to see thinking itself as structured in ways similar to the method or text of nature and to see those methods in operation in each moment.

What comes of transferring one method to the other, from life in the biotext to life with literary texts? To answer this, I will go back to *Nature,* its chapter called "Prospects," and its concept of the "best read naturalist": "The savant becomes unpoetic. But the best read naturalist who lends an entire and devout attention to truth, will see that there remains much to learn of his relation to the world, and that it is not to be learned by any addition or subtraction or other comparison of known quantities, but is arrived at by untaught sallies of the spirit, by a continual self-recovery, and by entire humility."[86] Thinking about this passage, I see where a natural philosophy of reading might be heading. "The savant becomes unpoetic": the "learned scholar," the expert, the one who already knows things loses his or her poetic aspect—which does not mean that he or she can no longer write poetry, but that she or he is cut off from persistent relations and instead is resting in repose. "But the best read naturalist . . . lends an entire and devout attention to truth": the poetic reader who has read the text the best and who has been read the best by the text "lends" (or provides momentarily something "on the condition that it or its equivalent will be returned") a—not *the*—whole and devoted attention to (the search of, not the search for) truth, to the manifold meaning of the text.

The poetic reader "will see that there remains much to learn of his relation to the world" and thus to the text: such a reader will see the complexity of her or his relation to the world and see also that such a vision is not enough, for there always remains much more to be seen. What remains to be learned "is not to be learned by any addition or subtraction or other comparison of known quantities": the relation is not *given*, objectively out there, to be received and described by the quantifying savant according to preset formulations. To the contrary, it is to be perceived by an active patience, by transitional perseverance, and by recognition of the limits of the self as something that perceives. Vision of the manifold meaning of one's relation to the text "is arrived at by untaught sallies of the spirit, by a continual self-recovery, and by entire humility": by virtue of an anticonventional venturing forth, perpetual going over of the grounds of what is called the "self," and a deep-rooted acknowledgment of one's *humus* or earthiness, the natural philosopher is prepared to read.

Having returned to earth, the scholar is better suited to begin his or her work as a bringer of hope. Thus situated, one can read for the lustres that will illuminate the text one reads, one's standing in relation to that text, the biotext wherein one reads, and one's standing in it. Reading for the lustres can enlighten the process of reading itself, however briefly. It is in the light of such reading that we attain a prospect of the best ways onward. The scholar's hope lies in envisioning a new moment, another beginning, reading's only end. With no end to beginning in sight, how can I finish *this* moment except by glimpsing in Emerson's "Experience" an albeit elliptical (necessarily so) commencement? "Onward and onward! In liberated moments, we know that a new picture of life and duty is already possible. . . ."[87] To try to inspire others to see their own potential for newness is the best answer I know to our preposterous use of literature.

Notes

Introduction

1. James B. Thayer, *A Western Journey with Mr. Emerson* (Boston: Little, Brown, 1884), 95.

2. Cyrus R. K. Patell notes the use of fragments from "Self-Reliance" to peddle Reebok athletic shoes ("Emersonian Strategies: Negative Liberty, Self-Reliance, and Democratic Individuality," *Nineteenth-Century Literature* 48, no. 4 [1994]: 440–79). More recently, Emersonisms have been deployed in the ad campaigns of Target department stores and of American General, in which viewers are reminded to "Hitch your wagon to a star" and purchase life insurance.

3. Ralph Waldo Emerson, *The Collected Works of Ralph Waldo Emerson*, ed. Alfred R. Ferguson et al., 5 vols. to date (Cambridge, Mass.: Harvard University Press, 1971–), 1:56; hereafter *CW*.

4. Ibid.

5. In so doing I follow Nietzsche (who followed Eckhart), *mutatis mutandi:* "Hasn't the time come to say of morality what Master Eckhart said: "'I ask God to rid me of God'" (Friedrich Nietzsche, *The Gay Science* [New York: Vintage Books, 1974], 235).

6. Emerson, *CW*, 1:57.

7. Ibid., 2:165.

8. Ibid., 1:54.

9. Ibid., 1:55.

10. Ibid., 1:53.

11. Ibid., 1:56.

12. Ibid.

13. Ibid.

14. Ibid., 2:95 ("Spiritual Laws").

15. Ralph Waldo Emerson, *The Works of Ralph Waldo Emerson*, ed. James Elliot Cabot, 14 vols. (Boston: Houghton Mifflin, 1883), 9:22; hereafter *W*.

16. Emerson, *CW*, 2:80.

17. Ibid., 2:83.

18. Ibid., 2:77.

19. Ibid., 2:81.

Chapter 1: The Consumption of Emerson

1. Milton R. Konvitz and Stephen E. Whicher, *Emerson: A Collection of Critical Essays* (Englewood Cliffs, N.J.: Prentice-Hall, 1962), v.

2. Lawrence Buell, "The Emerson Industry in the 1980s: A Survey of Trends and Achievements," *ESQ* 30, no. 2 (1984): 117–36.

3. Oliver Wendell Holmes, *Ralph Waldo Emerson* (Boston: Houghton Mifflin, 1884; reprint, Boston: Houghton Mifflin, 1898), 181.

4. H. L. Mencken, *Prejudices: First Series* (New York: Knopf, 1919), 194.

5. Kenneth Burke, "I, Eye, Ay—Emerson's Early Essay 'Nature': Thoughts on the Machinery of Transcendence," in *Transcendentalism and Its Legacy*, ed. Myron Simon and Thornton Parsons (Ann Arbor: University of Michigan Press, 1966), 3.

6. Ibid., 11.

7. Steven Mailloux, "The Use and Abuse of Fiction: Readers Eating Books," *Reception Histories: Rhetoric, Pragmatism, and American Cultural Politics* (Ithaca: Cornell University Press, 1998), 128.

8. Cf. Georges Bataille's *The Accursed Share* (trans. Robert Hurley, New York: Zone Books, 1988), especially the discussion of a consciousness that "reduces the objects of thought to *things*" (74).

9. Richard Huber, *The American Idea of Success* (New York: McGraw-Hill, 1971), 124.

10. For histories of New Thought, see Huber, *American Idea*, 124–85, 307–40; Richard Weiss, *The American Myth of Success: From Horatio Alger to Norman Vincent Peale* (Urbana: University of Illinois Press, 1969), 128–234 (especially 128–53); Gail Thain Parker, *Mind Cure in New England: From the Civil War to World War I* (Hanover, N.H.: University of New England Press, 1973); and Donald Meyer, *The Positive Thinkers: A Study of the American Quest for Health, Wealth, and Personal Power from Mary Baker Eddy to Norman Vincent Peale* (New York: Doubleday, 1965). Huber summarizes its tenets thus: "Since you are divine and one with God, by thinking you are one with God, you cannot be sick because God cannot be sick. New Thought developed a wing of success writers who picked up the limitless proposition and put it this way: Since you are divine and one with God, by thinking you are one with God, you cannot be poor" (124). By humorously stringing together some New Thought titles, Huber makes his summary even pithier: "If you will put yourself in tune with the infinite, your power of positive

thinking can be your guide to confident living and bring you health, happiness, and prosperity" (124).

11. Regarding the other Ralph Waldo, Meyer points out that "certainly Trine was conversant with the seer so admired by his parents" (*Positive Thinkers*, 61).

12. Huber notes that *In Tune with the Infinite* "has sold over a million and a half hardbound copies" (*American Idea*, 126) and that Peale's *The Power of Positive Thinking*, "that titan of money-makers, settled into the best-seller lists and started growing roots" (316). Indeed, the "statistics mounted to over 2,000,000 hardcover copies with serialization in more than 85 newspapers and 13 national magazines" (316–17). Regarding Marden, Huber cites Mencken's "mournful estimation" in 1926 that, "'altogether, his writings in book-form must have reached a total sale of 20,000,000 copies, including 3,000,000 in twenty-five tongues other than English'" (164).

13. Weiss, *American Myth*, 161.

14. Huber, *American Idea*, 131.

15. John G. Cawelti, *Apostles of the Self-Made Man* (Chicago: University of Chicago Press, 1965), 97.

16. Parker, *Mind Cure*, 58.

17. Weiss, *American Myth*, 134.

18. Parker, *Mind Cure*, 58.

19. Irvin G. Wyllie, *The Self-Made Man in America: The Myth of Rags to Riches* (New Brunswick, N.J.: Rutgers University Press, 1954), 128.

20. Ibid., 128, quoting *The Dial* 20 (1896): 143.

21. Orison Swett Marden, *Peace, Power, and Plenty* (New York: Thomas Crowell, 1909); Ralph Waldo Trine, *In Tune with the Infinite; or, Fulness of Peace, Power, and Plenty* (New York: Dodge, 1897). Examples of this borrowing are many: the "Law of Prosperity" in Trine becomes the "Law of Opulence" in Marden; the "Infinite Spirit of Life back of all" becomes the "Great Within." Trine claims that "if one hold himself in the thought of poverty, he will be poor, and the chances are that he will remain in poverty" (176). Compare Marden: "Holding the poverty thought keeps us in touch with poverty-stricken, poverty-producing conditions; and the constant thinking of poverty, talking poverty, living poverty, makes us mentally poor" (23), hence poverty is a "mental disability" (*Peace*, 17); this exact wording reappears in his *Pushing to the Front* (Petersburg, N.Y.: Success Co., 1911), 705. Parker points out that the borrowing was mutual (*Mind Cure*, 71–72).

22. Parker, *Mind Cure*, 59.

23. Trine, *In Tune*, 176.

24. Ibid., 12.

25. Ibid., 16 (emphasis in original).

26. Ibid., 176.

27. This is illustrated in Trine's account of the "young lady who a short time ago wanted some money very badly. . . . She took and held herself in the attitude of mind we have just pointed out. In the morning she entered into the silence for a

few moments. In this way she brought herself into a more complete harmony with the higher powers. Before the day closed a gentleman called, a member of a family with which she was acquainted. He asked her if she would do for the family some work that they wanted done. . . . She undertook the work. *She did it well.* When she had completed it there was put into her hands an amount of money far beyond what she had expected" (*In Tune,* 182). Note that the most salient point, or at least the passage that Trine italicizes, involves doing one's work—referring, perhaps, to Emerson's "But do your work, and I shall know you" from "Self-Reliance" (*CW,* 2:32).

28. Trine, *In Tune,* 32.
29. Ibid., 163–64.
30. Ibid., 166.
31. Ibid., 164.
32. Emerson, *CW,* 2:34.
33. Trine, *In Tune,* 165.
34. Ibid.
35. Ibid., 190.
36. Ibid.
37. Ibid., 192.
38. Napoleon Hill's *Think and Grow Rich* (Meriden, Conn.: Ralston Society, 1937) was reprinted in *The Think and Grow Rich Action Pack* (New York: Hawthorn Books, 1972), which adds to Hill's work the *Think and Grow Rich Action Manual.*
39. Cawelti, *Apostles,* 209.
40. Ibid., 210.
41. Hill, *Think,* 38.
42. Ibid., 211. The list of sex gods includes George Washington, Napoleon Bonaparte, Shakespeare, Lincoln, Robert Burns, Jefferson, Elbert Hubbard, financier and lawyer Elbert H. Gary, Woodrow Wilson, salesman and manufacturer John H. Patterson, Andrew Jackson, Enrico Caruso, and Emerson (211). Women serve as a receptacle for men's sex energy (when the latter are not transmuting it); the good woman is "the woman who understands man's nature and tactfully caters to it" (224).
43. Ibid., 246.
44. Ibid., 246–47.
45. Ibid., 249.
46. Ibid., 252.
47. Ibid., 251.
48. Ibid., 253–54.
49. James Russell Lowell, *My Study Windows* (New York: Dutton, 1900), 360.
50. Ibid.
51. Ibid., 355–56.
52. Ibid., 356.
53. Emerson, *CW,* 3:3–4.

54. Lowell, *My Study Windows*, 357.

55. Emerson, *W,* 11:9.

56. Ibid., 11:10–11.

57. Ibid., 11:13.

58. Ralph Waldo Emerson, *Journals and Miscellaneous Notebooks of Ralph Waldo Emerson,* ed. William H. Gilman et al., 16 vols. (Cambridge, Mass.: Harvard University Press, 1960–84), 3:318–19; hereafter *JMN.*

59. Emerson, *W,* 11:28.

60. Ibid., 11:14.

61. Ibid., 11:19.

62. Ibid., 11:20.

63. Ibid., 11:16.

64. Ibid., 11:21–22.

65. Emerson, *JMN,* 7:525. Critics have made much of this dream. Joel Porte, for example, combining biblical interpretation with psychologizing, uses the dream scene to define a cohering trait of Emerson's opus: an "inspired" sense of power, a religious strength and drive to comprehend the "complex totality" of the world (*Representative Man: Ralph Waldo Emerson in His Time* [New York: Oxford University Press, 1979]). Moving away from biblical interpretations, Michael Lopez insists that "whatever reference this dream may have to Adam or the Book of Revelation, the imagery can clearly be interpreted according to the contrary terms of floating, powerless, versus controlling or mastering circumstances by incorporating 'the world'" ("Transcendental Failure: 'The Palace of Spiritual Power,'" in *Emerson: Prospect and Retrospect,* ed. Joel Porte [Cambridge, Mass.: Harvard University Press, 1982], 152).

66. See Emerson, *JMN,* 7:524–26.

67. Ibid., 7:526.

68. Ibid., 7:524.

69. Emerson refers to the line that will appear in "Self-Reliance" as "A foolish consistency is the hobgoblin of little minds, adored by little statesmen and philosophers and divines" (Emerson, *CW,* 2:33).

70. Emerson, *JMN,* 7:524.

71. Ibid.

Chapter 2: Writing in the Name of *Emerson*

1. Although what follows is mainly concerned with success writing from Emerson's day to the first half of the twentieth century and the appropriation of Emerson by success writers, I will note in passing that even at the end of the twentieth century Emerson still figures prominently in the discourse of success—primarily as the "ultimate authority on the subject" of self-reliance. See, for example, George Gallup Jr., Alec M. Gallup, and William Proctor, *The Great American Success Story: Factors That Affect Achievement* (Homewood, Ill.: Dow Jones-Irwin,

1986), 62. "Self-reliance" is listed among the "12 Success Characteristics" (56), and, after quotations from Emerson's essay "Self-Reliance," is defined as "the courage to take definitive action to get things moving in your life," "the ability to set goals, and . . . plain old will power" (62–63).

2. Elbert Hubbard, *A Message to Garcia and Other Essays* (Westwood, N.J.: Fleming H. Revell, 1959), 17.

3. In *Art and Glory: The Story of Elbert Hubbard* (New York: Crown, 1968), Freeman Champney recounts the infamous "Mousetrap" episode, in which Hubbard falsely attributed one of his own epigrammatic offerings to Emerson; Champney quotes an explanation from a later Hubbard publication (*Philistine*, June 1911): "It was a little strain on [Hubbard's] ego to let this thing go under his own stamp, so he saved his modesty and at the same time gave the epigram specific gravity, by attributing it to Ralph Waldo Emerson." The apology goes on to admit that "it is simply one of the things that Emerson would have said if it had occurred to him," and adds that although Hubbard may have claimed for himself the authorship of some thoughts that were actually written by Emerson, "the debt is more than offset by things which he has attributed to Emerson that Emerson never wrote" (205–6).

4. Stephen Crane, among others, reproved Hubbard for greatly distorting the deed in his glorification, writing to Hubbard, "I object strongly to your paragraphs about Rowan. You are more wrong than is even common on our humble incompetant [sic] globe. He didn't do anything worthy at all" (qtd. in John Berryman, *Stephen Crane* [New York: William Sloane Associates, 1950], 245; see also Champney, *Art,* 223).

5. Hubbard, *Message,* 11.

6. Ibid., 12, 15, 14.

7. Ibid., 17.

8. Ibid., 16.

9. See Champney, *Art,* 87–92. Corporations ordered massive reprints of "A Message to Garcia" and distributed them to their employees.

10. Hubbard, *Message,* 12.

11. Ibid., 14.

12. On a similar note, Hubbard writes that his "heart goes out" to "the man who, when given a letter . . . , quietly takes the missive, without asking any idiotic questions, and with no lurking intention of chucking it into the nearest sewer, or of doing aught else but deliver it, never gets 'laid off,' nor has to go on a strike for higher wages" (16–17).

13. John Cawelti, *Apostles of the Self-Made Man* (Chicago: University of Chicago Press, 1965), 4, 87. For other historical overviews of Emerson's importance to the myth of success, see Wyllie, *Self-Made Man;* Huber, *American Idea;* Weiss, *American Myth;* and Meyer, *Positive Thinkers.*

14. Mary Kupiec Cayton's "The Making of an American Prophet: Emerson, His Audiences, and the Rise of the Culture Industry in Nineteenth-Century America" (*American Historical Review* 92, no. 3 [1987]: 597–620) provides a fine account

of how Emerson's complicated presentations to such groups were received during a lecture tour to the Midwest.

15. Wyllie, *Self-Made Man*, 201.

16. Freeman Hunt, *Worth and Wealth: A Collection of Maxims, Morals, and Miscellanies for Merchants and Men of Business* (New York: Stringer and Townsend, 1856), 82–83.

17. Emerson, *CW*, 2:43 (emphasis in the original).

18. Cawelti, *Apostles*, 88.

19. Emerson, *CW*, 2:45.

20. Ibid., 2:32.

21. Ibid., 2:29.

22. Ibid., 2:44.

23. Ibid.

24. Ibid., 2:49.

25. Hunt, *Worth*, 83; Emerson, *CW*, 2:44.

26. Emerson, *CW*, 2:32.

27. Ibid.

28. Ibid.

29. Ibid., 2:45–46.

30. Ibid., 2:46.

31. Ibid., 2:36.

32. Hunt, *Worth*, 83.

33. Gary Taylor, "The Renaissance and the End of Editing," in *Palimpsest: Editorial Theory in the Humanities,* ed. George Bornstein and Ralph G. Williams (Ann Arbor: University of Michigan Press, 1993), 129.

34. Ralph Williams, "I Shall Be Spoken: Textual Boundaries, Authors, and Intent," in *Palimpsest,* 54.

35. William Mathews, *Getting on in the World; or, Hints on Success in Life* (Chicago: S. C. Griggs, 1874), 104. Mathews (1818–1909) was, among other things, the editor of a financial weekly, a public lecturer, a professor of rhetoric at the University of Chicago, and the author of several works on success and rhetoric. In the quite popular work I am currently discussing, he cites Emerson at least a dozen times, on topics ranging from "concentration" (66, 69, 70) to "preparatory training" (236).

36. Edward Bok, *The Americanization of Edward Bok: The Autobiography of a Dutch Boy Fifty Years After* (New York: Scribner's Sons, 1920; reprint, New York: Scribner's Sons, 1923), 34.

37. Ibid., 55.

38. Edward Bok, *Successward: A Young Man's Book for Young Men,* 3d ed. (New York: Fleming H. Revell, 1896), 8.

39. Ibid., 21.

40. Ibid., 17–18.

41. Emerson, *CW*, 2:28.

42. Bok, *Successward*, 49. The young man must answer to his boss's spirit because "The idea that an employer has no control over a young man's time away from the office is a dangerous fallacy" (71).

43. Ibid., 18.

44. Ibid., 31.

45. Bok, *Americanization*, 58–59.

46. Anthony Grafton, *Forgers and Critics: Creativity and Duplicity in Western Scholarship* (Princeton: Princeton University Press, 1990), 9.

47. Ibid., 23.

48. Ibid., 124.

49. Ibid., 126.

50. Ibid.

51. Emerson, *CW*, 2:44.

52. Stanley Cavell argues something similar in "Being Odd, Getting Even": "Your work, what is yours to do, is exemplified, when you are confronted with Emerson's words, by reading those words—which means . . . subjecting yourself to them as the writer has by undertaking to enact his existence in saying them" (*In Quest of the Ordinary: Lines of Skepticism and Romanticism* [Chicago: University of Chicago Press, 1988], 118).

53. Henry David Thoreau, *Walden*, ed. J. Lyndon Shanley (Princeton: Princeton University Press, 1971), 61.

54. Ibid., 29.

55. Emerson, *CW*, 2:33.

56. Ibid., 2:32.

57. Ibid., 2:30.

58. Ibid., 2:40.

59. Ibid., 2:35.

60. Ibid., 2:33.

61. Cavell arrives at a similar observation but from a slightly different direction and understanding different consequences. He writes of "Emerson's textuality" that "every sentence of an essay from him may be taken as its topic, and there is no end to reading it. Put otherwise . . . , an Emersonian essay is a finite object that yields an infinite response" (*This New Yet Unapproachable America* [Albuquerque, N.M.: Living Batch Press, 1989], 101).

Chapter 3: Waldo, Inc.

1. Cf. Joel Porte's observation that "the meaning and value of Emerson's work have typically been overshadowed, and frequently undermined, by an emphasis on his example and personal force" ("The Problem of Emerson," in *The Uses of Literature*, ed. Monroe Engel [Cambridge, Mass.: Harvard University Press, 1973], 86).

2. As such, these versions always constitute a form of "writing in Emerson's name" (see chapter 2). Most biographies devote attention to the subject's adolescent preference for his middle name; Gay Wilson Allen's *Waldo Emerson: A Biography* (New York: Viking, 1981) is the most dogged in its reliance on the moniker and begins with an explanation of the title. Observing that "Ralph Waldo Emerson disliked his first name, and his family and friends called him 'Waldo' after he requested them to do so while he was in college" (vii), Allen evidently considers himself a friend or family member, or at least attempts to reproduce the atmosphere of enjoying such an acquaintance. He goes on to write, in a hopeful vein, that "the name Waldo Emerson should also have more favorable connotations for readers of this biography than the forbidding three names, which carry associations with the trinomial New England contemporaries" Longfellow, Whittier, Lowell, and Holmes. Allen desires that when we think of Waldo, we think of other, more interesting binomials—e.g., Whitman, Dickinson, and Melville, overlooking the transcendentally problematic case of Henry Thoreau (aka Henry David Thoreau, née David Henry Thoreau). The other nicknames noted above come from Phillips Russell's *Emerson: The Wisest American* (New York: Brentano's, 1929); Moncure Daniel Conway's *Emerson at Home and Abroad* (Boston: James R. Osgood, 1882), 175; and Holmes's *Ralph Waldo Emerson,* 103.

3. This is from the flyleaf of Brooks's *The Life of Emerson* (New York: Dutton, 1932) and more directly refers to his expansive effort to bring to life "all the episodes of our literary history, and dozens of its representative men." Frederic Ives Carpenter, in his *Emerson Handbook* (New York: Hendricks House, 1953), labels Brooks's work a "sympathetic biography, 'written largely in Emerson's own words'" (46), and observes that this peculiar approach "described the man with unusual insight, and inspired several other scholars of Emerson . . . to employ the same method" (44).

4. Brooks, *Life,* 7. Cf. Robert D. Richardson Jr.'s *Emerson: The Mind on Fire* (Berkeley: University of California Press, 1995), which begins thus: "On March 29, 1832, the twenty-eight-year-old Emerson visited the tomb of his young wife, Ellen, who had been buried a year and two months earlier" (3).

5. Brooks, *Life,* 7.

6. Richardson deploys a similar juxtaposition at the conclusion of his first chapter, which is a study of Emerson and his encounters with his first wife's corpse: "In the months immediately ahead he continued to walk to Ellen's grave every day, but now his concentration on death was broken and he wrote a sermon called 'The God of the Living'. . . . He would live no longer with the dead. 'Let us express our astonishment,' he wrote in his journal in May, 'before we are swallowed up in the yeast of the abyss. I will lift up my hands and say Kosmos'" (5).

7. Brooks, *Life,* 91.

8. Ibid., 312. Brooks here has incorporated the work of another Emersonian biographer, Moncure Daniel Conway, who wrote in his *Emerson at Home and*

Abroad: "There are notable instances in which his voice, his manners, and the very expression of his face, could be recognised moving about Concord in persons unrelated to him by blood" (276).

9. Brooks, *Life,* 315. Edward Emerson believes that the closing phrase initially referred to members of the Saturday Club—see the later edition of *Emerson in Concord: A Memoir* (Boston: Houghton Mifflin, 1890), 258. As with much of Brooks's book, this phrasing is snatched from Emerson and inserted into a new narrative (without quotation marks or any form of citation); Brooks uses Emerson's words to tell the Emerson story, but makes those words his own. As Floyd Stovall asserts, "Van Wyck Brooks's [*Life*] has the charm of Emerson's own style, in addition to the considerable gifts of the biographer, for it is largely presented in the language of the journals. Its impressionistic manner holds the reader's interest and gives him the sense of reality, with many side glances at personalities, places, and moods of the time" ("Emerson," in *Eight American Authors: A Review of Research and Criticism,* ed. Floyd Stovall [New York: Modern Language Association, 1956], 54). Carpenter complains that although it is "an informal, readable biography, full of psychological insights," Brooks's work lacks "sharp criticism or discussion of ideas (*Emerson Handbook,* 46). The reader is thus given the direct presentation of the reality of Emerson's psyche rather than an intellectual or critical representation of specific elements of Emerson's writing qua writing.

10. Edward Emerson, *Emerson in Concord: A Memoir* (Boston: Houghton Mifflin, 1888), 2.

11. Edward Emerson, *Emerson* (1890), xlii.

12. George Willis Cooke, *Ralph Waldo Emerson: His Life, Writings, and Philosophy* (Boston: James R. Osgood, 1881), v.

13. Sarah K. Bolton, *Ralph Waldo Emerson* (New York: Thomas Y. Crowell, 1889; reprint, New York: Thomas Y. Crowell, 1904), 27.

14. Edward Emerson, *Emerson* (1888), 247.

15. Ibid., 58.

16. Ibid., 56.

17. Cooke, *Ralph Waldo Emerson,* 343.

18. Bolton, *Ralph Waldo Emerson,* 2.

19. Edward Emerson, *Emerson* (1888), 193.

20. Ibid., 28.

21. Conway, *Emerson,* 8.

22. Ibid., 377.

23. Conway provides numerous examples of this attitude of passive acceptance: "There was no need that [Emerson] should talk; simply to be with him was to me joy enough, and I put no questions" (ibid., 356).

24. Ibid., 229.

25. Ibid., 3–4. The Emerson offered by the bookstore was most likely Frederick (1788–1857), who was not of immediate relation to Ralph.

26. Edward Emerson, *Emerson* (1888), 188.

27. Ibid., 189.

28. Nancy Craig Simmons holds that James Elliot Cabot served as the most important single link in the chain of transmission between Emerson and the future" ("Arranging the Sibylline Leaves: James Elliot Cabot's Work as Emerson's Literary Executor," in *Studies in the American Renaissance, 1983*, ed. Joel Myerson [Charlottesville: University Press of Virginia, 1983], 335). Not only should Cabot's methods concern us, but so should their effects on "the shaping of Emerson's modern reputation" and "our understanding of [Emerson's] work" (337).

29. James Elliot Cabot, *A Memoir of Emerson in Two Volumes* (Boston: Houghton Mifflin, 1887, 1889), 1:iii–iv.

30. Ibid., 1:iv.

31. Ibid., 1:6. Cabot is quoting Rufus Dawes, a "school-fellow" of Emerson. He also cites William Henry Furness's recollection that Emerson never "engaged in boys' plays; not because of any physical inability, but simply because, from his earliest years, he dwelt in a higher sphere" (1:5–6).

32. Ibid., 2:673.

33. Ibid., 1:v–vi.

34. Ibid., 1:56–57.

35. Ibid., 1:56.

36. Ibid., 1:230, 237, 287, 2:649.

37. Emerson, *W*, 8:iv.

38. Cabot, *Memoir*, 2:421.

39. Ibid., 1:152.

40. Ibid., 1:303.

41. Ibid., 1:253.

42. Ibid., 1:315.

43. *Nature* is discussed beneath "Transcendentalism," while the two addresses fall beneath the "Religion" heading. This does not mean simply that these works are put into neat categories by Cabot (or, more likely, his publisher) and therefore dispensed with; it does mean, however, that the framework of Religion is the one in which readers are to make sense of Emerson. Religion, in this edition of Emerson's life, is to inform our reading of Emerson.

44. For example, Cabot holds that Holmes's remark—that Emerson was "an iconoclast without a hammer, who took down our idols from their pedestals so tenderly that it seemed like an act of worship"—was "well said; but I am not sure that he took them down, or even thought it important that they should come down, so long as they were really objects of worship" (1:262). Iconoclastic effects of Emerson's writing are repeatedly rendered nugatory by Cabot's insistence on Emerson's worshipful intentions.

45. Ibid., 1:153.

46. Although it cannot be claimed that he "thinks play radically," David Shimkin does offer an interesting counter to the conservation of Emerson that I am describing. See "Emerson's Playful Habit of Mind," *ATQ* 62 (Dec. 1986): 3–16. Shimkin

involves himself less with the play of signification than with metaphorizing Emerson's essays as playgrounds.

47. Cf. Glen M. Johnson, "Emerson's Essay, 'Immortality': The Problem of Authorship," in *On Emerson: The Best from* American Literature, ed. Edwin H. Cady and Louis J. Budd (Durham: Duke University Press, 1988), 245–62.

48. Emerson, *W,* 8:i.

49. Ibid.

50. Ibid.

51. Ibid., 8:ii.

52. Regarding the conflagration and its relation to the author and his work, Conway cites Louisa May Alcott's remembrance of the fire, during which the contents of his study, including his writings, "'were tumbled out of the window. . . . As I stood guarding the scorched wet pile, Mr. Emerson passed by, and surveying the devastation with philosophic calmness, only said in answer to my lamentations, "I see my library under a new aspect. Could you tell me where my good neighbors have flung my boots?"'" (142).

53. Emerson, *W,* 8:ii, iii. The executor observes that "sentences, even whole pages, were repeated, and there was a confusion of order beyond what even he would have tolerated" (8:ii).

54. Ibid., 8:iii.

55. Ibid., 8:v.

56. Ibid., 8:25.

57. Ibid., 8:25–26.

58. Ibid., 8:20.

59. Ibid.

60. Ibid., 8:68–69.

61. Ibid., 8:58.

62. George Woodberry, *Ralph Waldo Emerson* (New York: Macmillan, 1907), 187.

63. Emerson, *W,* 8:14.

64. Ibid.

65. Ibid., 8:10.

66. Ibid., 8:11–12.

67. Ibid., 8:25.

68. Ibid., 8:15.

69. Ibid., 8:40.

70. See, for example, George J. Stack, *Nietzsche and Emerson: An Elective Affinity* (Athens: Ohio University Press, 1992) and Walter Kaufmann, "Translator's Introduction," in *The Gay Science* (New York: Vintage Books, 1974), 3–26. Kaufmann reports that "Emerson was one of Nietzsche's great loves ever since he read him as a schoolboy" (7).

71. Kaufmann, "Translator's Introduction," 7. He translates the quotation thus:

"To the poet and sage, all things are friendly and hallowed, all experiences profitable, all days holy, all men divine."

72. Ibid., 8–10.

73. Ibid., 10; Emerson, *W*, 10:250.

74. Kaufmann, "Translator's Introduction," 7.

75. Nietzsche, *The Gay Science,* 32 (first and second quotes), 36 (third quote; emphasis in the original), 37 (fourth quote), 74 (fifth quote).

76. Ibid., 171.

77. Ibid., 121–22.

78. Ibid., 238 (emphasis in the original).

79. Ibid., 232.

80. Ibid., 76–77 (emphasis in the original).

81. Ibid., 336 (emphasis in the original).

82. Emerson, *W*, 8:45.

83. Ibid., 8:44.

Chapter 4: Foolish Consistencies

1. Emerson, *CW*, 1:83–84.

2. Ibid., 1:82 (emphasis in the original).

3. Ibid.

4. Ibid., 1:76.

5. Ibid., 1:81.

6. Ibid.

7. Ibid., 1:82.

8. Ibid., 1:76–77.

9. Emerson, *W*, 12:182.

10. Ibid., 181.

11. Immanuel Kant, *The Critique of Pure Reason,* trans. J. M. D. Meiklejohn (London: Everyman, 1991), 3.

12. Emerson, *W*, 12:180.

13. Ibid., 12:181.

14. Ibid.

15. Ibid.

16. Emerson, *CW*, 2:46.

17. Cheryl Walker, for example, responding to "'death of the author' critics," promotes "persona criticism, a form of analysis that focuses on patterns of ideation, voice, and sensibility linked together by a connection to author" ("Persona Criticism and the Death of the Author," in *Contesting the Subject: Essays in the Postmodern Theory and Practice of Biography and Biographical Criticism,* ed. William H. Epstein [West Lafayette, Ind.: Purdue University Press, 1991], 109). Valerie Ross claims that "structuralists and poststructuralists" have "contamin-

at[ed] biography as the domain of the naive, essential, humanist unsophisticate," which she finds "an essentially conservative gesture that keeps our circles small and our discourse elevated" ("Too Close to Home: Repressing Biography, Instituting Authority," in *Contesting the Subject*, 157, 158).

18. Gay Wilson Allen, "On Writing *Waldo Emerson*," in *Essaying Biography: A Celebration for Leon Edel*, ed. Gloria G. Fromm (Honolulu: University of Hawaii Press, 1986), 78.

19. Ibid., 76.

20. Ibid., 77.

21. Ibid., 76.

22. Ibid., 90.

23. W. K. Wimsatt Jr. and Monroe Beardsley, *The Verbal Icon: Studies in the Meaning of Poetry* (Louisville: University of Kentucky Press, 1954), 3–18. As the final sentence of the essay puts it, "Critical inquiries are not settled by consulting the oracle" (18).

24. Paul de Man, "Form and Intent in the American New Criticism," *Blindness and Insight: Essays in the Rhetoric of Contemporary Criticism* (New York: Oxford University Press, 1971), 27.

25. Roland Barthes, "The Death of the Author," *Image—Music—Text,* trans. Stephen Heath (New York: Noonday Press, 1977), 142–48; Stanley Fish, "Biography and Intention," in *Contesting the Subject,* 13.

26. Fish, "Biography and Intention," 12.

27. Nietzsche, *The Gay Science,* 316.

28. De Man, "Form and Intent," 33.

29. Frank Bergon, introduction to *A Sharp Lookout: Selected Nature Essays of John Burroughs* (Washington, D.C.: Smithsonian Institution Press, 1987), 9.

30. Bill McKibben, introduction to *Birch Browsings: A John Burroughs Reader* (New York: Viking Penguin, 1992), ix.

31. Emerson, *CW,* 1:10.

32. Ibid., 1:7.

33. Ibid., 1:9.

34. Ibid., 1:14.

35. Ibid., 1:39.

36. Ibid., 1:43.

37. Ibid., 1:44–45.

38. Ibid., 1:39.

39. John Burroughs, *The Writings of John Burroughs,* 20 vols. (Boston: Houghton Mifflin, 1904–19), 4:32; hereafter *WJB.*

40. Burroughs, *WJB,* 10:116, 117.

41. Ibid., 10:149.

42. Emerson, *CW,* 1:23.

43. Burroughs, *WJB,* 4:38. These lines immediately succeed the one that serves as this section's epigraph.

44. Robert E. Spiller, editor's introduction, *CW*, 1:117.

45. Emerson, *CW*, 1:120. Emerson quotes Proverbs 29:18.

46. Ibid., 1:121.

47. Ibid., 1:123 (emphasis in the original).

48. Ibid., 1:121.

49. The *OED* includes the following as definitions of *method:* "A way of doing anything, esp. according to a defined and regular plan; a mode of procedure in any activity, business, etc."; "systematic arrangement, order"; and "a regular, systematic arrangement of literary materials."

50. Emerson, *CW*, 1:124.

51. Ibid.

52. Ibid., 1:125.

53. Ibid., 1:125.

54. Ibid., 1:127.

55. Ibid., 1:131.

56. Ibid., 1:131–32.

57. Ibid. (emphasis added).

58. Ibid., 1:129 (emphasis in the original).

59. Burroughs, *WJB*, 10:26. Note the similarity with Emerson's observations in "The Method of Nature." The significant difference is that while Burroughs here prohibits study, Emerson urges a particular method of (textual) study as essential.

60. Ibid., 10:26–27 (emphasis in the original).

61. Ibid., 10:29.

62. Ibid., 10:89.

63. Ibid., 10:61.

64. Ibid.

65. Ibid., 10:15 (first quote), 16 (second and third quotes), 25 (fourth and fifth quotes).

66. Ibid., 3:157.

67. Ibid., 10:8.

68. Ibid., 10:81.

69. "I rave no more 'gainst time or fate, / For lo! my own shall come to me" (Burroughs, "Waiting," *WJB*, 17:v).

70. Ibid., 10:66.

71. Ibid., 8:269.

72. Ibid., 8:265.

73. Ibid., 3:185.

74. Ibid., 8:169.

75. Ibid., 3:180, 186, 194, 201. My claim is not that Burroughs is simply a bad reader or that his reading of Emerson is empty of merit because it is engrossed with the person of the writer. Burroughs provides us with insight into some of the cultural effects of Emerson in the late 1800s and early 1900s and in the process offers telling phrases suggestive of the power of Emerson's text. Emerson is described

as having an electrical quality that "is abrupt, freaky, unexpected, and always communicates a little wholesome shock" (3:187). "He stands among other poets like a pine-tree amid a forest of oak and maple" (3:194). "He would find a more powerful fulminant than has yet been discovered. He likes to see two harmless elements come together with a concussion that will shake the roof" (8:84).

76. Ibid., 10:149.

77. Clifton Johnson, *John Burroughs Talks* (Boston: Houghton Mifflin, 1922), 176–77 (emphasis added). Burroughs presents several accounts of the episode: the 17 April 1900 entry in his journal, in which he notes that he first "steeped" himself in Emerson "while at the Old Home" (*The Heart of Burroughs' Journals,* ed. Clara Barrus [Boston: Houghton Mifflin, 1928], 217); "Autobiographical Sketches," in which the prevailing metaphor is the biting of an apple (Clara Barrus, *Our Friend John Burroughs* [Boston: Houghton Mifflin, 1914], 105); and "An Egotistical Chapter," in which Burroughs describes how he "fed upon" and "steeped" himself in several of Emerson's works (*WJB* 8:267).

78. Burroughs, *WJB,* 12:231.

79. Ibid., 15:236.

80. Ibid., 12:233.

81. Ibid., 12:238.

82. James Russell Lowell's "A Fable for Critics" contains perhaps the most famous portrait of these contradictions, and it is customary in Emersonian criticism to cite the following passage: "A Greek head on right Yankee shoulders, whose range / Has Olympus for one pole, for t'other the Exchange;" this is followed by the description of Emerson as "A Plotinus-Montaigne" (James Russell Lowell, *The Complete Poetical Works of James Russell Lowell,* ed. Horace E. Scudder [Boston: Houghton Mifflling, 1897], 127).

83. That is, the contradictions, like Emerson's skepticism (Cabot, *Memoir,* 326), are depicted as means to a higher end.

84. Holmes, *Ralph Waldo Emerson,* 189. In his *Emerson Handbook* Carpenter places Holmes's work among the "notable" biographies, though "often poor as criticism" (47). Floyd Stovall notes that Holmes's work was "the first book-length biography" and "is valuable to the modern reader of Emerson chiefly as it reflects the friendly but somewhat skeptical Bostonian attitude towards the Concord transcendentalist at the time of his death" ("Emerson" 52).

85. Holmes, *Ralph Waldo Emerson,* 103.

86. Ibid., 369.

87. Ibid., 72.

88. Ibid., 411.

89. Ibid., 398.

90. Ibid., 397.

91. Ibid., 396.

92. Ibid., 37.

93. Ibid., 235–36.

94. Lowell, on the other hand, claims that "our favourite teacher's practicality is not in the least of the Poor Richard variety. If he have any Buncombe constituency, it is that unrealized commonwealth of philosophers which Plotinus proposed to establish; and if he were to make an almanack, his directions to farmers would be something like this: 'OCTOBER: *Indian Summer;* now is the time to get in your early Vedas.'" In this rendition of Emerson, Montaigne seems to be losing ground to Plotinus: "above all . . . his mysticism gives us a counterpoise to our super-practicality" (*My Study Windows* 353).

95. Holmes, *Ralph Waldo Emerson,* 231.

96. Ibid., 409.

97. Ibid., 166.

98. Ibid., 181.

99. Ibid., 179.

100. Ibid., 252; cf. Emerson, W, 7:32–33.

101. Holmes, *Ralph Waldo Emerson,* 238.

102. Ibid., 358.

103. Jonathan Bishop, *Emerson on the Soul* (Cambridge, Mass.: Harvard University Press, 1964), 234. Bishop observes that "the first generation of Emersonians, taking up the definition [of Emerson's essence] surviving from the age that knew Emerson chiefly as an exemplary person, tended to regard the works as a kind of transparent medium through which to make contact with a distinguished spirit" (2).

104. Carpenter, *Emerson Handbook,* 44, 2.

105. That Perry sees such a deposit occurring is clear; his essay "Emerson's Saving Bank" (*In Praise of Folly and Other Papers* [Boston: Houghton Mifflin, 1923], 114–29) picks up Emerson's own trope for the journals and frames the revivification of Emerson in the discourse of capital and currency: writing then becomes "a kind of perpetual balancing of his bank-books." Adding that experiencing the journals is "essential to a full realization of Emerson's character," Perry opines that "more perfectly than he could have imagined, his diaries have thus become his Bank" (116). Emerson lives again in the coins that bear his image.

106. Bliss Perry, *Emerson Today* (Princeton: Princeton University Press, 1931), 1.

107. Ibid., 1–2.

108. Ibid., 16.

109. Ibid., 1.

110. Ibid., 59.

111. Ibid., 103–4.

112. Ibid., 21.

113. Ibid., 83.

114. Ibid., 20.

115. Ibid., 2.

116. Ibid., 83.

117. Ibid., 56. Although Perry suggests that "the only way to discover the truth or falsity of Emerson's utterances is to read and re-read, with prosaic fidelity, ev-

erything he wrote" (104), the emphasis falls squarely on the unpublished, personal papers, which connect the utterances to the utterer.

118. For other examples of critical approaches to Emerson that orient around the subject (or tie the writing to the writer), see Vivian C. Hopkins, *Spires of Form: A Study of Emerson's Aesthetic Theory* (Cambridge, Mass.: Harvard University Press, 1951); Sherman Paul, *Emerson's Angle of Vision: Man and Nature in American Experience* (Cambridge, Mass.: Harvard University Press, 1952); Bishop, *Emerson on the Soul;* Leonard Neufeldt, *The House of Emerson* (Lincoln: University of Nebraska Press, 1982); Eric Cheyfitz, *The Trans-Parent: Sexual Politics in the Language of Emerson* (Baltimore: Johns Hopkins University Press, 1981); B. L. Packer, *Emerson's Fall: A New Interpretation of the Major Essays* (New York: Continuum, 1982); Julie K. Ellison, *Emerson's Romantic Style* (Princeton: Princeton University Press, 1984); and Evelyn Barish, *Emerson: The Roots of Prophecy* (Princeton: Princeton University Press, 1989).

119. Stephen E. Whicher, *Freedom and Fate: An Inner Life of Ralph Waldo Emerson* (Philadelphia: University of Pennsylvania Press, 1953), 29. Emerson's "writings, and particularly his journals, record a genuine drama of ideas, a little known story that adds a new dimension of interest to his thought" (vii).

120. Ibid., vii.

121. Ibid., 57–58.

122. Ibid., 58 (emphasis in the original).

123. Ibid., 26.

124. Ibid., 52.

125. Ibid., 159.

126. Ibid.

Chapter 5: American Scholars and the Objects of Criticism

1. See Charles Feidelson Jr., *Symbolism and American Literature* (Chicago: University of Chicago Press, 1953), 124–28.

2. Emerson, *CW,* 1:10.

3. Ibid.

4. Feidelson, *Symbolism,* 132.

5. Ibid., 128.

6. Emerson, *CW,* 1:7.

7. Ibid., 1:39.

8. Ibid., 1:8.

9. Ibid., 1:28.

10. Ibid., 1:10.

11. Ibid.

12. Ibid., 1:15.

13. Ibid., 1:10.

14. Ibid., 1:44.

15. Ibid., 1:30–31.

16. Ibid., 1:31.

17. Ibid., 1:14.

18. Ibid.

19. Feidelson, *Symbolism,* 3. He qualifies his condemnation with a nod to "Matthiessen's *American Renaissance,* which is 'primarily concerned with *what* these books were as works of art. . . .' Yet even in this magnificent work, which reorients the entire subject, the sociological and political bent of studies in American literature makes itself felt indirectly" (3).

20. Ibid., 5.

21. Harold Bloom, *A Map of Misreading* (New York: Oxford University Press, 1975), 171.

22. Henry Steele Commager, *The American Mind: An Interpretation of American Thought and Character Since the 1880's* (New Haven: Yale University Press, 1950), 98.

23. H. L. Mencken, *Prejudices: First Series* (New York: Knopf, 1919), 191.

24. Ibid., 192. Mencken's egalitarianism is, of course, open to question (as is his brand of "Nietzscheism"). The brief essay under consideration, "An Unheeded Law-Giver," is marked by misogynist references to "vassarized old maids" (192) hungering for a "Transcendentalism rolled into pills" (194).

25. Ibid., 193.

26. Ibid., 191.

27. Ibid., 192.

28. Ibid.

29. Ibid.

30. Ibid., 193.

31. Ibid., 192.

32. Ibid., 193.

33. Ibid., 191.

34. Ibid.

35. Ibid., 193. Richard Ruland, in *The Rediscovery of American Literature: Premises of Critical Taste, 1900–1940* (Cambridge, Mass.: Harvard University Press, 1967), finds that "it was Emerson the rebel, Emerson the independent, revolutionary thinker and champion of forthright action that Mencken valued. Insofar as Emerson swam against the tide, Mencken did him honor" (124).

36. Charles A. Beard and Mary R. Beard, *The Rise of American Civilization,* vol. 1 (New York: Macmillan, 1927; reprint, New York: Macmillan, 1936), 780.

37. Ibid., 780–84. When compared to Poe just nine pages later, the serene and optimistic Emerson returns (793). The alternations between a benign Emerson and an Emerson in revolt are not explained.

38. Vernon Louis Parrington, *Main Currents in American Thought,* 3 vols. (New York: Harcourt Brace, 1927–58), 3:50. David R. Shumway notes the "overwhelmingly positive" reception of Parrington's work, "the impact that *Main Currents* had

on so many of its readers," and the Pulitzer Prize it was awarded (*Creating American Civilization: A Genealogy of American Literature as an Academic Discipline* [Minneapolis: University of Minnesota Press, 1994], 167).

39. Parrington, *Main Currents,* 2:295.

40. Ibid., 2:377.

41. Ibid., 2:312.

42. Lewis Mumford, *The Golden Day: A Study in American Experience and Culture* (New York: Boni and Liveright, 1926), 96.

43. Ibid., 94 (first, second, and third quotes), 94–95 (fourth quote).

44. Ibid., 95.

45. Ibid., 96.

46. Lowell, *My Study Windows,* 354. As Joel Porte suggests in *Representative Man,* Emerson's writings demonstrate an interest in a "spermatic economy." See "Economizing," especially 257–82. For an extended discussion of Emerson framed by questions of sexuality, see Cheyfitz's *The Trans-Parent.* In some ways, Cheyfitz's interest in a masculine-feminine dynamics at work in both Emerson's writing and that of his commentators resembles this investigation of practical idealism.

47. Mumford, *Golden Day,* 91.

48. Parrington, *Main Currents,* 2:379.

49. Ibid., 3:75.

50. Ibid., 3:70.

51. Ibid., 2:384.

52. Ibid., 3:319.

53. Cf. W. C. Brownell's *American Prose Masters* (New York: Scribner's Sons, 1909), which, as Shumway points out, in making "the strongest claims for Emerson's Americanness," resorts to "mentioning merely his individualism and democracy" (*Creating* 83). For another example of Emerson's centrality to America and especially American literature, see *The Cambridge History of American Literature,* ed. William Peterfield Trent, John Erskine, Stuart P. Sherman, and Carl Van Doren (New York: Putnam, 1917–21). "While this centrality is nowhere directly proclaimed, Emerson is ubiquitous in this history, being the most frequently mentioned author according to the indexes of three volumes" (Shumway, *Creating,* 94).

54. John Jay Chapman, *Emerson, and Other Essays* (New York, Scribner's Sons, 1898), 151. Chapman's selection comes from "Considerations by the Way" (Emerson, *W,* 6:237) and begins with "Leave this hypocritical prating about the masses." (The last sentence of the excerpt is "Away with this hurrah of masses, and let us have the considerate vote of single men spoken on their honor and their conscience.") It is noteworthy that Chapman chooses this as the central Emerson work. Published when Emerson was in his late fifties, the volume is usually characterized by Emersonian critics as among his more pragmatic efforts.

55. Chapman, *Emerson,* 150.

56. Ibid.

57. Ibid., 151.

58. Ibid., 164.

59. Ibid.

60. Ibid., 162. If we should, however, accidentally stumble upon a volume of the sage and fumble with the pages, this is what would happen (according to Chapman): The reader "is perhaps unable to see the exact logical connection between two paragraphs of an essay, yet he feels they are germane. He takes up Emerson tired and apathetic, but presently he feels himself growing heady and truculent, strengthened in his most inward vitality, surprised to find himself again master in his own house" (163).

61. Ibid., 155.

62. Ibid., 167.

63. Ibid.

64. Ibid., 172.

65. Ibid., 183.

66. Ibid., 175.

67. Quoted by Jacques Barzun in his introduction to *The Selected Writings of John Jay Chapman* (New York: Farrar, Strauss and Cudahy, 1957), xiii.

68. Chapman, *Emerson*, 163.

69. See Yvor Winters, *In Defense of Reason* (New York: Swallow Press, 1947). Bothered by, among other things, what he viewed as Emerson's abandonment of Christianity for the sake of personal whim (267), Winters rejected Emerson "as a fraud and a sentimentalist, and his fraudulence impinges at least lightly upon everything he wrote" (279). Winters apparently had read "everything he wrote," albeit with a certain distaste.

70. Irving Babbitt, *The Masters of Modern French Criticism* (Boston: Houghton Mifflin, 1912), 391.

71. Ibid., 348.

72. Ibid., 355.

73. Ibid., 352–53.

74. Ibid., 353.

75. Ibid., 359.

76. Ibid., 350.

77. Ibid., 362.

78. Walter Sutton, in *Modern American Criticism* (Englewood Cliffs, N.J.: Prentice Hall, 1963), records Edmund Wilson's questioning of "Babbitt's scholarship in his essay in *Humanism and America*, in which, according to Wilson, Babbitt misrepresents a Greek text in order to turn Sophocles into a Harvard Humanist" (45).

79. Irving Babbitt, *Democracy and Leadership* (Boston: Houghton Mifflin, 1924), 240. The quotation comes from a chapter titled "Democracy and Standards" (239–317).

80. In a fascinating association, Walter Sutton refers to More as "Thoreau to Babbitt's Emerson" (*Modern American Criticism*, 33). It is also noteworthy that

Merle Curti, in *The Growth of American Thought* (New York: Harper and Brothers, 1943), characterizes Babbitt and More as sophisticated versions of the success writer Elbert Hubbard in their preaching of "a doctrine of the elite" (643).

81. Paul Elmer More, *Shelburne Essays: First Series* (Boston: Houghton Mifflin, 1904), 79.

82. Ibid., 81.

83. Ibid., 73.

84. Ibid., 74.

85. Ibid., 80, 81, 75.

86. Emerson, *W*, 6:49.

87. See More's *Shelburne Essays: Eleventh Series: A New England Group and Others* (Boston: Houghton Mifflin, 1921): "Now Emerson certainly recognized the double nature of experience, but it is a fair question whether he realizes its full meaning and fateful seriousness. He accepts it a trifle too jauntily; is sometimes too ready to wave aside its consequences, as if a statement of the fact were an escape from its terrible perplexities. To be reconciled so cheerfully to this dark dilemma is not a reconciliation of the dilemma itself, but argues rather some deep-lying limitation of spiritual experience" (89). More here seems to miss the significance of paradox and the consequence of irreconcilable dilemmas.

88. Ibid., 94. This line of critique is not uncommon. James Truslow Adams, in his 1930 essay "Emerson Re-read" (collected in Milton R. Konvitz, *The Recognition of Ralph Waldo Emerson: Selected Criticism since 1837* [Ann Arbor: University of Michigan Press, 1972], 182–93], confesses that (to return briefly to metaphors of consumption) he had an appetite for Emerson as a lad, but lost his stomach for him with age and wisdom. After the myriad disappointments that beset a fellow in the "gulf between a man of fifty and the boy of sixteen" (190), Adams finds Emerson "lacking in depth and virility" (193), even dangerously feminine ("a siren voice, a soft Lydian air" [189]). At once too easy and too hard ("His doctrine contains two great flaws, one positive, the other negative, and both as typically American as he himself was in everything" [188]), this Emerson just won't do. Cf. D. H. Lawrence's short "Emerson" from the May 1923 *Dial* (in Konvitz's *Recognition*, 168–69): "The fact of the matter is, all those gorgeous inrushes of exaltation and spiritual energy which made Emerson a great man, now make us sick" (169).

89. Arnold L. Goldsmith, *American Literary Criticism: 1905–1965* (Boston: Twayne, 1979), 44. Shumway argues that "Foerster was more influential than his theoretical masters, Babbitt and More, because Foerster read American literature more sympathetically than they did" (145). He adds that Foerster's influence can still be felt throughout the discipline, and that "the effect of Foerster's program for study of American literature was to render such study more conservative and to limit the possibilities for other interpretations" (144).

90. Norman Foerster, *American Criticism: A Study in Literary Theory from Poe to the Present* (Boston: Houghton Mifflin, 1928), 223.

91. Ibid., 259.

92. Ibid., 257.

93. "For our best examples of sound art, which gives to ample materials firmness of inner meaning and of outward form, in other words fuses quality and quantity of beauty, we must still return to the ancients" (Ibid., 250).

94. Ibid., 241–49.

95. Ibid.

96. Ibid., 107.

97. Ibid., 64.

98. Harold Bloom, *The Ringers in the Tower: Studies in Romantic Tradition* (Chicago: University of Chicago Press, 1971), 226.

99. Harold Bloom, *Agon: Towards a Theory of Revisionism* (New York: Oxford University Press, 1982), 19.

100. Bloom, *Agon,* 42.

101. Harold Bloom, *Figures of Capable Imagination* (New York: Seabury Press, 1976), 75.

102. Bloom, *Ringers,* 269.

103. Bloom, *Agon,* 170 (emphasis in the original).

104. Bloom, *Ringers,* 269.

105. Ibid., 305.

106. Harold Bloom, *The Anxiety of Influence: A Theory of Poetry* (New York: Oxford University Press, 1973), 103.

107. Bloom, *Map,* 64.

108. Bloom, *Agon,* 167.

109. Ibid.

110. Ibid., 145.

111. Harold Bloom, ed., *Ralph Waldo Emerson* (New York: Chelsea House, 1985), 2.

112. Bloom, *Map,* 172.

113. Ibid., 9, 63.

114. Harold Bloom, *Poetry and Repression: Revisionism from Blake to Stevens* (New Haven: Yale University Press, 1976), 254.

115. Bloom refers to Chapman's piece on Emerson as "a great essay" (*Emerson,* 2) and "still the best introductory essay on Emerson" (*Ringers,* 269). Mumford's *The Golden Day* "still is the best guide as to *why* Emerson was and is the central influence upon American letters," and Bloom cites the trope of "nakedness" to substantiate this claim (*Emerson,* 10–11).

116. Bloom, *Emerson,* 8.

117. Ibid., 8.

118. "It would lead to something more intense than quarrels if I expressed my judgment upon 'black poetry' or the 'literature of Women's Liberation'" (Bloom, *Map,* 36). I interpret this statement and Bloom's (at best) indifference to works by women and African Americans in his major critical volumes as an exclusion of these

groups from the Great Tradition, the literature of "our fathers," and hence his circle. After all, Bloom surmises, "everyone who now reads and writes in the West, of whatever racial background, sex or ideological camp, is still a son or daughter of Homer." Bloom fears what will happen "if the burgeoning religion of Liberated Woman spreads from its clusters of enthusiasts to dominate the West" (33). Cf. Robert Moynihan's *A Recent Imagining: Interviews with Harold Bloom, Geoffrey Hartman, J. Hillis Miller, Paul de Man* (Hamden, Conn.: Shoe String Press, 1986), in which Bloom quips, "Most feminist poetry, of course, is like most black poetry. It isn't poetry. It isn't even verse. It isn't prose. It is just . . . I have no term for it" (30). Such works "would have a certain number of readers for awhile, but these are not readers, of course. These are just dyslexiads" (31). For more on the sanctity of the canon, see Bloom's *The Western Canon: The Books and School of the Ages* (New York: Harcourt Brace, 1994).

119. Bloom, *Emerson,* 10.

120. Bloom, *Figures,* xii.

121. Bloom, *Anxiety,* 11.

122. Ibid., 12.

123. Bloom, *Map,* 5, 9.

124. Ibid., 79.

125. Bloom, *Agon,* 16.

126. Ibid., 17. Bloom continues in this passage that reading is more than a will to power over texts, but a longing "to be yet another Demiurge," using Emerson to substantiate this claim.

127. Bloom, *Agon,* 19.

128. Ibid., 58.

129. Bloom, *Poetry,* 240 (emphasis in the original).

130. Bloom, *Map,* 27 (emphasis in the original).

131. Bloom, *Agon,* 41.

132. For other examples of pragmatic renderings of the Emerson object, see Richard Poirier, *The Renewal of Literature: Emersonian Reflections* (New York: Random House, 1987); Cornel West, *The American Evasion of Philosophy: A Genealogy of Pragmatism* (Madison: University of Wisconsin Press, 1989); and David Jacobson, *Emerson's Pragmatic Vision: The Dance of the Eye* (University Park: Pennsylvania State University Press, 1993).

133. Bloom, *Emerson,* 1.

134. Bloom, *Map,* 77.

135. Bloom, *Agon,* viii.

136. Ibid., 42.

137. Ibid., 21 (emphasis in the original).

138. Ibid., 19.

139. Bloom, *Map,* 176.

140. Ibid., 176.

141. Emerson, *CW,* 2:188.

142. Ibid., 2:188.

143. Ibid., 2:182.

144. Ibid., 2:189.

145. Bloom, *The Western Canon,* 17. Bloom follows his memorializing of hope with an elitist brand of pragmatism: "We need to teach more selectively, searching for the few who have the capacity to become highly individual readers and writers. The others, who are amenable to a politicized curriculum, can be abandoned to it. Pragmatically, aesthetic value can be recognized or experienced, but it cannot be conveyed to those who are incapable of grasping its sensations and perceptions."

146. Woodberry, *Ralph Waldo Emerson,* 183.

Chapter 6: Toward a Natural Philosophy of Reading

1. Emerson, *CW,* 2:181.

2. Ibid., 2:185.

3. Ibid., 2:188–89.

4. Ibid., 1:69.

5. Emerson, *W,* 10:135–36.

6. *The Oxford Dictionary of English Etymology,* ed. C. T. Onions (Oxford: Oxford University Press, 1966), reminds us that expecting has to do with waiting (for), with looking for in anticipation: *ex + spectare.* As I remarked earlier, this involves looking out; but it involves more: "From the orig. sense of going out or forth (cf. EXIT), sometimes with the additional notion of being raised (cf. EXTOL), the prefix acquired that of changing condition (cf. EFFERVESCE) and of completion (cf. EFFECT, EXCRUCIATE, EXHAUST)" (333). *Expect,* then, can mean a changing of the conditions from which we see or make sense of nature and our places in it or the completion or finish of one way of thinking in order to move on to others.

7. Emerson, *CW,* 1:58.

8. Ibid., 2:196.

9. Ibid., 1:64.

10. Merton M. Sealts Jr., *Emerson on the Scholar* (Columbia: University of Missouri Press, 1992), 267.

11. For examples of such exceptions, see David Van Leer, *Emerson's Epistemology: The Argument of the Essays* (Cambridge: Cambridge University Press, 1986), and John Michael, *Emerson and Skepticism: The Cipher of the World* (Baltimore: Johns Hopkins University Press, 1988).

12. Stanley Cavell, "Thinking of Emerson," *The Senses of Walden,* expanded ed. (San Francisco: North Point Press, 1981), 129.

13. Cavell refers to a sentence from Emerson's essay "History": "So all that is said of the wise man by stoic or oriental or modern essayist, describes to each reader his own idea, describes his unattained but attainable self" (*CW,* 2:5).

14. Stanley Cavell, *Conditions Handsome and Unhandsome: The Constitution of Emersonian Perfection* (Chicago: University of Chicago Press, 1990), 12.

15. Much of Cavell's philosophy entails thinking about reading. *The Senses of Walden,* for example, is devoted to a thorough reading of a book that Cavell claims is itself about a book; *Disowning Knowledge in Six Plays of Shakespeare* (Cambridge: Cambridge University Press, 1987) consists primarily of readings; and other works include interpretive meditations (or, better yet, meditative interpretations) on various films. In this latter category, see particularly *Pursuits of Happiness: The Hollywood Comedy of Remarriage* (Cambridge, Mass.: Harvard University Press, 1981) and *The World Viewed: Reflections on the Ontology of Film,* enlarged ed. (Cambridge, Mass.: Harvard University Press, 1979). For bibliographies of Cavell's works and works on Cavell, see Peter Wasel, "A Working Bibliography on Stanley Cavell," in *The Senses of Stanley Cavell,* ed. Richard Fleming and Michael Payne (Lewisburg, Pa.: Bucknell University Press, 1989), and "Stanley Cavell: A Bibliography, 1958–1994," in Cavell's *Philosophical Passages: Wittgenstein, Emerson, Austin, Derrida* (Oxford: Blackwell, 1995).

16. Cavell, *The World Viewed,* xii.

17. Thoreau, *Walden,* 225.

18. Stanley Cavell, *The Claim of Reason: Wittgenstein, Skepticism, Morality, and Tragedy* (New York: Oxford University Press, 1979): "Part of the reason I want the word 'read' [to function in this particular reading of Wittgenstein's *Investigations*] is, I feel sure, recorded in its history: it has something to do with being advised, and hence with seeing" (361).

19. Stanley Cavell, *In Quest of the Ordinary: Lines of Skepticism and Romanticism* (Chicago: University of Chicago Press, 1988), 17.

20. Thoreau, *Walden,* 121–22.

21. Bruce Kuklick, *The Rise of American Philosophy: Cambridge, Massachusetts, 1860–1930* (New Haven: Yale University Press, 1977).

22. Cavell, *In Quest,* 14. In a father-figuring gesture similar to that made by Bloom, Cavell calls Emerson "the founder of American thinking" (*Philosophical Passages,* 15).

23. Cavell, *Conditions,* 21.

24. Cavell, *In Quest,* 115.

25. Ibid., "The Philosopher in American Life," 3–26.

26. Cavell, *In Quest,* 116.

27. Samuel Beckett, *Waiting for Godot* (New York: Grove Press, 1954), 41.

28. Samuel Beckett, *Worstward Ho* (New York: Grove Press, 1983), 7.

29. Emerson, *CW,* 4:43–44.

30. Cavell, *Senses,* 152.

31. Cavell, *In Quest,* 36.

32. Stanley Cavell, *Themes out of School: Effects and Causes* (San Francisco: North Point Press, 1984), 52.

33. Emerson, *CW,* 2:6–7.

34. Emerson, *W*, 8:160.

35. Edwin Way Teale, in his introduction to a volume of Muir's writing, *The Wilderness World of John Muir* (Boston: Houghton Mifflin, 1954), notes that "Emerson was one of the great admirations of Muir's life." Emerson, in turn, included Muir on "his list of 'My Men,' the ones who had influenced him most" (xi).

36. Muir, *Wilderness World*, 162. The excerpt comes from *Our National Parks* (Boston: Houghton Mifflin, 1902), 131–36.

37. Muir, *Wilderness World*, 164. Teale informs us that "it was this book [of Emerson's prose] that John Muir carried with him, read and reread, during his mountain days in the high Sierra" (xi), and presents one example of a discrepancy in reading the land: "in *Nature*, Emerson observes: 'There is in woods and waters a certain enticement and flattery, together with a failure to yield a present satisfaction. This disappointment is felt in every landscape.' Muir dissents: 'No— always we find more than we expect'" (xi).

38. Muir, *Wilderness World*, 163.

39. Ibid., 164.

40. Ibid.

41. Alfred North Whitehead, *The Concept of Nature* (Cambridge: Cambridge University Press, 1930), 5.

42. Emerson, *CW*, 1:123 (emphasis in the original).

43. Whitehead, *Concept*, 14–15.

44. Shunryu Suzuki, *Zen Mind, Beginner's Mind*, ed. Trudy Dixon (New York: Weatherhill, 1970; reprint, New York: Weatherhill, 1984), 21, 22. Compare this with Cavell's sense that "what stands in the way of further knowledge is knowledge itself, as it stands, as it conceives of itself," which leads him to "my concept of acknowledgment" (*In Quest*, 8).

45. See, for example, *In Quest*: "To acknowledge that I am known by what this text knows does not amount to agreeing with it, in the sense of believing it, as if it were a bunch of assertions or as if it contained a doctrine. *To be known by it is to find thinking in it that confronts you*" (118; emphasis added).

46. Emerson, *CW*, 2:188.

47. "What I write, whilst I write it, seems the most natural thing in the world: but, yesterday, I saw a dreary vacuity in this direction in which now I see so much; and a month hence, I doubt not, I shall wonder who he was that wrote so many continuous pages" (ibid., 182).

48. Ibid., 189.

49. Ibid.

50. Ibid. Cavell surmises something similar from a passage of "Experience": "if we are to think anew it must be from a new stance, one essentially unfamiliar to us; or, say, from a further perspective that is uncontrollable by us" (Stanley Cavell, "Time after Time," *London Review of Books*, 12 Jan. 1995, 6).

51. Emerson, *CW*, 2:93.

52. Ibid., 2:95. The actual sentences are largely concerned with biography, and

run thus: "Byron says of Jack Bunting,—'He knew not what to say, and so he swore.' I may say it of our preposterous use of books,—He knew not what to do, and so, *he read*. I can think of nothing to fill my time with, and I find the Life of Brant. It is a very extravagant compliment to pay to Brant, or to General Schuyler, or to General Washington. My time should be as good as their time,—my facts, my net of relations as good as theirs, or either of theirs. Rather let me do my work so well that other idlers, if they choose, may compare my texture with the texture of these and find it identical with the best."

53. Emerson, *W*, 8:152–53.

54. Cavell, *Philosophical Passages*, 24.

55. Friedrich Nietzsche, *Twilight of the Idols; or, How One Philosophizes with a Hammer*, in *The Portable Nietzsche*, ed. and trans. Walter Kaufmann (New York: Penguin, 1954; reprint, New York: Penguin, 1968), 522. I attach the prelude to these lines, as a treat for those yet interested in metaphorical consumption: "*Emerson*. Much more enlightened, more roving, more manifold, subtler than Carlyle; above all, happier. One who instinctively nourishes himself only on ambrosia, leaving behind what is indigestible in things." Nietzsche adds that "Carlyle, who loved [Emerson] very much, nevertheless said of him: 'He does not give us enough to chew on'—which may be true, but is no reflection on Emerson."

56. Emerson, *CW*, 2:39.

57. Ibid., 3:32.

58. I borrow these measurements from *The New Grolier Multimedia Encyclopedia* (Boston: Grolier, 1993).

59. Emerson, *CW*, 3:27.

60. Ibid., 3:27, 28.

61. Ibid., 3:29.

62. Stanley Cavell, *This New Yet Unapproachable America: Lectures after Emerson after Wittgenstein* (Albuquerque: Living Batch Press, 1989), 86.

63. Emerson, *CW*, 3:30.

64. Ibid., 3:47: "I know better than to claim any completeness for my picture. I am a fragment, and this is a fragment of me."

65. Ibid., 3:38.

66. Ibid., 3:37.

67. Emerson, *W*, 8:273–74.

68. Cavell also makes something of transit in Emerson, although he keeps it to progress down the "philosophical path" (see *This New*, 27–28). For more on transitory reading, cf. H. Meili Steele's notion that "transitional words" (e.g., those linking paragraph to paragraph) are suppressed in Emerson's writing, "so that the relationship among the sentences is often reduced to their contiguity or to the tenuous connections of his farfetched analogies or to theme and variation. If the reader is to follow the essay, he must leap from sentence to sentence without the comforting links of traditional discourse, much as he would in a lyric poem" ("Ro-

mantic Epistemology and Romantic Style: Emerson's Development from *Nature* to the *Essays,*" in *Studies in the American Renaissance,* 197).

69. Werner Heisenberg, *Philosophical Problems of Quantum Physics,* trans. F. C. Hayes (Woodbridge, Conn.: Ox Bow Press, 1979), 11.

70. Ibid., 12.

71. Emerson, CW, 3:35.

72. Ibid., 3:49.

73. Ibid., 3:49. "Experience" contrasts these moments with larger temporal chunks: "It takes a good deal of time to eat or to sleep, or to earn a hundred dollars" (3:49).

74. Ibid., 3:41.

75. Ibid., 3:48–49.

76. Emerson, W, 10:132.

77. Emerson, CW, 2:193.

78. Ibid.

79. Ibid.

80. Ibid., 2:196.

81. Ibid., 2:202.

82. Ibid.

83. Ibid., 2:200–201.

84. Ibid., 3:137.

85. Ibid., 3:201.

86. Ibid., 1:39.

87. Ibid., 3:43.

Index

Adams, James Truslow, 172
Alcott, Louisa May, 162
Alger, Horatio, 37
Allen, Gay Wilson, 76–77, 159
America: nature of, 2, 89–91, 103–4, 107, 114–18; and New Humanism, 111–12; and success, 21, 34–37, 46
Arnold, Matthew, 125

Babbitt, Irving, 110–13, 118, 171, 172
Bacon, Francis, 15
Barish, Evelyn, 168
Barrus, Clara, 166
Barthes, Roland, 77
Barzun, Jacques, 171
Bataille, Georges, 152
Beard, Charles A., 106
Beard, Mary R., 106
Beardsley, Monroe, 77, 164
Beckett, Samuel, 129
Bergon, Frank, 164
Berryman, John, 156
Biographical criticism, 8, 51–64, 72–78, 87–97
Bishop, Jonathan, 91, 167, 168
Bloom, Harold, 103–4, 114–20, 125, 173–74, 175, 176
Bok, Edward, 42–45, 158

Bolton, Sarah K., 55
Brooks, Van Wyck, 52–53, 159, 160
Brownell, W. C., 170
Buell, Lawrence, 13
Burbank, Luther, 23
Burke, Kenneth, 14
Burroughs, John, 78–80, 83–86, 165–66

Cabot, James Elliot, 58–64, 67, 88, 90, 118, 161, 162
Carnegie, Andrew, 22–23
Carnegie, Dale, 21
Carpenter, Frederic Ives, 159, 166
Carson, Johnny, 137
Cavell, Stanley, 125–30, 136, 138, 141, 158, 175, 176, 177, 178
Cawelti, John G., 16, 21, 37
Cayton, Mary Kupiec, 156
Champney, Freeman, 156
Chapman, John Jay, 108–10, 116, 170, 171, 173
Cheyfitz, Eric, 168, 170
Christian Science, 16, 111–12
Commager, Henry Steele, 104
Consumption: of Emerson, 7, 13–33, 131, 178; and incorporation, 51, 55; and "Self-Reliance," 38, 46–50
Conway, Moncure, 56–58, 63, 159–60, 162

Cooke, George Willis, 54, 58
Crane, Stephen, 156
Curti, Merle, 172

Dawes, Rufus, 161
de Man, Paul, 77–78

Eckhart, Meister, 151
Ellison, Julie, 168
Emerson, Edward Waldo, 54–56, 58, 160
Emerson, Mary Moody, 52
Emerson, Ralph Waldo: and American culture, 8–9, 14–15, 32, 34, 41, 45, 51, 58, 112; "The American Scholar," 3–6, 62, 124–25; autograph of, 42–45; "Circles," 1, 31, 120, 122–23, 136–37; "The Comic," 63, 132, 138; and Concord, 44, 54–58, 60, 62, 71, 77, 88, 94; The Conduct of Life, 17, 108, 112; "Considerations by the Way," 170; Divinity School Address, 62, 72–74; "Education," 123, 145; "Experience," 131, 139–46, 148, 177, 179; "Fate," 43, 112; "History," 131, 175; "Inspiration," 142; "Intellect," 146–47; journals of, 29, 31–32, 53, 92; Letters and Social Aims, 59, 61–64; life of, 25–26, 51–56, 58–62, 76–77, 89, 91, 94; "The Lord's Supper," 7, 27–32; "Man the Reformer," 31; "The Method of Nature," 72, 80–82, 87, 133–34, 165; Nature, 8, 14, 62, 72, 79–80, 87–88, 98–102, 115, 132–33, 146, 148–49, 161, 177; "The Over-Soul," 5; "Persian Poetry," 63; as Plotinus-Montaigne, 88–94, 104, 166, 167; "The Poet," 26; "Poetry and Imagination," 8, 63–70, 72, 74; "Progress of Culture," 64; "Quotation and Originality," 41, 47, 63–64; Representative Men, 129; "The Scholar," 68–69; "Self-Reliance," 7–8, 31, 35, 37–41, 43, 46, 48–50, 61, 75, 128, 139, 151, 154, 155–56; "The Sphinx," 130–31; "Spiritual Laws," 11, 137; "Thoughts on Modern Literature," 75–76, 97, 122, 129; "The Transcendentalist," 17; "Uriel," 9

Feidelson, Charles, Jr., 98, 101–2
Fish, Stanley, 77
Foerster, Norman, 111, 113, 172, 173
Ford, Henry, 23

Franklin, Benjamin, 37, 88–89, 109
Furness, William Henry, 161

Goldsmith, Arnold L., 172
Grafton, Anthony, 45–46

Heisenberg, Werner, 142–43
Hill, Napoleon, 21–25, 89, 154
Holmes, Oliver Wendell, 1, 14, 88–92, 95, 104, 113, 161, 166
Hopkins, Vivian C., 168
Hubbard, Elbert, 35–36, 156, 172
Huber, Richard, 16, 152–53
Hunt, Freeman, 37–41, 48

Incorporation, 51–64, 69–71

Jacobson, David, 174
James, William, 104–5
Jesus Christ, 27–30, 72–73
Johnson, Clifton, 85
Johnson, Glen M., 162

Kaufmann, Walter, 68–69, 162

Lawrence, D. H., 172
Lopez, Michael, 155
Lowell, James Russell, 13, 25–26, 107, 166, 167

Mailloux, Steven, 15
Marden, Orison Swett, 16–17, 153
Mathews, William, 41, 157
Matthiessen, F. O., 169
McKibben, Bill, 164
Mencken, H. L., 14, 16, 104–6, 153, 169
Meyer, Donald, 152–53
Michael, John, 175
More, Paul Elmer, 111–13, 171–72
Moynihan, Robert, 174
Muir, John, 132–34, 177
Mumford, Lewis, 107, 116, 173

Natural philosophy of reading, 122–25, 129–35, 138–49
Nature: as adversary, 117; and American scholars, 5–7, 124; and "Circles," 123; conquest of, 95–96; and Divinity School Address, 72–74; and "Experience," 139–40; and Nature, 98–102; and Representative Men, 129; as text, 10–11, 66–67, 71, 78–82, 86–87, 131–35, 143;

and "Thoughts on Modern Literature,"
75–76; as trope, 65
Neufeldt, Leonard, 168
New Criticism, 46, 77
New Humanism, 110–14
New Testament, 27–32
New Thought: compared to success tracts,
34, 41; histories of, 152; Mencken's
view of, 14, 104–6; and Ralph Waldo
Trine, 16–21
New York Times, 15
Nietzsche, Friedrich, 8, 68–71, 78, 138,
151, 162, 178

Objective criticism, 97–104, 108–21
Onions, C. T., 175

Packer, B. L., 168
Palimpsest, 40–42, 45, 47, 50, 131
Parker, Gail Thain, 17
Parrington, Vernon Louis, 106–9, 169–70
Patell, Cyrus R. K., 151
Paul, Sherman, 168
Peale, Norman Vincent, 16, 21, 153
Perry, Bliss, 91–93, 95, 104, 167–68
Poirier, Richard, 174
Porte, Joel, 155, 158, 170
Practical idealism, 90–93, 96, 104–8, 120
Pragmatism, 89–90, 105, 118–19, 125
Preposterousness: Emerson on, 7, 137,
178; and hope, 119–22; and interpreta-
tion, 9–10, 24, 50, 97, 128, 132, 136–
38; and nature, 71

Richardson, Robert D., Jr., 159
Rorty, Richard, 119
Ross, Valerie, 163
Ruland, Richard, 169

Russell, Phillips, 159
Ryder, Annie H., 15

Sealts, Merton, Jr., 125
Shimkin, David, 161–62
Shumway, David R., 169–70, 172
Simmons, Nancy Craig, 161
Spiller, Robert E., 165
Stack, George J., 162
Steele, H. Meili, 178–79
Stovall, Floyd, 160, 166
Structuralism, 78
Sutton, Walter, 171
Suzuki, Shunryu, 136

Taylor, Gary, 40
Teale, Edwin Way, 177
Thayer, James, 1
Thoreau, Henry David, 15, 48–49, 126–
27, 171
Trine, Ralph Waldo, 16–21, 24–25, 34, 43,
153–54

Van Leer, David, 175

Walker, Cheryl, 163
Webster, Daniel, 106
Weiss, Richard, 17
West, Cornel, 174
Whicher, Stephen, 13, 94–96, 168
Whitehead, Alfred North, 134–35
Whitman, Walt, 78
Williams, Ralph, 40
Wilson, Edmund, 171
Wimsatt, W. K., Jr., 77, 164
Winters, Yvor, 110, 171
Wyllie, Irvin G., 153
Woodberry, George, 66, 120

T. S. MCMILLIN is an associate professor of English at Oberlin College. He has published articles on diverse literary matters, including Emerson and interpretation, Thoreau and transcendentalism, nature writing, and self-help books.

Typeset in 10/13 Sabon
with Nofret display
Designed by Dennis Roberts
Composed by Jim Proefrock
at the University of Illinois Press
Manufactured by Thomson-Shore, Inc.

University of Illinois Press
1325 South Oak Street
Champaign, IL 61820-6903
www.press.uillinois.edu